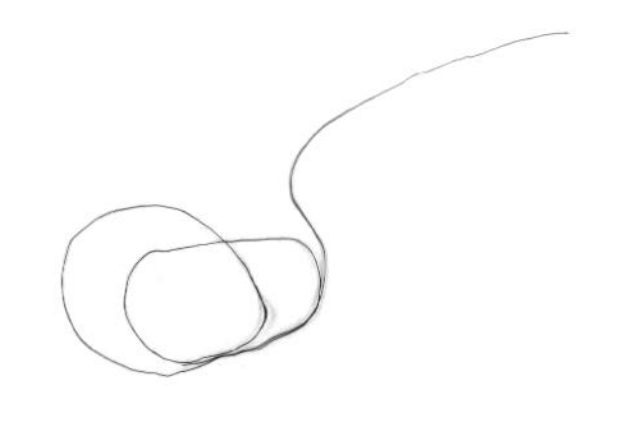

Jurisdiction of the International Court of Justice

The Composition of the Curatorium of the Xiamen Academy of International Law

The titles published in this series are listed at *brill.com/ccxa*

Jurisdiction of the International Court of Justice

Xiamen Academy of International Law Summer Courses, July 27–31, 2015

VOLUME 10

By

Xue Hanqin

BRILL

LEIDEN | BOSTON

Library of Congress Cataloging-in-Publication Data

Names: Xue, Hanqin, 1955-, author.
Title: Jurisdiction of the International Court of Justice / By Xue Hanqin.
Description: Leiden : Brill Nijhoff, 2017. | Series: Collected courses of the Xiamen academy of international law ; 10 | Includes bibliographical references and index.
Identifiers: LCCN 2017012465 (print) | LCCN 2017016574 (ebook) | ISBN 9789004342767 (E-book) | ISBN 9789004342750 (hardback : alk. paper)
Subjects: LCSH: International Court of Justice. | Jurisdiction.
Classification: LCC KZ6283 (ebook) | LCC KZ6283 .X84 2017 (print) | DDC 341.5/52--dc23
LC record available at https://lccn.loc.gov/2017012465

Typeface for the Latin, Greek, and Cyrillic scripts: "Brill". See and download: brill.com/brill-typeface.

ISSN 1875-4678
ISBN 978-90-04-34275-0 (hardback)
ISBN 978-90-04-34276-7 (e-book)

This book is printed on acid-free paper and produced in a sustainable manner.

To He Jin and Xiaoxue

∵

Contents

CHAPTER I

Introduction*

Peaceful settlement of international disputes, as enshrined in Article 2, paragraph 3, of the Charter of the United Nations, is one of the basic norms and fundamental principles of international law. Under Article 33 of the Charter, there are various peaceful means for the settlement of international disputes, namely, negotiation, enquiry, mediation, conciliation, arbitration, judicial settlement, resort to regional agencies or arrangements, or other peaceful means of States' own choice. All these methods are regarded as peaceful and equally important in law. They may be adopted singly or jointly, consecutively or alternatively, depending on the specific circumstances of each case. There is no requirement under general international law as to the order in which they may be used, unless otherwise specifically provided for or agreed to by the parties. It is up to the State parties concerned to decide which means is the most suitable and appropriate to use for the settlement of their dispute.

Although in practice most of international disputes are settled directly through negotiations, without resort to a third party, judicial settlement has attracted most attention and study. This is largely due to the fact that judicial settlement is based on a highly structured and well-defined procedure. By producing binding decisions, it provides legal certainty, stability and predictability. Its consistent and continuous jurisprudence has general effect on the interpretation and application of international law. Therefore, advocacy of judicial settlement is often regarded as an effective means to promote the rule of law in international relations.[1]

* The author wishes to express her profound appreciation and gratitude to her assistants, Mr. Jiang Bin, Ms Shang Weiwei, Ms Solène Guggisberg and Ms Barbara Dalsbaek, for their valuable research assistance. On top of their work at the Court, they each graciously lent their support to the project, particularly during the final stage of proof-reading and indexing. Their dedication and diligence are highly commendable and appreciated. The author of course remains solely responsible for any mistake or error that may be found in the monography.

1 For example, in the United Nations Decade of International Law, the General Assembly adopted resolutions calling on States to promote the means and methods for the peaceful settlement of international disputes, including resort to and full respect for the International Court of Justice and to accept its jurisdiction in accordance with its Statute. UN doc. A/Res/45/40, 28 November 1990. The 2005 World Summit Outcome, in particular, in the part on the rule of law, emphasizes "the important role of the International Court of Justice, the principal judicial organ of the United Nations, in adjudicating disputes among States and

 | DOI 10.1163/9789004342767_002

The theme of this special course focuses on the jurisdiction of the International Court of Justice ("the ICJ," or "the Court"), the principal judicial organ of the United Nations. The purpose in choosing such a topic is two-fold.

First, the question of jurisdiction is an essential matter for international judicial adjudication. In international law, it directly bears on the sovereignty of States. It determines the competence of the Court, both in general terms as well as in each specific case. In a way, it is the cornerstone of the legal institution and a departure point for any legal proceedings. This is a unique feature of the international judicial practice.

Secondly, notwithstanding its world-wide impact, the Court is largely influenced by the practice of two major legal systems—European civil law and English common law.[2] Although States attach great importance to the work of the Court, only a small number of Asian States have accepted the jurisdiction of the Court or submitted their disputes to the ICJ for settlement.[3] Apparently advocacy of the rule of law alone is not sufficient to persuade States to resort to the Court. Their confidence and trust in the judicial settlement have to be supported by their technical competence in, and genuine understanding of, the legal system. Such technical matters as jurisdiction and admissibility, unfortunately, are seldom taught in international law courses in many Asian countries. It is therefore necessary to fill the gap.

---

the value of its work," and "call[s] upon *States that have not yet done so to consider accepting the jurisdiction of the Court* in accordance with its Statute and consider means of strengthening the Court's work." UN doc. A/RES/60/1, 24 October 2005, p. 29, para. 134. The same expression was adopted in the following years' General Assembly "rule of law" resolutions. See UN doc. A/Res/61/39, 18 December 2006; UN doc. A/Res/62/70, 8 January 2008; UN doc. A/Res/63/128, 15 January 2009; UN doc. A/Res/64/116, 15 January 2010; UN doc. A/Res/65/32, 10 January 2011; UN doc. A/Res/66/102, 13 January 2012; UN doc. A/Res/67/97, 14 January 2013; UN doc. A/Res/68/116, 18 December 2013; UN doc. A/Res/69/123, 18 December 2014; see also Declaration of the high-level meeting of the General Assembly on the rule of law at the national and international levels, UN doc. A/Res/67/1, 30 November 2012, p. 5, para. 31.

2 The ICJ is the only organ in the United Nations system that uses French and English as its official languages, a tradition passed on from its predecessor, the Permanent Court of International Justice.

3 6 out of 72 States that have accepted compulsory jurisdiction of the Court under Article 36, paragraph 2, of the Statute of the Court are from Asia: Cambodia accepted the compulsory jurisdiction of the ICJ on 19 September 1957; Pakistan on 13 September 1960; the Philippines on 18 January 1972; India on 18 September 1974; Japan on 9 July 2007 (renewed on 6 October 2015); Timor-Leste on 21 September 2012. So far there are 15 Asian States that have appeared before the Court as a party in a contentious case. They are Bahrain, Cambodia, Georgia, India, Indonesia, Iran, Israel, Japan, Lebanon, Malaysia, Pakistan, Qatar, Singapore, Thailand, and Timor-Leste. Moreover, among the counsels that appear before the Court, only a few of them come from Asia.

1 A Historical Review

Under the Westphalian system, the right to resort to war for the settlement of international disputes constituted part of traditional international law. In the modern era, judicial settlement of international disputes was preceded by many efforts and attempts in looking for possible peaceful ways to resolve inter-State disputes so that wars could be avoided. Among such endeavours, the practice of international arbitrations in the 19th century and the early 20th century had a direct impact on the formation and establishment of the World Court.[4]

a *European Arbitrations in the 19th Century and the Permanent Court of Arbitration*

The origin of peaceful settlement of disputes through mediation and arbitration dates back ages to the ancient times in both eastern and western civilizations. Modern practice of international arbitrations is, nevertheless, primarily derived from the western culture, given the nature of the international legal order.

According to historical records, arbitration was long practiced by the ancient Greeks as an alternative to war for settlement of inter-State disputes, and later it was also used in Roman times.[5] However, international arbitration

4 The first court of international justice inspired by the Hague Peace Conferences for the pacific settlement of international disputes was the Central American Court of Justice which was set up in 1907 and operated for ten years. It was revived in 1991 and began its work again in 1994. See Rosa Riquelme Cortado, "Central American Court of Justice (1907–18)," *Max Planck Encyclopedia of Public International Law*, http://opil.ouplaw.com/view/10.1093/law:epil/9780199231690/law-9780199231690-e15, 7 April 2016; Corte Centroamericana de Justicia, "Historia del Tribunal," http://portal.ccj.org.ni/ccj2/Historia/tabid/57/Default.aspx, 7 April 2016.

5 It is said that it was in the ancient Greece that the peaceful adjudication of international disputes had its true origin and earliest development. As is recorded, arbitration was used throughout the Hellenic period for five hundred years from the 7th to the middle of the 2nd century B.C. Nevertheless, war remained the ultimate and effective means for settlement of disputes. Usually when there was a certain equilibrium obtained among the Greek states, arbitration was more referred to. In the Roman times, as a militant republic and a world empire, Rome herself was never a party to an arbitration, which was mainly used to settle differences among the peoples of the Italian peninsula. Before the 12th century in the Middle Ages, among the lords and princes, war was the rule rather than the exception to settle their disputes and quarrels. That does not mean arbitration did not exist then. Popes, kings, emperors and even law professors would play the role of arbitrator to settle disputes between the sovereigns. Henry S. Fraser, "Sketch of the History of International Arbitration," *Cornell Law Quarterly*, Vol. 11, 1925–1926, pp. 185–190.

became meaningful for international law studies only from the late 18th century.[6]

It is generally believed that the Jay Treaty concluded between the United States and the United Kingdom in 1794 in the wake of the American Independence War was a milestone for the commencement of international arbitration,[7] as numerous treaties followed suit, including arbitration clauses for the settlement of disputes. Substantively, the Jay Treaty arbitration contributed to modern international arbitration in three aspects: the right of the commissioners to determine their own jurisdiction; the right to take decisions by a majority vote and; the right to settle disputes on the basis of international law.[8]

Notwithstanding, institutionally the impact of the Jay Treaty was rather limited for general practice of arbitration, as the mixed commissions thus formed under the Jay Treaty worked, to a large extent, in a diplomatic and accommodating way by the application of equity through negotiations. In the 19th century there was a resurgence of State practice to settle disputes by international arbitration, especially in the last two decades, where more arbitral awards were rendered than those put together in the first half of that century.[9]

6 Theoretically, from 15th century onwards, there were many scholarly writings and advocacy for international arbitration in Europe. According to Grotius, for instance, wars could be evaded by arbitral decisions as well. From the 16th to the 18th century, however, with the great discovery of the world and the expansion of European powers with trade and subsequent colonization, there was a clear retreat of arbitration. The rising nationalism among European States promoted the doctrine of balance of power and non-intervention, leaving little room for the idea of amicable arbitration among States. See *ibid.*, pp. 179–185, 198. It is also interesting and revealing to note that arbitration practically disappeared from interstate relations in the decades following the Peace of Westphalia in 1648, a point that supposedly marked the beginning of modern international law.

7 The Treaty of Amity, Commerce, and Navigation was concluded between the United States and the United Kingdom on 19 November 1794, with an aim to improve the bilateral relations between the two countries that had deteriorated after the signing of the 1783 Treaty of Paris, which ended the American War of Independence. It is called Jay Treaty after the name of John Jay, the then U.S. Secretary of State. The Jay Treaty included, among others, the provision on the establishment of three mixed claims commissions for dispute settlement to deal with the issues left over from the War. Each commission was composed of members of equal number appointed by each of the two States with an umpire chosen by them or drawn by lot. The three commissions settled many claims to the satisfaction of the parties. See Vanda Lamm, *Compulsory Jurisdiction in International Law*, Edward Elgar, 2014, p. 5.

8 Kaj Hobér, *Essays on International Arbitration*, Huntingdon and JurisNet, LLC, 2006, pp. 3–8.

9 There were more than 100 international arbitrations during those two decades. See Vanda Lamm, *op. cit. supra* footnote 7, p. 4, footnote 13.

The *Alabama Claims* Arbitration held in Geneva in 1871–1872 is often regarded as another landmark for third-party dispute settlement to prevent war.

During the American Civil War, the Southern Confederacy ordered the *Alabama* war vessel to be made at the shipyards in Liverpool, Great Britain. Although having declared its neutrality at the outset of the Civil War and thus under the obligation to refrain from providing any military equipment to either belligerent, the British government nevertheless knowingly let the vessel be delivered to the South. During the Civil War, the *Alabama* vessel caused considerable damage to the Northern economy, capturing more than 60 Northern freight vessels. After the War, the United States initially proposed to submit their dispute to arbitration, but Great Britain refused. In 1871 the two governments ultimately signed the Washington Treaty and agreed to have recourse to arbitration. The Tribunal rendered its award the next year, deciding that Great Britain should pay the United States $15,500,000 in gold as compensation. Great Britain eventually recognized the award as valid in its entirety and paid the sum accordingly.

The *Alabama Claims* Arbitration produced a number of rules and practice which were gradually to gain general acceptance. First, the Tribunal consisted of five members. Three neutral arbitrators were appointed respectively by the heads of State of Italy, Switzerland and Brazil, highlighting the neutrality of the bench. The national members were rather regarded as the representatives of their own country.[10] Secondly, the arbitrators of the Tribunal were allowed to append their separate and dissenting opinions to the award, underscoring the importance of the reasoning of the award and the independence of the arbitrators.[11] Thirdly, the parties chose the applicable law for the Tribunal. In this case the applicable law was the so-called "Washington rules" on the duties of neutrals, which had a higher standard on neutrality than the British law applicable at that time. The arbitral settlement of the *Alabama* case impressed the world as a possible universal remedy against further wars.

This background explains that by the end of the 19th century arbitration had become a widely accepted method for settling disputes. Such practice, of course, was mainly confined to Western "civilized nations," not including those

---

10 There were five members of the Tribunal, two appointed by the United States and Great Britain respectively, three appointed by the King of Italy, the President of the Swiss Confederation and the Emperor of Brazil.

11 The British arbitrator actually dissented from the award, although the British government ultimately accepted it. See Tom Bingham, "Alabama Arbitration," *Max Planck Encyclopedia of Public International Law*, October 2006, http://opil.ouplaw.com/view/10.1093/law:epil/9780199231690/law-9780199231690-e89?prd=EPIL, 8 April 2016.

still under colonial and foreign domination. In 1899, in the face of fierce arms race and maritime rivalry among the major European powers for the expansion of their spheres of influence and overseas colonies, Russian Czar Nikolas II called for the convening of the first Hague Peace Conference to discuss about disarmament and peaceful settlement of international disputes. One of the major outcomes of this Conference was the signing of the Convention for the Pacific Settlement of International Disputes, under which the Permanent Court of Arbitration (PCA) was established.[12] The PCA was set up in 1900 and began its operation in 1902. It is the oldest standing international institution for the peaceful settlement of international disputes. After six dormant decades in the 20th century, it got revived in the post-Cold War era.

One of the important contributions of the PCA is to provide standard rules of procedure for international arbitration. In case the parties to a dispute fail to agree on the procedural rules of arbitration, they may resort to the PCA rules. Apart from a permanent Bureau,[13] the PCA, however, is largely an institutional structure or framework, waiting for States to initiate its services. It maintains a roster of arbitrators appointed by the contracting State parties. Each State party is entitled to appoint up to four members.[14] States who wish to resort to arbitration may select arbitrators from that roster.

At the Hague Conferences, the proposal to provide compulsory arbitration under the PCA was raised. It was, however, not accepted by the contracting State parties. The PCA left considerable discretion to the parties in the conduct of international arbitration. During the Second Hague Peace Conference, the idea to set up an international judicial court to render decisions on the basis of international law by salaried judges was put forward. Largely

---

12 27 States signed the 1899 Convention at the first Hague Peace Conference and 46 signed the 1907 Convention at the second Hague Peace Conference. The latter had made some minor changes to the former. See Kaj Hobér, *op. cit. supra* footnote 8, pp. 23–28.

13 Article 22 of the 1899 Hague Convention for the Pacific Settlement of International Disputes.

14 Under Article 44 of the 1907 Hague Convention for the Pacific Settlement of International Disputes, and Article 23 of the 1899 Hague Convention for the Pacific Settlement of International Disputes, each contracting power should select four persons at the most, of known competency in questions of international law and of the highest moral reputation. Those persons constitute "national groups" for the purpose of the Convention. Many contracting States have these members to form their national groups for other purposes, a point to be discussed later. If any contracting parties wished to have recourse to the PCA, they could jointly choose arbitrators from that list. Failing to do so by agreement, each party shall appoint two arbitrators and these two together choose a presiding member. See Articles 23 and 24 of the 1899 Convention.

due to lack of confidence in the impartiality and independence of the judges, States could not reach an agreement on the method of appointment of judges,[15] an issue that was only to be resolved subsequently by the League of Nations.

b *The First World Court—PCIJ*

The creation of the PCA, of course, did not prevent the outbreak of the First World War. Despite the pacifist movement in Europe, the right to war for the settlement of disputes or for the pursuit of national policy was not prohibited in international law until much later.[16] In the wake of WWI, the League of Nations was founded, and the idea to establish a permanent world court for the settlement of international disputes resurfaced. By then, the idea of judicial settlement of inter-State disputes was received more favourably by States. Members of the League of Nations agreed that, "if there should arise between them any dispute likely to lead to a rupture, which could not be satisfactorily settled by diplomacy, they would submit the matter either to arbitration or judicial settlement or to enquiry by the Council."[17] For that purpose, Article 14 of the Covenant of the League provided that:

15 At the second Hague Peace Conference, a recommendation for a Judicial Arbitration Court was adopted. As is recorded, in his instructions to the American delegates to the 1907 Hague Peace Conference, Elihu Root, the American Secretary of State, said, "There can be no doubt that the principal objection to arbitration rests not upon the unwillingness of nations to submit their controversies to impartial arbitration, but upon an apprehension that the arbitrations to which they submit may not be impartial. It has been a very general practice for arbitrators to act, not as judges deciding questions of fact and law upon record before them under a sense of judicial responsibility, but as negotiators effecting settlements of the questions brought before them in accordance with the traditions and usages and subject to all the considerations and influences which affect diplomatic agents…." See Kaj Hobér, *op. cit. supra* footnote 8, p. 26.

16 The 1899 Hague Convention for the Pacific Settlement of International Disputes restrained the right to use force, encouraging the resort to peaceful settlement through good offices or mediation. The same was contained in the 1907 Hague Conventions, restraining the use of war to seek the recovery of debts. But these provisions were not mandatory, with limited control over States' actions. The Covenant of the League of Nations further restrained the member States' right to resort to war with certain limitations in terms of both time and conditions. Under the 1928 Kellogg-Briand Pact, the contracting parties "condemn[ed] recourse to war for the solution of international controversies, and renounce[d] it, as an instrument of national policy in their relations with one another." They undertook to settle their disputes by pacific means. The Pact outlawed war without indicating any exceptions. The parties, however, reserved their position in case of self-defence. See Kellogg-Briand Pact 1928.

17 See Article 12, paragraph 1 and Article 13, paragraphs 1 and 2, of the Covenant of the League of Nations.

> The Council shall formulate and submit to the Members of the League for adoption plans for the establishment of a Permanent Court of International Justice. The Court shall be competent to hear and determine any dispute of an international character which the parties thereto submit to it. The Court may also give an advisory opinion upon any dispute or question referred to it by the Council or by the Assembly.

In order to fulfil that objective, the Council of the League, in 1920, appointed a Committee of ten jurists of different nationalities to prepare a plan for the preparation of the Permanent Court. The Committee in due course submitted the plan, "draft scheme," to the Council for adoption and approval. The text of the "draft scheme" was approved by the Council and the Assembly respectively. In order to enter into force, the text was still subject to the ratifications of the Protocol of 16 December 1920 attached thereto by the majority of the member States of the League. The Protocol entered into force in September 1921. As a result, the text acquired the status of an international convention; it could not be amended without the consent of the member States. The "draft scheme" thus became the Statute of the Permanent Court of International Justice (PCIJ), the first World Court. The PCIJ met for the first time in January 1922.

The PCIJ set up a number of important precedents, which are, to a large extent, still carried on by the ICJ today.

The Permanent Court was composed of fifteen judges of different nationalities.[18] The candidates for the election to the Permanent Court were not nominated by State governments, but by the national groups of the State parties to the League. The national group of each State was formed by the four arbitrators that that State had designated to the PCA.[19] The national group should consult with its highest national court of justice and academic society of international law before the nominations were made. Each group could nominate four candidates, but no more than two could be of their own nationality. States which

18 Under the 1920 Statute, the PCIJ consisted of 11 judges, and 4 deputy-judges. Deputy-judges would not sit on the bench unless any of the judges could not perform his functions. The Statute was revised once in 1929 with two major changes. The first was to expand the number of judges from 11 to 15. Secondly, it added a new chapter to deal with the question of advisory opinions. The right to institute the advisory proceedings was confined to the Council and the Assembly. In 1930, the Assembly decided to elect 15 judges and 4 deputy-judges. The deputy-judges ceased to exercise their function when the revised Statute came into force in 1936.

19 To date, there are 120 States who are members to the PCA. See PCA, "Member States," https://pca-cpa.org/en/about/introduction/member-states/, 14 June 2016.

were not parties to the PCA could form special national groups for that purpose. This method was apparently designed to ensure the quality and integrity of the candidates.

The members of the Permanent Court were elected by the Council and the Assembly separately. Those who got absolute majority votes in both organs were elected.[20] This procedure was presumably to safeguard the interests of the big powers in the Council and that of the members of the Assembly.

Each member had a nine-year term and could be re-elected. Judges received annual salaries and pensions budgeted from the League,[21] and at the same time they were subject to strict rules regarding the holding of incompatible offices.[22] Every three years, one third of the members would be elected. The term of the President and the Vice-President was also three years.[23]

Under the Statute, the Permanent Court as a whole should represent the main forms of civilization and the principal legal systems of the world, but in fact it was comprised of judges primarily from Europe and America, with a very small number of judges from Asia,[24] and none from Africa. In each case, the parties might also appoint judges *ad hoc*, if there were no members on the bench who were of their nationality. Judges *ad hoc* took part in the Court's decision on terms of complete equality with the members of the Court.[25] This judge *ad hoc* mechanism safeguarded the same interest that States had in the appointment of arbitrators.

The PCIJ was seated in The Hague at the Peace Palace with its registry headed by the Registrar. Its official languages were French and English.

By virtue of Article 14 of the League Covenant, the PCIJ had two kinds of jurisdiction: contentious and advisory. In other words, it was to settle disputes between States and give advisory opinion on issues of international law

---

20 The election procedure was much more complicated than this. In case the two bodies could not agree, after three meetings, a joint committee of the two bodies may be called upon to choose one name for each place still vacant, a procedure that was rarely used. See Articles 11 and 12 of the Statute of the PCIJ.

21 Although institutionally the PCIJ was not part of the League, the election of the judges and the budget of the Court were controlled by the League. See Articles 32 and 33 of the Statute of the PCIJ.

22 See Articles 16 and 17 of the Statute of the PCIJ. All these mechanisms were to ensure the independence of the judges.

23 See Article 21 of the Statute of the PCIJ.

24 Japan was an exception. For China, its first member, Judge Wang Chonghui was deputy-judge from 1922 to 1930. None of the members from major powers served as deputy-judges.

25 See Article 31 of the Statute of the PCIJ.

referred to it by the Council or the Assembly of the League. Only States could bring their disputes to the PCIJ for settlement.

On the judicial competence, the Statute provided for compulsory jurisdiction of the Court. States could by accepting the Optional Clause of the Statute or by acceding to the General Act (for the Pacific Settlement of Disputes) adopted by the League Assembly on 26 September 1928 accept the jurisdiction of the PCIJ in all or any of certain classes of legal disputes. Besides, they could also accept the jurisdiction of the Court through special and separate international agreements.[26] In case of a dispute over the jurisdiction of the Court, the matter was to be decided by the Court.

On the advisory function, both the Council and the Assembly might request an advisory opinion from the Court. In practice, only the Council requested such opinions from the Court on matters relating to the disputes referred to it by the member States, or matters transmitted from individual States or international organizations.

The Permanent Court received 63 cases (36 contentious cases and 27 requests for advisory opinions) on its docket in the 18 years of its judicial function from 1922 to 1940.[27] Because the peace treaties concluded at the end of WWI entrusted the Court with special responsibilities in respect of the pacific settlement of disputes, one half of the contentious cases and more than half of the requests for advisory opinions brought to the Court were ascribed to the territorial transfers effected by the 1919–1920 peace treaties.[28] Many of the advisory opinions in fact concerned disputes between States. Instead of directly instituting contentious proceedings in the Court, the relevant States would submit the dispute to the Court by way of the Council's request for an advisory opinion. That explains why the PCIJ in its short lifespan received so many requests for advisory opinions.

Due to the outbreak of WWII, the Court ceased to function after 1940. It had its last public sitting on 4 December 1939. Its judgments, advisory opinions and orders were published in Series A, B and A/B of its official publications

26 In December 1938 there were 38 States that had accepted the Optional Clause and 23 States having acceded to the General Act. Apart from those two general treaties, there were over 500 international agreements with clauses on compulsory jurisdiction of the Court for disputes arising from the interpretation and application of the treaties. The lists of these agreements are given in Series D of the PCIJ's publications.

27 From 1922 to 1936, during its initial 14 years, the Court met in annual ordinary sessions and, if summoned by the President, also in extraordinary sessions. After the Statute was revised in 1929 and entered into force in 1936, the Court sat permanently in session except during the judicial vacations. See Article 23 of the Statute of the PCIJ.

28 Registry of the International Court of Justice, *The International Court of Justice*, United Nations, 2006, p. 29.

in 76 volumes.[29] The continuous and consistent jurisprudence as developed through the judgments still has a direct bearing on the work of the ICJ to the present day. Their contribution to the development of international law is generally recognized. These series of cases have become a valuable and rich source for the study and research on the PCIJ's work.

c *The World Court under a New Order*

In the political life of the League of Nations, the PCIJ's role in settling international disputes was far from people's expectation, as it was not involved in dealing with the main political issues of the day.[30] Its establishment nevertheless was taken as a positive move. As Judge Hudson observed, "the Court's bolstering of the structure of peace was accomplished through its advisory opinions, through the confidence which it inspired, and through the encouragement which it gave to the extension of the law of pacific settlement, rather than through its disposition of particular disputes."[31]

At the end of the Second World War, at the Moscow conference in 1943, the Allied Powers decided to establish a general international organization for the maintenance of world peace and security for the future world order. A new world court was envisaged in the general framework.[32] During the preparations, two aspects were raised concerning the prospective court: its place in the general structure of the Organization and the organization of the court itself.

29 During the period from 1922–1940, the PCIJ rendered 34 judgments (11 on jurisdiction or other preliminary questions, 23 on merits) and 27 advisory opinions, with one request for advisory opinion withdrawn by the Council, six cases withdrawn by the parties and two cases whose proceedings were discontinued. The numbers of cases and judgments are differently presented in the official publications of the Registry of the Court. One different account is 29 contentious cases and 27 requests for advisory opinions. See *ibid.*, p. 29; Registry of the International Court of Justice, *The Permanent Court of International Justice: 1922–2012*, 2012, pp. 55–67, 201.

30 In Spiermann's words, the work of the PCIJ was "but a footnote." Ole Spiermann, *International Legal Argument in the Permanent Court of International Justice: The Rise of the International Judiciary*, Cambridge University Press, 2005, p. 132.

31 Shabtai Rosenne, *The Law and Practice of the International Court, 1920–2005, Vol. 1, The Court and the United Nations*, 4th edition, Martinus Nijhoff Publishers, 2006, p. 1, citing Manley O. Hudson, *International Tribunals: Past and Future*, Carnegie Endowment for International Peace, 1944, pp. 238–239.

32 Already in 1942, the United States and the United Kingdom declared themselves in favour of creating or re-establishing an international court after the war. In 1943, at the Moscow conference, the Joint Four Nations Declaration referred to the need to establish a general international organization. At the 1944 Dumbarton Oaks conference, the principles of the world organization were laid down. At the 1945 Yalta conference, the voting procedure at the Security Council was agreed upon.

Based on the discussions of the Allied Powers, the Proposals for the Establishment of a General International Organization, known as the Dumbarton Oaks Proposals, were announced in October 1944. Following that, a committee of jurists representing 44 States held its meetings to prepare the draft Statute of the International Court of Justice for submission to the San Francisco Conference. As the Charter of the United Nations was adopted at the San Francisco Conference, each of the major organs took its definitive form.

In the general structure of the Organization, among others, the Security Council bears the primary responsibility for the maintenance of peace and security, while the General Assembly is entrusted with the task for the general welfare of the world. The Court is the principal judicial organ of the United Nations with two jurisdictions: contentious jurisdiction and advisory competence. By virtue of Article 92 of the Charter of the United Nations, the ICJ largely continues the practice of its predecessor as its Statute is based on the Statute of the PCIJ. The new Court, nonetheless, possesses several distinctive features.

First, the ICJ constitutes one of the six major organs of the United Nations, alongside the General Assembly, the Security Council, the Economic and Social Council, the Trusteeship Council and the Secretariat. The PCIJ, although organically linked with the League of Nations for the election of its members and the budget of its function, was not part of the League.

The Court is the only major organ of the United Nations that is not situated in the Headquarters of the Organization in New York, but seated in the same site as was the PCIJ—the Peace Palace in The Hague.[33]

Secondly, the Statute of the ICJ, although based on the Statute of the PCIJ, is annexed to the Charter and constitutes an integral part of it. All the UN member States are *ipso facto* parties to the ICJ Statute. States that are not members of the United Nations may become parties to the Statute on conditions to be determined in each case by the General Assembly upon the recommendation of the Security Council. Institutionally the Court is closely linked with the decision-making organs of the United Nations.

Thirdly, according to Article 94 of the Charter, member States are obliged to comply with the decisions of the Court in any case to which they are parties. If any party to a case fails to perform the obligations incumbent upon it under a judgment rendered by the Court, the other party may have recourse to the Security Council. Should the circumstances so require, the Security Council may be called upon to consider taking measures to ensure compliance.

33 During the war time, as there were no more judicial business and no further elections of judges, the Court moved to Geneva in 1940, with one single judge sitting in The Hague assisted by a few Registry officials of Dutch nationality. Systematically, the two institutions are often conveniently referred to as "the World Court."

The PCIJ met for the last time in October 1945 when it decided to take all appropriate measures to transfer its archives and effects to the ICJ. The judges of the PCIJ all resigned on 31 January 1946. The election of the first members of the ICJ took place six days later at the First Session of the UN General Assembly and Security Council on 6 February 1946.[34] Months later, the Court elected Judge Jose Gustavo Guerrero (El Salvador), the last President of the PCIJ, as its first President, symbolically ensuring the continuity between the two Courts.

2 A Hindsight—70 Years' Experience

By the end of June 2016, there have been 135 contentious cases filed before the Court and 26 requests submitted to it for advisory opinions, making a total of 161 cases placed on its General List.[35] Given the time span of seven decades, the Court's work, in terms of the number of cases it has received, does not seem particularly impressive, even compared with its predecessor: the Permanent Court had 63 cases before it in the course of its eighteen operational years. Of course, it goes without saying that quantity is but one of the factors to gauge the success of the work of the Court. Moreover, as a judicial organ, the Court cannot solicit its clients. In other words, it is up to the States and international organizations to decide when to come to the Court. Unlike its predecessor, the PCIJ, the Court was not entrusted to deal with any particular category of issues left over by WWII.

As the principal judicial organ, the Court does not function in a vacuum. What took place in the wake of WWII and what has happened in international affairs since then has equally left its footprint on the work of the Court, albeit in a unique way.

Professor Shabtai Rosenne, a generally recognized authority on the work of the Court, in his work on the *Law and Practice of the International Court*, made the following observation:

> Whatever the present Court's superficial resemblances to and descent from the Permanent Court, it cannot be regarded as being the same institution under a new name, or as meeting the same needs. From many points of view the League of Nations represented a transitional stage from the international law and organization of the nineteenth century based

34 Because of that, now each newly elected member at the regular change of composition of the Court starts his/her term on that very date.

35 It is to be noted that in different academic sources, different statistics are given.

> upon the Westphalian European State-system, with its emphasis on the individualist conception of national sovereignty, to the highly integrated world of the end of the twentieth century, in which the independent state is not the only actor on the international plane. This is experiencing a vast extension of the scope of international law accompanying the slow development of a new conception of sovereignty in which the emphasis is placed upon the collective duties of States and their interdependence, alongside their independent existence in which State sovereignty is still a potent political factor. It is also witnessing, in all parts of the world, new types of State organization and new conceptions of the role of government in human affairs.[36]

This fundamental change has taken several stages in the Court's development.[37]

a *The Initial Success—1946 to 1965*

The first twenty years as the initial period for the Court, on the whole, was quite productive and fruitful, regardless of the increasing tensions between the two superpowers in the aftermath of the War. A year after it started its work in April 1946, the Court received its first case instituted by the United Kingdom against Albania, the *Corfu Channel* case.[38] In this case, the Court not only made important pronouncements on State responsibility, but also set some precedents on the rules of evidence and expert testimony. This initial period lasted until the Court delivered its judgment in the "Second Phase" of the *South West Africa* cases in 1966. During this period, there were 37 contentious cases and 12 requests for advisory opinions filed in the Court. The Court rendered 32 judgments and 13 advisory opinions. 16 cases were removed from the Court's list as a result of lack of jurisdiction or by agreement of the parties.

---

36 Shabtai Rosenne, *op. cit. supra* footnote 31, *Vol. I, The Court and the United Nations,* p. 7.

37 Some scholars have different appreciations of the Court's work and divided it into different phases. For example, Shabtai Rosenne counted the whole period starting from the time of the PCIJ and divided it into five periods, while Hugh Thirlway considers that the period between the mid-1960s to the late 1970s was a special period for the Court, and since 1989 till the present date, the Court has entered a new phase. See Shabtai Rosenne, *op. cit. supra* footnote 31, *Vol. I, The Court and the United Nations,* pp. 16–32; Hugh Thirlway, "The International Court of Justice 1989–2009: At the Heart of the Dispute Settlement System?," *Netherlands International Law Review*, Vol. 57, December 2010, pp. 347–395. The author thinks that this is mainly a matter of appreciation.

38 The date of a case is that on which the case is instituted in the Court, rather than that on which the judgment is delivered.

This stage bears a couple of attributes. First, the composition of the Court was affected by the fact that, against the backdrop of the Cold War, Europe was divided into two blocs. The increased number of UN members from the Eastern Bloc reflected the changing political landscape in Europe. In the Permanent Court, although there were members from the eastern part of Europe, for example, Romania, Poland and Yugoslavia, they did not represent any particular legal or social system of their region.[39] The Soviet Union and the other socialist countries took quite a different approach towards the Court as well as international law.[40] Some cases brought up against them during this period deepened their concern that the Court was a political instrument of the West.[41] Their negative attitude towards the jurisdiction of the Court was to a large extent responsible for the situation where for nearly fifty years there was an obvious disinclination among States to submit their disputes to the judicial procedure of the Court for settlement and general reluctance to accept its compulsory jurisdiction.

Secondly, under the Statute, the advisory competence of the Court was more restrictive than that of its predecessor, confined to answering legal questions to provide legal guidance for future actions rather than settling any concrete disputes before the General Assembly or the Security Council. In the League of Nations' time, the Council could act on the unanimity of its members to request an advisory opinion of the Permanent Court for the resolution of a particular dispute between the member States. Under Article 96 of the Charter, only the General Assembly and the Security Council may be, by a majority vote, entitled to make such requests of the ICJ. Such voting system would enable the General Assembly to request an advisory opinion of the Court even in the event that the General Assembly is faced with significant opposition from some States. Other organs of the United Nations or specialized agencies may,

39 On the political nature of the composition of the Court, see Edward McWhinney, "Judicial Opinion-Writing in the World Court and the Western Sahara Advisory Opinion," *Heidelberg Journal of International Law*, Vol. 37, 1977, pp. 1–42.

40 For some relevant reading, see Edward McWhinney, *The International Court of Justice and the Western Tradition of International Law*, Martinus Nijhoff, 1987, pp. 12–16.

41 A number of cases instituted in the mid-1950s by the United States or the United Kingdom against the Soviet Union or some other Eastern European countries for aerial incidents or treatment of their aircraft and crew showed the political confrontation of the two Camps in the Cold War. The so-called "unwilling respondent" was a noticeable phenomenon of the time. See Bardo Fassbender, "Article 9," in Andreas Zimmermann, Christian Tomuschat and Karin Oellers-Frahm (eds.), *The Statute of the International Court of Justice: A Commentary*, Oxford University Press, 2006, p. 273.

with the authorization of the General Assembly, also request advisory opinions of the ICJ on legal questions arising within the scope of their activities.[42]

Thirdly, the Court, acting as the principal judicial organ of the United Nations, delivered a number of important judgments and advisory opinions that proved to have a lasting effect on the development of international law, particularly in respect of the international personality of international organizations (*Reparation for Injuries Suffered in the Service of the United Nations, Advisory Opinion,* 1949), treaty reservations (*Reservations to the Convention on the Prevention and Punishment of the Crime of Genocide, Advisory Opinion,* 1951), fishery rights (*Fisheries* (*United Kingdom* v. *Norway*), 1951) and conditions for diplomatic protection (*Nottebohm case* (*Liechtenstein* v. *Guatemala*), 1953). Moreover, jurisprudence on the procedural rules and practice of the Court were further enriched.

b *A Dormant Period—1966 to 1984*

The second stage lasting from 1966 to 1984 can be described as "a dormant period" for the Court. Because of the position taken by the Court in the judgment of 18 July 1966 in the *South West Africa* cases (Second Phase),[43] the Court's reputation suffered great damage.[44] As a result, its workload was considerably decreased. During those 18 years, the Court received only 16 contentious cases and 6 requests for advisory opinions. It delivered 17 judgments and 5 advisory opinions. In between, in 1966, 1968, 1969, 1975 and 1977, there was no single case submitted to the Court. Out of 16 contentious cases, 9 cases related to maritime delimitation and fisheries matters.[45]

42 There are 16 specialized agencies within the United Nations family that are authorized to submit such requests.

43 *South West Africa cases* (*Ethiopia* v. *South Africa*), *Second Phase, Judgment of 18 July 1966, I.C.J. Reports 1966,* p. 6.

44 Following the decision, the General Assembly refused to pass certain budgetary estimates for the Court as a sign of its disproval. Shabtai Rosenne, *op. cit. supra* footnote 31, *Vol. 1, The Court and the United Nations*, p. 17, footnote. 27.

45 *North Sea Continental Shelf* (*Federal Republic of Germany/Netherlands*), 1967; *North Sea Continental Shelf* (*Federal Republic of Germany/Denmark*), 1967; *Fisheries Jurisdiction* (*Federal Republic of Germany* v. *Iceland*), 1972; *Fisheries Jurisdiction* (*United Kingdom of Great Britain and Northern Ireland* v. *Iceland*), 1972; *Aegean Sea Continental Shelf* (*Greece* v. *Turkey*), 1976; *Continental Shelf* (*Tunisia/Libyan Arab Jamahiriya*), 1978; *Delimitation of the Maritime Boundary in the Gulf of Maine Area* (*Canada/United States of America*), 1981; *Continental Shelf* (*Libyan Arab Jamahiriya/Malta*), 1982; *Application for Revision and Interpretation of the Judgment of 24 February 1982 in the Case concerning the* Continental Shelf (Tunisia/Libyan Arab Jamahiriya) (*Tunisia* v. *Libyan Arab Jamahiriya*), 1984.

Given its negative impact on the work of the Court, it is worthwhile to recall the ruling of the Court in the *South West Africa* cases in the present context. In 1960, Ethiopia and Liberia respectively instituted proceedings before the Court against the Union of South Africa for a dispute concerning the interpretation and application of the Mandate under the League of Nations.[46] The Applicants claimed that South West Africa, the then South Africa-administered former German colony, was a Territory under the League of Nations, which was entrusted to South Africa as a Mandate. In the opinions of Ethiopia and Liberia, although the League ceased to exist, the Mandate as an international treaty in force continued to govern the Territory. South Africa therefore remained bound by the international obligations set forth in Article 22 of the League Covenant and those in the Mandate, in particular obligations to submit to the supervision and control of the General Assembly with regard to the exercise of the Mandate, to transmit to the United Nations petitions from the inhabitants of the Territory, as well as to submit annual reports to the satisfaction of the United Nations in accordance with Article 6 of the Mandate. South Africa's practice of *apartheid* was in violation of its obligations under Article 2 of the Mandate and Article 22 of the Covenant. It had failed to promote to the utmost the material and moral well-being and the social progress of the inhabitants of the Territory as required by Article 2 of the Mandate, had treated the Territory in a manner inconsistent with its international status, and had

46 These cases were instituted against a rather complicated history with regard to the Mandate system set up under the League of Nations in South West Africa (now Namibia) which was entrusted to South Africa. Since South Africa refused to convert the Mandate into a trusteeship agreement under the United Nations and failed to maintain its international obligations in the Territory, the General Assembly had requested three times, in 1949, 1954 and 1955, the Court for advisory opinions on the legal status of the Mandate system in South West Africa and the obligations of South Africa in that regard. In its first advisory opinion, the Court found that the Mandate system was still in force, and the obligations arising therefrom were still binding on South Africa. In the second and third opinions, the Court clarified the voting procedure on questions relating to reports and petitions concerning the Territory and the admissibility of hearings of petitioners by the Committee on South West Africa. As these advisory opinions had no binding force and South Africa refused to cooperate, the General Assembly adopted resolution 1361 (XIV) on 17 November 1959, and drew the attention of the member States to the possibility of their bringing a contentious case against South Africa. This calling was answered during the Second African States Conference held in 1960. Ethiopia and Liberia decided to institute proceedings in the Court against South Africa. By then, the decolonization process was well under way.

thereby impeded opportunities for self-determination by the inhabitants of the Territory.[47]

The Union of South Africa, the respondent, for its part, argued that the Mandate for South West Africa had lapsed on the dissolution of the League of Nations, and that it was, in consequence, no longer subject to any legal obligations thereunder.[48]

By the Order of 20 May 1961, the two actions were joined as the Court considered that the submissions of the two cases were almost identical for the protection of the same interest.

As South Africa subsequently raised four preliminary objections to the jurisdiction of the Court in the case, under Article 79, paragraph 5, of the Rules of Court, the proceedings on the merits were suspended. The Court had to first determine the issue of jurisdiction. On 21 December 1962, the Court delivered its judgment on the preliminary objections. By eight votes for and seven against, the Court found that it had jurisdiction to adjudicate upon the merits of the dispute.[49] In other words, it rejected South Africa's preliminary objections, upholding that, among others, the Mandate for South West Africa was a treaty or convention in force and despite the dissolution of the League, Ethiopia and Liberia had *locus standi* under Article 7, paragraph 2, of the Mandate to invoke the jurisdiction of the Court.

The cases thus continued. After written pleadings, the Court carried on oral hearings in 1965, which lasted for several months, with 14 witnesses and experts called to testify before the Court. Although the parties pleaded on the merits of the cases, namely, whether the *apartheid* policy imposed by South Africa in the Territory was contrary to international law and whether South Africa was in breach of its international obligations, the Court, however, finally reached a finding relating to the question of the applicants' standing in the present cases.

On 18 July 1966, the Court delivered its judgment, rejecting the claims submitted by Ethiopia and Liberia on the ground that they failed to have established any legal right or interest appertaining to them in the subject-matter of their claims.[50] With 14 votes equally divided, President Spender cast the

---

47 See *South West Africa* (*Ethiopia* v. *South Africa; Liberia* v. *South Africa*), *Second Phase, Judgment of 18 July 1966, I.C.J. Reports 1966*, pp. 10–13, 15–16.

48 See *ibid.*, pp. 14, 16–17.

49 *South West Africa cases* (*Ethiopia* v. *South Africa; Liberia* v. *South Africa*), *Preliminary objections, Judgment of 21 December 1962: I.C.J. Reports 1962*, p. 347.

50 See *South West Africa* (*Ethiopia* v. *South Africa; Liberia* v. *South Africa*), *Second Phase, Judgment of 18 July 1966, I.C.J. Reports 1966*, pp. 19–51, paras. 9–99.

deciding vote.[51] The Court, by taking a strict legal positivist approach to the interpretation and application of international obligations under the Mandate, managed to get around the legal findings of the 1962 judgment that had been delivered only four years earlier, and virtually sanctioned the extension of the *apartheid* regime of racial segregation in South West Africa. Dissenting opinions appended to the judgment equally demonstrated intellectually how the Court was divided on the subject.[52]

This decision was rightfully condemned by the General Assembly and the international community at large. The General Assembly on 27 October 1966, three months after the judgment, adopted resolution 2145 (XXI) and decided that South Africa was in breach of the Mandate and the General Assembly, by terminating the Mandate, assumed direct responsibility for the Territory of South West Africa until its independence.[53]

The *South West Africa* cases are regarded by many as the most frustrating piece of litigation ever conducted by the World Court. One thing is clear: the judicial division in the Court was just a reflection of the changing time. By the time of the judgment of 18 July 1966, six years after the adoption of the General Assembly resolution 1514 (XV) on the Declaration on the Granting of Independence to Colonial Countries and Peoples in 1960,[54] most former colonies in Asia and Africa had gained independence and become members of the United Nations. That had exerted significant impact on the functional structure

51 Sir Gerald Fitzmaurice is known to have been the principal author of the majority opinion in the *South West Africa* cases (Second Phase), signed on behalf of the Court's majority by President Spender. See Edward McWhinney, *op. cit. supra* footnote 40, p. 39.

52 In this regard, it is particularly helpful to read the dissenting opinions of Vice-President Wellington Koo and Judge Jessup, *I.C.J. Reports 1966*, p. 216, and p. 325; Edward McWhinney, "'Internationalizing' the International Court: the Quest for Ethno-cultural and Legal-systemic Representativeness," in Emmanuel G. Bello and Bola A. Ajibola (eds.), *Essays in Honour of Judge Taslim Olawale Elias,* Martinus Nijhoff Publishers, 1992, Vol. I, pp. 279–280.

53 Politically there were a series of significant actions taken by the United Nations that condemned the continued presence of the South African authorities in Namibia. In addition to General Assembly resolution 2145(XXI), on 20 March 1969, the Security Council adopted resolution 264, calling on the Government of South Africa to withdraw immediately its administration from the Territory. On 30 January 1970, by its resolution 276, the Security Council declared that continued presence in Namibia by South African authorities was illegal.

54 On 14 December 1960, the General Assembly adopted resolution 1514 (XV) on the Declaration on the Granting of Independence to Colonial Countries and Peoples.

of the Organization, particularly with regard to the practice of geographical distribution. Against this political background, the Court's judgment in the *South West Africa* cases was unsurprisingly perceived as "an exercise in legal Eurocentrism by a Western-dominated, 'Western' tribunal."[55] Most African and Asian States considered that the Court's composition was partly responsible for the decision in the *South West Africa* cases. Derived from their dissatisfaction over the judgment was the heightened interest of States in the election processes of the members of the Court. In addition to attending regular, triennial elections of the Court, they began to more rigorously scrutinize national candidacies for election to the Court, and regional geographic distribution of the Court became a hot issue in the United Nations. The change of regional distribution of the Court was incremental and progressive, but the *South West Africa* cases definitely served as a catalyst in speeding up the process.[56]

In July 1970, in light of the situation in South West Africa, the Security Council adopted resolution 284, requesting an advisory opinion from the Court on the same subject-matter as presented by Ethiopia and Liberia in 1960, namely, what are the legal consequences for States of the continued presence of South

55 Edward McWhinney, *op. cit. supra* footnote 52, p. 278. See also Victor Kattan, "Decolonizing the International Court of Justice: The Experience of Judge Sir Muhammad Zafrulla Khan in the South West Africa Cases", *Asian Journal of International Law*, Vol. 5, issue 2, July 2015, pp. 310–355.

56 The immediate result from the political backlash against the judgment was the defeat of the Australian candidate, Sir Kenneth Bailey, who was running for the election to succeed the retiring President Percy Spender, who had resigned, on behalf of the Court's majority, for the judgment in that case. See Edward McWhinney, *op. cit. supra* footnote 52, p. 278. In 1963, by General Assembly resolution 1991 (XVIII), which entered into force on 31 August 1965, the Security Council was expanded from 11 to 15 members, with the regional distribution as follows: Asia: three; Africa: three; Latin-America: two, Eastern Europe: two; Western Europe and others: five. The five permanent members are China, France, Russia (former U.S.S.R.), United Kingdom and the United States. In the 1969 election of the members of the Court, the same regional distribution of the Security Council applied to the Court and such practice was gradually accepted as a general principle. Out of the three members from Africa, the understanding is that one should come from Arab countries, and the two others should come from Sub-Sahara, one from the Anglophonic common law system and the other from the Francophonic civil law system. With the election of Judge Shahabuddeen to the Court in 1987, the Caribbean was considered a possible sub-group within the Latin-American group. In the 2014 triennial election, Judge Robinson from Jamaica was elected. As a result, there is currently no member from the Spanish-speaking countries of Latin America in the Court. For details, see Shabtai Rosenne, *The World Court, What It Is and How It Works*, 5th completely revised edition, Martinus Nijhoff Publishers, 1995, pp. 54–62.

Africa in Namibia (South West Africa). In its Opinion, the Court by an overwhelming majority gave the following answers:

(1) the continued presence of South Africa in Namibia being illegal, South Africa is under obligation to withdraw its administration from Namibia immediately and thus put an end to its occupation of the Territory;
(2) States Members of the United Nations are under obligation to recognize the illegality of South Africa's presence in Namibia and the invalidity of its acts on behalf of or concerning Namibia, and to refrain any acts and in particular any dealings with the Government of South Africa implying recognition of the legality of, or lending support or assistance to, such presence and administration;
(3) it is incumbent upon States which are not Members of the United Nations to give assistance, within the scope of subparagraph (2) above, in the action which has been taken by the United Nations with regard to Namibia.[57]

Notwithstanding this lopsided, reversed position, damage to the Court was done. The result was a substantial falling off in all the business of the Court, both contentious and advisory. In 1970 the Court delivered the judgment in the *Barcelona Traction* case, in which it drew a distinction between the obligations of a State towards the international community as a whole, obligations *erga omnes*, and those bilateral obligations arising vis-à-vis another State.[58] This important pronouncement was perceived as an attempt on the part of the Court to mend the judicial "self-inflicted wound" left over by the *South West Africa* cases, by underscoring the importance of communal common interests. The effect of this effort was only to be felt much later.

c *Towards a Revival—1985 to 1990*

The third phase is relatively short as it was marked as a transitional period before the Court was fully revived. This period possesses a number of features.

First of all, the workload of the Court was modestly but discernibly on the rise. During this short time span, there were 9 contentious cases filed before the Court and 2 requests for advisory opinions.

Moreover, disputes in the contentious cases before the Court covered a wider scope of international legal issues, displaying a reviving general interest in

57 *Legal Consequences for States of the Continued Presence of South Africa in Namibia (South West Africa) notwithstanding Security Council Resolution 276 (1970), Advisory Opinion, I.C.J. Reports 1971*, p. 58, para, 133.

58 Case concerning the *Barcelona Traction, Light and Power Company, Limited (Belgium v. Spain), Second Phase, Judgment, I.C.J. Reports 1970*, p. 32, para. 33.

judicial settlement by the Court. In addition to its traditional types of cases concerning land disputes and maritime delimitation, a number of cases concerned the use of force,[59] and sovereignty over natural resources.[60] In *Certain Phosphate Lands in Nauru* (*Nauru* v. *Australia*), although the case was ultimately withdrawn by the agreement of the parties, the Court rendered its judgment on the question of jurisdiction. Among the cases involving use of force, the case concerning *Military and Paramilitary Activities in and against Nicaragua* (*Nicaragua* v. *United States of America*) was the most complicated one.

The United States, as the unwilling respondent, raised objections to the jurisdiction of the Court and the admissibility of the application. After the Court delivered its judgment on jurisdiction and admissibility, rejecting the United States' objections,[61] the United States withdrew from the legal proceedings.[62] Subsequently the Court rendered its judgment on the merits of the case, declaring that the United States was in breach of its obligations not to violate the sovereignty of another State, not to interfere in the internal affairs of another State, and not to use force against another State under customary international law.[63]

The judgment was severely assailed by the United States government as a "political decision," but regarded as a watershed judgment by international law scholars.[64] It was the first case that involved current use of force and direct interference in the internal affairs of one party. The judgment was mainly perceived as a judicial response to the foreign policy of the Reagan Administration.[65] The negative attitude of the United States towards the legal proceedings

---

59 *Military and Paramilitary Activities in and against Nicaragua* (*Nicaragua* v. *United States of America*), *Merits, Judgment, I.C.J. Reports 1986*, p. 14. A month after the delivery of the decision by the Court in the *Military and Paramilitary Activities* case, Nicaragua instituted two separate proceedings in the Court against Costa Rica and Honduras respectively for border and transborder armed actions against the sovereignty of Nicaragua. Thanks to the 1987 Agreement signed by the Presidents of five States of Central America, Nicaragua ultimately discontinued the legal proceedings against Costa Rica.

60 For example, the case concerning *Certain Phosphate Lands in Nauru* (*Nauru* v. *Australia*) filed by Nauru against Australia in 1989.

61 *Military and Paramilitary Activities in and against Nicaragua* (*Nicaragua* v. *United States of America*), *Jurisdiction and Admissibility, Judgment, I.C.J. Reports 1984*, p. 442, para. 113.

62 "Statement of Department of State on US Withdrawal from Nicaragua Proceedings, 18 January 1985," in "Contemporary Practice of the United States," *American Journal of International Law*, Vol. 79, 1985, p. 438.

63 *Military and Paramilitary Activities in and against Nicaragua* (*Nicaragua* v. *United States of America*), *Merits, Judgment, I.C.J. Reports 1986*, pp. 146–149, para. 292.

64 Edward McWhinney, *op. cit. supra* footnote 52, p. 281.

65 It is also considered that the Indian Presidency played a role for the Court to reach its decision. See Abram Chayes, "Nicaragua, The United States, and the World Court," *Columbia*

indicated a shift of its position on the jurisdiction of the Court. On 7 October 1985, after the Court delivered its judgment on jurisdiction and admissibility, the United States withdrew its declaration accepting the compulsory jurisdiction of the Court under Article 36, paragraph 2, of the Statute, which it had deposited on 26 August 1946.[66]

In addition to the above-discussed two features, proceedings during this period were also getting more complicated. In November 1981, Canada and the United States, by a Special Agreement, submitted their maritime dispute to the Court, requiring their case to be heard by an *ad hoc* chamber instead of the full Court.[67] That was the first time in the history of the Court that the parties to a dispute resorted to the chamber procedure, a possibility embodied in the Statute and the Rules of Court. Under the Statute of the Court, there are three types of chambers. One is the Chamber of Summary Procedure, a standing mechanism for States to use for the speedy despatch of settlement. In practice, there was only one instance in 1924 when this mechanism was invoked. The second type is the special chamber that may be set up for particular kinds of cases, for instance, cases relating to labour, transit and communication. This was designed under the Statute of the PCIJ and continued by the ICJ. By the amendment of Article 26, paragraph 2, of the Statute in 1945, the third kind of chamber, the *ad hoc* chamber, was added. The Court may establish an *ad hoc* chamber to deal with a particular case. The number of judges is to be determined by the Court with the agreement of the parties.[68]

Subsequently in 1983 during the border conflict between Burkina Faso and Mali, with the intervention of the Organization of African Unity (currently the African Union), the two countries agreed to submit their dispute to an *ad hoc*

Law Review, Vol. 85, 1985, pp. 1445–1482; Paul Reichler, "Holding America to Its Own Best Standards: Abe Chayes and Nicaragua in the World Court," *Harvard International Law Journal*, Vol. 42, 2001, pp. 15–46.

66 Twenty five years after the delivery of the judgment on the merits, the then American judge on the bench of the Court still expressed strong criticism against the Court for upholding its jurisdiction. See Stephen Schwebel, "Celebrating a Fraud on the Court," *American Journal of International Law*, Vol. 106, 2012, pp. 102–105; Stephen Schwebel, "The *Nicaragua* Case: A Response to Paul Reichler," *American Journal of International Law*, Vol. 106, 2012, pp. 582–583.

67 *Delimitation of the Maritime Boundary in the Gulf of Maine Area (Canada/United States of America), Judgment, I.C.J. Reports 1984*, p. 246.

68 Shabtai Rosenne, *op. cit. supra* footnote 56, pp. 75–76. The Court set up a special chamber for environmental law cases, but as the mechanism was not resorted to, it has not been recomposed since 2006.

chamber of the ICJ for settlement.[69] In 1986, El Salvador and Honduras again chose to use an *ad hoc* chamber to settle their territorial disputes.[70] The following year, the United States instituted proceedings against Italy concerning the acquisition of the American assets by the Italian authorities, *Elettronica Sicula S.p.A.* (*ELSI*), also resorting to a chamber of five judges.[71]

Given the *ad hoc* nature of a chamber procedure, the choice of the members of the chamber gave rise to heated debates. The selection of the members of the aforementioned chambers, although with a certain discretion left to the parties, did not reflect the geographical distribution that the full Court possesses.[72] If such procedure becomes the normal practice of the Court, the legal and geographical representation of the Court, as required by Article 9 of the Statute, could in fact be evaded.

Another procedural novelty during this period was the third party intervention in contentious cases. Albeit in the Statute, such procedure was rarely invoked in contentious cases during the early practice of the World Court.[73] In the 1986 *Land, Island and Maritime Frontier Dispute* between El Salvador and Honduras, Nicaragua intervened as a third party. In this case, for the first time, the Court accorded permission to a third State to intervene under Article 62 of the Statute. In its judgment, the Court discussed at length the extent of procedural rights acquired by the intervening State as a result of that permission. The Court made it clear that "the intervening State does not become party to the proceedings, and does not acquire the rights, or become subject to the obligations, which attach to the status of a party, under the Statute and Rules of Court, or the general principles of procedural law."[74] This is a landmark case for the third party intervention procedure in the Court's practice.

---

69 *Frontier Dispute (Burkina Faso/Republic of Mali), Judgment, I.C.J. Reports 1986*, p. 554.

70 *Land, Island and Maritime Frontier Dispute (El Salvador/Honduras: Nicaragua intervening), Judgment, I.C.J. Reports 1992*, p. 351.

71 *Elettronica Sicula S.p.A. (ELSI) (United States of America* v. *Italy), Judgment, I.C.J. Reports 1989*, p. 15. It is said that the United States submitted the case as an attempt to mollify domestic criticism of the Administration's attitude towards the Court in the *Military and Paramilitary Activities* case. Shabtai Rosenne, *op. cit. supra* footnote 31, *Vol. I, The Court and the United Nation*. p. 22.

72 The *ad hoc* chamber for the *Delimitation of the Maritime Boundary in the Gulf of Maine Area (Canada/United States of America)* case was composed of five Judges: Judge Ago (Italy), *President of the Chamber*; Judges Gros (France), Mosler (Germany), Schwebel (United States), and Judge *ad hoc* Cohen.

73 It is observed that although the procedure was written in the Statute of the PCIJ as well as in that of the ICJ, in the first 60 years since 1922 there was only one occasion where third party intervention in a contentious case was instituted.

74 *Land, Island and Maritime Frontier Dispute (El Salvador/Honduras: Nicaragua intervening), Application to Intervene, Judgment, I.C.J. Reports 1990*, pp. 135–136, para. 102.

d *New Challenges—1991 to the Present*

Since the beginning of the 1990s, the Court has entered a new phase with considerable changes of its work, in terms of both its clientele and the scope of the subject-matters of the cases before it.

In the first place, with the end of the Cold War, international relations became propitious to international cooperation and promoting international law. Recourse to the ICJ for the peaceful settlement of international disputes was gaining momentum. Such willingness not only came from its traditional clients from the West and Latin America, but also spread to other regions. Among various factors, the changed political landscape, particularly in Europe, exerted direct impact in this area. With the dissolution of the Soviet Union and expansion of the European Union, many Eastern European countries accepted the jurisdiction of the Court.

In the last 25 years, there have been 75 contentious cases filed in the Court and 6 requests for advisory opinions. In the past two decades, the Court's workload has grown significantly, frequently with 10 to 20 pending cases on the docket.[75] The Court has rendered in this period more judgments than in its first 44 years of existence.

Furthermore, during this period the parties appearing before the Court have come from all five continents. Between 1946 and June 2016, nearly 90 States have pleaded in the Court in contentious cases and about 120 States have submitted to the Court their statements in written and oral proceedings in advisory opinion proceedings.[76] In those contentious cases, among the parties,

75 It is noted that in 1989 there were only four cases pending, while in 2010, there were 14 cases, and currently there are 14 cases pending.

76 *The International Court of Justice: Handbook*, 6th edition (available on the ICJ's website), pp. 43–44. A list of States is available at pp. 44–45. It states that "[i]n practice, since the creation of the ICJ [till December 2013] 86 States have been parties to contentious proceedings." It is notable that among these 86 States, Iceland and Turkey never took part in the proceedings against them. Therefore, for the purposes of this lecture, they are not considered as having pleaded in the Court. In addition, in December 2013, Timor-Leste instituted proceedings against Australia on questions relating to the seizure and detention of certain documents and data; in 2014, Marshall Islands took legal actions in the Court against nine nuclear weapons States; the cases against India, Pakistan and the United Kingdom are now pending before the Court; Somalia submitted its maritime dispute with Kenya to the Court for delimitation. This is the first time that these four States (Timor-Leste, Marshall Islands, Somalia and Kenya) have resorted to the jurisdiction of the ICJ.

The number of States which have submitted written or oral statements during advisory proceedings between 1946 and 2013 is 120 (including Palestine). The list of these States can be found in the same book at pp. 87–88. This number has not changed till today, as there has been no advisory proceeding since 2013.

25 States come from Africa, 16 from Latin-America, 13 from Asia, and 34 from Europe and other regions, being either the applicant or the respondent.[77]

Meanwhile, the subject-matters of the cases vary considerably. In terms of scope, they cover a large variety of areas, ranging from traditional domains of territorial[78] and maritime disputes,[79] and use of

77 In the past 25 years, in those contentious cases, 19 cases were instituted by or against African States, 12 cases by or against Asian States, 19 cases by or against Latin-American States, 18 cases by or against Eastern European States and, 35 cases by or against Western States. The high number of cases from Eastern Europe is largely due to the cases concerning *Legality of Use of Force* instituted by Yugoslavia (Serbia and Montenegro) against ten NATO member States for their use of force in Kosovo.

78 For cases on territorial disputes, see *Frontier Dispute* (*Burkina Faso/Republic of Mali*), 1983; *Land, Island and Maritime Frontier Dispute* (*El Salvador/Honduras: Nicaragua intervening*), 1986; *Territorial Dispute* (*Libyan Arab Jamahiriya/Chad*), 1990; *Maritime Delimitation and Territorial Questions between Qatar and Bahrain* (*Qatar* v. *Bahrain*), 1991; *Land and Maritime Boundary between Cameroon and Nigeria* (*Cameroon* v. *Nigeria: Equatorial Guinea intervening*), 1994; *Kasikili/Sedudu Island* (*Botswana/Namibia*), 1996; *Sovereignty over Pulau Ligitan and Pulau Sipadan* (*Indonesia/Malaysia*), 1998; *Territorial and Maritime Dispute between Nicaragua and Honduras in the Caribbean Sea* (*Nicaragua* v. *Honduras*), 1999; *Territorial and Maritime Dispute* (*Nicaragua* v. *Colombia*), 2001; *Frontier Dispute* (*Benin/Niger*), 2002; *Application for Revision of the Judgment of 11 September 1992 in the Case concerning the* Land, Island and Maritime Frontier Dispute (El Salvador/Honduras: Nicaragua intervening) (*El Salvador* v. *Honduras*), 2002; *Sovereignty over Pedra Branca/ Pulau Batu Puteh, Middle Rocks and South Ledge* (*Malaysia/Singapore*), 2003; *Frontier Dispute* (*Burkina Faso/Niger*), 2010; *Request for Interpretation of the Judgment of 15 June 1962 in the Case concerning the* Temple of Preah Vihear (Cambodia *v.* Thailand) (*Cambodia* v. *Thailand*), 2011; *Alleged Violations of Sovereign Rights and Maritime Spaces in the Caribbean Sea* (*Nicaragua* v. *Colombia*), 2013.

79 In the maritime area, the Court remains the mostly used recourse for settling fisheries and maritime delimitation disputes. Its jurisprudence has been well respected by other courts and tribunals. Since 1949 there have been 26 cases on maritime disputes submitted to the Court for adjudication: *Fisheries* (*United Kingdom* v. *Norway*), 1949; *North Sea Continental Shelf* (*Federal Republic of Germany/Denmark*) *and* (*Federal Republic of Germany/ Netherlands*), 1967; *Fisheries Jurisdiction* (*Federal Republic of Germany* v. *Iceland*) *and Fisheries Jurisdiction* (*United Kingdom* v. *Iceland*), 1972; *Aegean Sea Continental Shelf* (*Greece* v. *Turkey*), 1976; *Continental Shelf* (*Tunisia/Libyan Arab Jamahiriya*), 1978; *Delimitation of the Maritime Boundary in the Gulf of Maine Area* (*Canada/United States of America*), 1981; *Continental Shelf* (*Libyan Arab Jamahiriya/Malta*), 1982; *Application for Revision and Interpretation of the Judgment of 24 February 1982 in the Case concerning the* Continental Shelf (Tunisia/Libyan Arab Jamahiriya) (*Tunisia* v. *Libyan Arab Jamahiriya*), 1984; *Land, Island and Maritime Frontier Dispute* (*El Salvador/Honduras: Nicaragua intervening*), 1986; *Maritime Delimitation in the Area between Greenland and Jan Mayen* (*Denmark* v. *Norway*), 1988; *Maritime Delimitation between Guinea-Bissau and Senegal* (*Guinea-Bissau*

force,[80] to contemporary issues of human rights,[81] international humanitarian law,[82] international criminal law,[83] environmental protection,[84] sovereign

v. *Senegal*), 1991; *Maritime Delimitation and Territorial Questions between Qatar and Bahrain* (*Qatar* v. *Bahrain*), 1991; *Land and Maritime Boundary between Cameroon and Nigeria* (*Cameroon* v. *Nigeria: Equatorial Guinea intervening*), 1994; *Fisheries Jurisdiction* (*Spain* v. *Canada*), 1995; *Sovereignty over Pulau Ligitan and Pulau Sipadan* (*Indonesia/Malaysia*), 1998; *Territorial and Maritime Dispute between Nicaragua and Honduras in the Caribbean Sea* (*Nicaragua* v. *Honduras*), 1999; *Territorial and Maritime Dispute* (*Nicaragua* v. *Colombia*), 2001; *Application for Revision of the Judgment of 11 September 1992 in the Case concerning the* Land, Island and Maritime Frontier Dispute (El Salvador/Honduras: Nicaragua intervening) (*El Salvador* v. *Honduras*), 2002; *Sovereignty over Pedra Branca/Pulau Batu Puteh, Middle Rocks and South Ledge* (*Malaysia/Singapore*), 2003; *Maritime Delimitation in the Black Sea* (*Romania* v. *Ukraine*), 2004; *Maritime Dispute* (*Peru* v. *Chile*), 2008; *Question of the Delimitation of the Continental Shelf between Nicaragua and Colombia beyond 200 nautical miles from the Nicaraguan Coast* (*Nicaragua* v. *Colombia*), 2013; *Maritime Delimitation in the Caribbean Sea and the Pacific Ocean* (*Costa Rica* v. *Nicaragua*), 2014; *Maritime Delimitation in the Indian Ocean* (*Somalia* v. *Kenya*), 2014.

80 See *Oil Platforms* (*Islamic Republic of Iran* v. *United States of America*), 1992; cases concerning *Legality of Use of Force* (instituted by Yugoslavia against ten NATO member States), 1999; cases concerning *Armed Activities on the Territory of the Congo* (filed by the Democratic Republic of the Congo against Burundi, Uganda and Rwanda respectively), 1999.

81 There have been a series of cases concerning consular and diplomatic protection: *Vienna Convention on Consular Relations* (*Paraguay* v. *United States of America*), 1998; *Ahmadou Sadio Diallo* (*Republic of Guinea* v. *Democratic Republic of the Congo*), 1998; *LaGrand* (*Germany* v. *United States of America*), 1999; *Avena and Other Mexican Nationals* (*Mexico* v. *United States of America*), 2003.

82 For example, the advisory proceeding: *Legal Consequences of the Construction of a Wall in the Occupied Palestinian Territory*, 2003.

83 Such cases are mainly related to interpretation and application of conventions against genocide, racial discrimination and torture: *Application of the Convention on the Prevention and Punishment of the Crime of Genocide* (*Bosnia and Herzegovina* v. *Serbia and Montenegro*), 1993; *Application of the Convention on the Prevention and Punishment of the Crime of Genocide* (*Croatia* v. *Serbia*), 1999; *Application for Revision of the Judgment of 11 July 1996 in the Case concerning* Application of the Convention on the Prevention and Punishment of the Crime of Genocide (Bosnia and Herzegovina *v.* Yugoslavia), Preliminary Objections (*Yugoslavia* v. *Bosnia and Herzegovina*), 2001; *Application of the International Convention on the Elimination of All Forms of Racial Discrimination* (*Georgia* v. *Russian Federation*), 2008; *Questions relating to the Obligation to Prosecute or Extradite* (*Belgium* v. *Senegal*), 2009.

84 There have been six cases concerning international environmental law: *Gabčíkovo-Nagymaros Project* (*Hungary/Slovakia*), 1993; *Pulp Mills on the River Uruguay* (*Argentina* v. *Uruguay*), 2006; *Aerial Herbicide Spraying* (*Ecuador* v. *Colombia*), 2008; *Whaling in the*

immunity,[85] nuclear weapons,[86] State secession and State succession,[87] etc. In the judgments, the Court has made many important pronouncements on the law. It is not exaggerating to say that never before has the Court been so dynamic in its function as the principal judicial organ of the United Nations, and at the same time, never before has it been faced with so much competition from other third-party dispute settlement mechanisms.[88]

In light of this new development, the Court has also improved its internal work and procedural rules with a view to enhancing the efficiency of its work.

Antarctic (*Australia* v. *Japan: New Zealand intervening*), 2010; *Certain Activities carried out by Nicaragua in the Border Area* (*Costa Rica* v. *Nicaragua*), 2010; *Construction of a Road in Costa Rica along the San Juan River* (*Nicaragua* v. *Costa Rica*), 2011.

85 See *Arrest Warrant of 11 April 2000* (*Democratic Republic of the Congo* v. *Belgium*), 2000; *Certain Criminal Proceedings in France* (*Republic of the Congo* v. *France*), 2003; *Certain Questions of Mutual Assistance in Criminal Matters* (*Djibouti* v. *France*), 2006; *Jurisdictional Immunities of the State* (*Germany* v. *Italy: Greece intervening*), 2008; *Questions relating to the Obligation to Prosecute or Extradite* (*Belgium* v. *Senegal*), 2009.

86 After the *Nuclear Tests* cases instituted by Australia and New Zealand against France in 1973, the general issue of nuclear arms was raised again in the 1990s. In 1993 the World Health Organization (WHO) submitted a request to the Court for an advisory opinion on the legality of the use by a State of nuclear weapons in armed conflict. The Court declined to exercise its advisory jurisdiction on the ground that the matter did not fall within the mandate of the WHO. In 1995, the General Assembly submitted a similar request for an advisory opinion of the Court on the legality of the threat or use of nuclear weapons. In 2014, Marshall Islands instituted a series of action against a number of nuclear States in the Court. See *Obligations concerning Negotiations relating to Cessation of the Nuclear Arms Race and to Nuclear Disarmament* (*Marshall Islands* v. *India*) (*Marshall Islands* v. *Pakistan*) *and* (*Marshall Islands* v. *United Kingdom*).

87 See *Application of the Convention on the Prevention and Punishment of the Crime of Genocide* (*Bosnia and Herzegovina* v. *Serbia and Montenegro*), 1993; cases concerning *Legality of Use of Force* (instituted by Yugoslavia against ten NATO member States), 1999; *Application of the Convention on the Prevention and Punishment of the Crime of Genocide* (*Croatia* v. *Serbia*), *1999*; *Application for Revision of the Judgment of 11 July 1996 in the Case concerning* Application of the Convention on the Prevention and Punishment of the Crime of Genocide (Bosnia and Herzegovina *v.* Yugoslavia), Preliminary Objections (*Yugoslavia* v. *Bosnia and Herzegovina*), 2001; *Accordance with International Law of the Unilateral Declaration of Independence in respect of Kosovo* (*Request for Advisory Opinion*), 2008.

88 The revival of the Court does not stand alone, as other courts and tribunals, e.g., the International Tribunal for the Law of the Sea (ITLOS), the Permanent Court of Arbitration (PCA), and *ad hoc* tribunals, are also more frequently resorted to for the settlement of disputes.

In addition to its amendments to the Rules of Court,[89] in October 2001 the Court adopted Practice Directions for use by States appearing before it. In no way alternating or departing from the Rules of Court, Practice Directions lay down specific rules and guidance on the procedural aspects of the legal proceedings for the purpose of good administration of justice.

In 2009, the General Assembly decided to create 15 posts of associate legal officers (P-2) for the Court. In the following year, for the first time each judge was provided with one law clerk to assist his/her research and legal work.[90] In addition, the Court also runs a university trainee programme.[91] Through extremely competitive examinations, a group of brilliant young lawyers and law students are selected to work for the Court. The Court is now better equipped to perform its judicial function.

This brief review of the historical development of the World Court reveals that in pursuing pacific means of settlement of international disputes, States have gone a long way in developing a full-fledged international judicial organ; by applying legal techniques, the Court manages to settle disputes through a "de-politicized process" in accordance with international law in the midst of political conflicts. Every step of the way, the question of jurisdiction, as an indicator, tests the effectiveness of the mechanism and affects the confidence of States in the judicial settlement of international disputes.

89 In 1946, the Court adopted, with only some minor amendments, the Rules of Court of the PCIJ of 11 March 1936. The Rules remained applicable until the 1970s when the Court undertook a complete revision. In 2001, amendments to Articles 79 and 80 entered into force and in 2005 amendments to Articles 43 and 52 entered into force.

90 The law clerkship is not a career track position. Each legal officer (P-2 level) is entitled to a two-year term contract and with one possible renewal for another two years.

91 The university trainees (UT) usually work at the Court for 9 to 10 months, depending on each particular case. At present, there are 15 UTs, each working for one judge.

CHAPTER II

The General Concepts

To understand the jurisdiction of the International Court of Justice, it is essential to distinguish the courts that we are familiar with in the national legal system from the international judicial organs that are empowered by States to settle international disputes. For that purpose, some general concepts about the jurisdiction of the ICJ should be introduced at the outset.

1 The Concept of Jurisdiction at International Level

In municipal systems, the intention of the parties does not play a significant role with regard to the jurisdiction of a court. Courts' jurisdictions are normally laid down in the statutory laws. Within the constitutional structure of a State, there is generally a schematic hierarchy of courts. At different instances, the courts serve different judicial functions. Their competence and jurisdiction are predetermined by law so as to ensure that they have the necessary power and legitimacy for their operation. An individual claimant has to seise the court in accordance with the procedural laws of the country to file his case. Rarely does a situation arise where no court has jurisdiction to adjudicate a particular case. Lack of jurisdiction of a court over a certain case is often due to the fact that the claimant has chosen a wrong court to present his grievance. In the *Anglo-Iranian Oil Co.* case (interim measures of protection), in addressing the Court's competence to render provisional measures, some dissenting judges made the following observation on the difference between municipal law and international law:

> The question of the jurisdiction of the national tribunal does not in practice arise; the application is made to the competent tribunal; if the tribunal has no jurisdiction it will not order interim measures. But, in municipal law, there is always some tribunal which has jurisdiction.
>
> In international law it is the consent of the parties which confers jurisdiction on the Court; the Court has jurisdiction only in so far as that jurisdiction has been accepted by the parties. The power given to the Court by Article 41 [of the Statute] is not unconditional; it is given for the purposes of the proceedings and is limited to those proceedings. If there

 | DOI 10.1163/9789004342767_003

> is no jurisdiction as to the merits, there can be no jurisdiction to indicate interim measures of protection.[1]

In international law, international courts and tribunals are not established within any constitutional framework of States with a schematic hierarchy. They are formed individually and separately with competence and jurisdiction defined and designed by special constitutive instruments on the basis of voluntary and collective acceptance by sovereign States. Ostensibly, these courts and tribunal are formed in a fragmented and random fashion, but in reality, their competence and jurisdiction seldom conflict or overlap. This is because the choice of the court lies with the parties. To give an example, if two States have a dispute over maritime delimitation, they may submit the dispute either to the ICJ or to the International Tribunal for the Law of the Sea (ITLOS) for settlement, depending on which jurisdiction they both have accepted. If the parties have accepted the jurisdiction of both the ICJ and the ITLOS, they could choose to go to either of them. If the respondent has objections to the jurisdiction of the forum thus chosen by the applicant State, the relevant court shall decide on the matter, normally through treaty interpretation. If there are several fora available that satisfy the conditions of jurisdiction, unless there are rules governing on the choice of forum, it is normally up to the applicant State to decide which forum it would like to seise for the settlement of the dispute. Institutionally there is no international court that has the competence to control the actions of other courts or tribunals as is the case in some national legal system, where a superior court can control the actions of a lower court or another tribunal.[2]

The relationship between different international courts and tribunals, of course, is not as simple as it may sound. This lecture will not deal with that matter.[3]

Within the United Nations system, the Charter confers on the ICJ institutional pre-eminence. All the major organs of the United Nations and its

1 *Anglo-Iranian Oil Co. Case (United Kingdom* v. *Iran), Order of July 5th, 1951: I.C.J. Reports 1951*, Dissenting opinion of Judges Winiarski and Badawi Pasha, pp. 96–97.

2 In the common law system, by way of writ of *certiorari*, a superior court can control the actions of a lower court or another tribunal. Shabtai Rosenne, *The Law and Practice of the International Court, 1920–2005, Vol. II, Jurisdiction*, 4th edition, Martinus Nijhoff Publishers, 2006, p. 518, citing David Walker (ed.), *The Oxford Companion to Law*, Oxford University Press, 1980, p. 197.

3 See Shabtai Rosenne, *op. cit. supra* footnote 2, *Vol. II, Jurisdiction*, pp. 519–522.

specialized agencies may, in accordance with Article 96 of the Charter, make requests to the Court for an advisory opinion on any legal question.

Although the ICJ enjoys high respect from other international courts and tribunals, such pre-eminence in terms of jurisdiction does not extend, and indeed, cannot extend, beyond the realm of the Organization. The Charter does not provide the Court with the exclusive power of judicial settlement of international disputes. States remain free to choose any means, or go to any other court or tribunal as they deem appropriate to settle their disputes. This freedom is recognized by Article 95 of the Charter:

> Nothing in the present Charter shall prevent Members of the United Nations from entrusting the solution of their differences to other tribunals by virtue of agreements already in existence or which may be concluded in the future.

This feature of the international judicial institution reflects the characteristics of the State system, under which States enjoy sovereignty and sovereign equality, with no jurisdiction over one another. Jurisdiction of the Court over sovereign States is subject to their consent.

2 Competence and Jurisdiction

In the English literature on international law, competence and jurisdiction both refer to the power of a court to make a decision. In the Charter and the Statute of the Court, they are often interchangeably used without clear distinction. The Statute limits the word *jurisdiction* to contentious cases,[4] while the word *competence* (in English) is sometimes used by the Court to refer to its power to render advisory opinions. One school suggests that so far as the Court is concerned, jurisdiction is a stricter concept than competence. It relates to the *power* or *capacity* of the Court to decide a particular case with final and binding force. Competence, on the other hand, refers to the "quality" of the court or tribunal to examine the complaints submitted to it. If the organ is not qualified, therefore, it is not competent to make a decision. It has a broader meaning. This element of qualification is not supposedly implied in the term "jurisdiction."[5]

The two terms in French language, however, are distinguished in another way, perhaps, the opposite way. According to French jurists, "*juridiction*" refers

4 See Articles 36 and 53 of the Statute.

5 Shabtai Rosenne, *op. cit. supra* footnote 2, *Vol. II, Jurisdiction*, p. 524.

to the general attributes of the judicial function rather than the judges' powers in a particular case. By contrast, "*compétence*" refers more to the concrete context in which the judges exercise their functions.[6] For instance, in the *Nuclear Tests* cases, France objected to the jurisdiction of the Court, claiming that the Court was manifestly "not competent" for dealing with such cases. This classification is clearly influenced by the municipal legal concepts.[7]

Notwithstanding such nuanced understandings, it is generally held that the distinction between the two terms, albeit notionally plausible, is of little practical relevance in international law, to the procedure of the Court.[8] They are frequently used as synonyms. They both refer to the power, general or specific, of the Court to render binding decisions in a legal dispute between States.

The concept of jurisdiction in international law can be used in two different contexts. One refers to national jurisdiction in international law as the power of a State deriving from its sovereignty in international law, or "the capacity of a State under international law to prescribe or enforce a rule of law"[9] notwithstanding its national constitutional basis. For example, under international law a State is entitled to prescribe laws and regulations governing its nationals with regard to their nationality, marriage, property rights, etc., and matters within or relating to its territory, such as security, transport, land uses, economic and trade activities, and environmental protection. It also has the right to enforce such laws and regulations in a way that is not incompatible with its international obligations. Although at the national level such State power (sovereignty) is neither determined by, nor derived from, international law, exercise of such sovereign power may directly affect the sovereignty of another State, such as nationality law, financial regulations, and trade restrictions. National jurisdiction is unavoidably a subject-matter under international law. Jurisdiction in that sense does not fall into the scope of this special course.

The jurisdiction we are concerned with in this context relates to the power of an international judicial organ, to be more specific, the power of the ICJ to

6 An authoritative French Dictionary draws the distinction of the two terms as follows: they are sometimes used as equivalents with a tendency to employ "*juridiction*" in a general and abstract sense, and "*compétence*" in relation to a particular decision or a particular incident in the course of a proceeding. Jules Basdevant (ed.), *Dictionnaire de la terminologie du droit international*, Sirey, 1960, pp. 133, 355.

7 This is an example to show the differences between the common law and the civil law.

8 Robert Kolb, *The International Court of Justice*, Hart Publishing, 2013, pp. 211–212.

9 American Law Institute, *Restatement of the Law, Second (1965): Foreign Relations Law of the United States,* Chapter 1, Section 6, p. 20, quoted in Hugh Thirlway, *The Law and Procedure of the International Court of Justice: fifty years of jurisprudence,* Vol. I, Oxford University Press, 2013, p. 691.

give a decision with binding force for the litigating parties. Jurisdiction is the essential element that enables the Court to act, and "to do justice," so to speak. Whenever a State institutes proceedings in the Court, it has to indicate in its application on what jurisdictional basis it has brought the case. The respondent State, for its part, either by word or by deed, has to accept such ground so that proceedings can further go ahead. Should the respondent State raise objections to the jurisdiction of the Court, proceedings on the merits have to be suspended until and unless the Court decides that it has jurisdiction in the case. Out of 137 contentious cases that the Court has received so far since 1946, in more than half of the cases, the respondent States have raised objections to the jurisdiction of the Court and the admissibility of the application. In more than 20 cases, the Court found that it had no jurisdiction or the case was not admissible. Currently, in seven pending cases the respondent States have raised objections to the jurisdiction of the Court and the admissibility of the application.[10]

Jurisdiction in this sense is not a purely procedural matter. It bears on the substance of international law relating to the sovereignty of States and the fundamental principles of international law governing judicial settlement of international disputes. As is pointed out:

> The question whether and to what extent the Court has jurisdiction is frequently of political importance no less than the decision on the merits, if not more. When a respondent raises a matter of jurisdiction…it frequently indicates the absence of political agreement that the Court should entertain the case. These are not mere technical issues.[11]

When one State unilaterally institutes proceedings in the Court, jurisdiction could serve as a "fire wall" to stop unduly-instituted lawsuits.

Jurisdiction in the narrow sense of the term also means the judicial power of the Court to control the legal proceedings of a case, for example, issuing orders to the parties for the conduct of the case; fixing the time-limit for the parties to

10 *Obligation to Negotiate Access to the Pacific Ocean* (*Bolivia* v. *Chile*); *Alleged Violations of Sovereign Rights and Maritime Spaces in the Caribbean Sea* (*Nicaragua* v. *Colombia*); *Question of the Delimitation of the Continental Shelf between Nicaragua and Colombia beyond 200 nautical miles from the Nicaraguan Coast* (*Nicaragua* v. *Colombia*); *Maritime Delimitation in the Indian Ocean* (*Somalia* v. *Kenya*); *Immunities and Criminal Proceedings* (*Equatorial Guinea* v. *France*); *Certain Iranian Assets* (*Islamic Republic of Iran* v. *United States of America*); *Application of the International Convention for the Suppression of the Financing of Terrorism and of the International Convention on the Elimination of All Forms of Racial Discrimination* (*Ukraine* v. *Russian Federation*).

11 Shabtai Rosenne, *op. cit. supra* footnote 2, *Vol. II, Jurisdiction*, p. 803.

submit written pleadings; deciding how many rounds of written pleadings are required; setting up the arrangements for the conduct of oral proceedings; deciding whether to have witnesses and experts appear before the Court to give testimony; deciding whether a certain document or evidence is admissible.[12] These matters are procedural in nature.

Jurisdiction of the Court is primarily governed by the following legal instruments: the Charter of the United Nations; the Statute of the International Court of Justice (the Statute of the Court); the Rules of Court; and the relevant resolutions adopted by the General Assembly and the Security Council.

Procedural matters are generally governed by the Rules of Court and Practice Directions. The Rules of Court were basically adopted on the model of the Rules of Court of the PCIJ, only materially amended and revised in 1976 and 1978. Practice Directions are the guidance for the States appearing before the Court as to how to participate in the written and oral proceedings in the Court. They are supplemental and additional to the Rules of Court.

In normal proceedings, the parties tend to disagree on some procedural matters, such as the necessary time limits for the submission of their written pleadings; appointment of technical experts; submission of additional evidence and documents. However trivial they may seem, they often give rise to concerns over procedural fairness and the good administration of justice. It is for the Court, after seeking the views of the parties, to take decisions on these matters.

As mentioned before, under the Statute, the Court has jurisdiction in two types of cases: cases concerning legal disputes between States—contentious cases—and requests for advisory opinions from certain international organizations. In the former case, the Court's judgment is binding and final on the parties and in respect of the case; while in the latter case, the Court's advisory opinion is not binding, but it has authoritative effect in international law.

Jurisdiction of the Court has to be specifically conferred on the Court by the States. It is not right to make any sweeping and general statement that the Court has jurisdiction over territorial and maritime disputes, or disputes over the question of *jus cogens*. Whether the Court has jurisdiction is a matter that has to be examined and decided in the concrete context of each specific case. As the Court said in the *Nottebohm* case, "[t]he Court is not concerned with defining the meaning of the word 'jurisdiction' in general. In the present case, it must determine the scope and meaning" of *the relevant title of jurisdiction*.[13] Under Article 38, paragraph 2, of the Rules of Court, in filing a case, the applicant State shall in its application "specify as far as possible the

12 See Article 48 of the Statute.

13 *Nottebohm case* (*Liechtenstein* v. *Guatemala*) (*Preliminary Objection*), *Judgment of November 18th, 1953: I.C.J. Reports 1953*, pp. 121–122.

legal grounds upon which the jurisdiction of the Court is said to be based." The Court shall examine and decide, either based on the applicant's claim, or by itself, *proprio motu*, whether it has jurisdiction in the case. As the question of jurisdiction is a matter of law, the ultimate decision rests with the Court.

In relation to the jurisdictional basis, three concepts are often referred to in the judgments of the Court: personal jurisdiction, *ratione personae*, subject-matter jurisdiction, *ratione materiae*, and temporal jurisdiction, *ratione temporis*. They are three necessary elements of jurisdiction. To establish the Court's jurisdiction, these elements must each be satisfied. Personal jurisdiction means that the parties appearing before the Court must have the capacity and the legal right to institute proceedings in the Court. Both parties must be qualified to have access to the Court. Subject-matter jurisdiction requires that the substance of the dispute falls within the jurisdiction of the Court. Lastly, temporal jurisdiction denotes that the Court's jurisdiction only extends to the facts that occurred during the relevant period of time when the parties have conferred jurisdiction on the Court. Proceedings on the question of jurisdiction of the Court all relate to these or any of these three aspects. In the following sections, these aspects will be discussed in detail in the context of specific cases.

3 Jurisdiction and Admissibility

Coupled with jurisdiction, admissibility is another ground on which the Court has to decide whether it is competent to adjudicate a dispute. The question of admissibility usually refers to the suitability of a claim or an application for judicial adjudication. In other words, admissibility is more related to the qualities of a claim or an application, whereas jurisdiction is more concerned with the power of the Court. An objection to the admissibility of a claim "consists in the contention that there exists a legal reason, even when there is jurisdiction, why the Court should decline to hear the case, or more usually, a specific claim therein."[14] In the case concerning *Oil Platforms* (*Islamic Republic of Iran* v. *United States of America*) the Court noted that:

> Objections to admissibility normally take the form of an assertion that, even if the Court has jurisdiction and the facts stated by the applicant

---

14 *Application of the Convention on the Prevention and Punishment of the Crime of Genocide* (*Croatia* v. *Serbia*), *Preliminary Objections, Preliminary Objections, Judgment, I.C.J. Reports 2008*, p. 456, para. 120.

> State are assumed to be correct, nonetheless there are reasons why the Court should not proceed to an examination of the merits.[15]

Admissibility could be a bar to a claim as well as to the jurisdiction of the Court.

With regard to the jurisdiction of the Court, the Court should first of all, either at the request of the parties, or by itself, *proprio motu*, ascertain whether it has jurisdiction in the case before proceeding to the merits. Regarding the question of admissibility, in most cases, it is up to the parties to raise the issue. The line between the question of jurisdiction and that of admissibility is not always clear-cut.[16] One observation is helpful for the understanding of their difference:

> The essential difference between the two concepts lies in the fact that, broadly speaking, jurisdiction is a question of the *propriety of the court's deciding the case*. This has to be considered in light of the personal capacity of the claimant to appear before the Court, the legal nature of the claim (since a Court can speak only to the law), and the bases upon which the parties can be said to have consented to the jurisdiction. Admissibility, by contrast, is essentially concerned with *formal or material defects in the claim as formulated*, on the supposition that the Court itself could, in principle, if there were no such defects, be seised of a case of the kind in question.[17]

In practice, the Court will first determine the question of jurisdiction before it turns to the question of admissibility. Even if the Court founds its jurisdiction, it may nevertheless decide that, by reason of some legal defects in an application or a claim, the application or the claim is inadmissible, and consequently the case should be dismissed. Notwithstanding a few established rules with regard to the admissibility of claims, it is hard to generalize the bases for the inadmissibility of claims. In practice, the parties before the Court have raised various kinds of reasons for the inadmissibility of an application or a claim. The Court has to consider them in the particular context in a specific case.

15 *Oil Platforms (Islamic Republic of Iran* v. *United States of America), Judgment, I.C.J. Reports 2003*, p. 177, para. 29.

16 Robert Kolb, *op. cit. supra* footnote 8, pp. 200–206.

17 *Ibid.*, p. 202, emphasis in the original.

If the Court finds that it has no jurisdiction, it need not go on to determine the question of admissibility.[18]

Admissibility and jurisdiction are two distinct, but often interrelated issues. The way in which the parties differentiate them does not bind the Court. It is always up to the Court to classify the issue. In the case where there are different objections to both jurisdiction and admissibility, the Court will decide for itself whether a question relates to jurisdiction or to admissibility. In the case concerning *Application of the Convention on the Prevention and Punishment of the Crime of Genocide* (*Croatia* v. *Serbia*), for instance, Croatia claimed that, from early 1991 to late 1992, the Federal Republic of Yugoslavia (FRY, later Serbia) committed crimes of genocide in the territory of Croatia, in breach of its international obligations under the Genocide Convention, to which both Croatia and Serbia were parties. In response, Serbia contended that the Court did not have jurisdiction *ratione temporis* over the alleged genocidal acts prior to 27 April 1992, the date on which the FRY proclaimed to be a State. Alternatively, it contended that should the Court found its jurisdiction in the case, those alleged acts were not admissible, because the FRY undertook its treaty obligations only from the date when it succeeded to the said treaty as a State party. The Convention did not have retroactive effect both pursuant to its terms and under general treaty law. Apparently Serbia treated the matter both as an issue of admissibility as well as jurisdiction. The Court said in its judgment that:

> In the view of the Court, the questions of jurisdiction and admissibility raised by Serbia's preliminary objection *ratione temporis* constitute two inseparable issues in the present case. The first issue is that of the Court's jurisdiction to determine whether breaches of the Genocide Convention were committed in the light of the facts that occurred prior to the date on which the FRY came into existence as a separate State, capable of being a party in its own right to the Convention; this may be regarded as a question of the applicability of the obligations under the Genocide Convention to the FRY before 27 April 1992. The second issue, that of

18 For example, in the case concerning *Armed Activities on the Territory of the Congo* (*New Application: 2002*) (*Democratic Republic of the Congo* v. *Rwanda*), the Court concludes that "from all of the foregoing considerations that it cannot accept any of the bases of jurisdiction put forward by the DRC in the present case. Since it has no jurisdiction to entertain the Application, the Court is not required to rule on its admissibility." *Armed Activities on the Territory of the Congo* (*New Application: 2002*) (*Democratic Republic of the Congo* v. *Rwanda*), *Jurisdiction and Admissibility, Judgment, I.C.J. Reports 2006*, p. 52, para. 126.

> admissibility of the claim in relation to those facts, and involving questions of attribution, concerns the consequences to be drawn with regard to the responsibility of the FRY for those same facts under the general rules of State responsibility.[19]

The Court considered Serbia's objections bearing on both the question of jurisdiction and that of admissibility. In its view, on the treaty status of Serbia to the Genocide Convention, the matter concerned jurisdiction, while the issue of attribution related to the question of admissibility.

Grounds to challenge admissibility are considerably varied. Many of them are not upheld by the Court.[20] These grounds either concern procedural aspects of the litigation or relate to the material aspects of the case.

On the procedural defects, the respondent may challenge the admissibility of the application alongside the question of jurisdiction during the preliminary objections stage. It may assert that the application is not admissible because between the parties there exists no dispute over the subject-matter of the case,[21] or the condition for initiating the judicial process has not yet been satisfied,[22] or the other party lacks legal standing to take action.[23]

In the incidental proceedings such as third party intervention, the question of jurisdiction is governed by the statutory rules, but an objection may still be raised to the admissibility of the request as to whether the requesting State genuinely has an interest of legal nature in the case.

In case of a request for interpretation of an existing judgment, two conditions must be satisfied, namely, the request must be aimed at clarifying the meaning and scope of the judgment, but not at getting a new judgment.[24]

19 *Application of the Convention on the Prevention and Punishment of the Crime of Genocide* (*Croatia* v. *Serbia*), *Preliminary Objections, Judgment, I.C.J. Reports 2008*, p. 460, para. 129.

20 Robert Kolb summarizes around 30 kinds of ground for the inadmissibility of a case. Robert Kolb, *op. cit. supra* footnote 8, pp. 219–223.

21 See, for example, *Land and Maritime Boundary between Cameroon and Nigeria* (*Cameroon* v. *Nigeria*), *Preliminary Objections, Judgment, I.C.J. Reports 1998*, pp. 313–317, paras. 84–94.

22 See *Alleged Violations of Sovereign Rights and Maritime Spaces in the Caribbean Sea* (*Nicaragua* v. *Colombia*), *Judgment, Preliminary Objections*, paras. 80–101.

23 See *Ahmadou Sadio Diallo* (*Republic of Guinea* v. *Democratic Republic of the Congo*), *Preliminary Objections, Judgment, I.C.J. Reports 2007*, pp. 602–607, 610–616, paras. 50–67, 77–95.

24 After the delivery of the judgment in the *Request for Interpretation of the Judgment of 15 June 1962 in the Case concerning the* Temple of Preah Vihear (Cambodia *v.* Thailand) (*Cambodia* v. *Thailand*), a question was asked why the Court did not decide on the boundary in

Secondly, the applicant must demonstrate that the parties had a dispute over the meaning and scope of the judgment concerned. In the *Request for Interpretation of the Judgment of 31 March 2004 in the Case concerning* Avena and Other Mexican Nationals, the Court stated that "[a]s is clear from the settled jurisprudence of the Court, a dispute must exist for a request for interpretation to be admissible."[25] If the applicant cannot demonstrate that it has such a dispute with the respondent, it does not have a case in the Court. In other words, such a request is not admissible.

The question of admissibility may also be pertinent to a new claim raised by a party during the proceedings. Procedurally the applicant State may present new facts and amend its claims after the filing of its application. However, such new facts and claims must have been implicit in the application and must arise directly out of the question which is the subject of the application.[26] If a new claim changes the subject-matter of the dispute and transforms it into a new dispute, it is not admissible.[27] In the case concerning *Land and Maritime Boundary between Cameroon and Nigeria*, the Court recalled that

> it has become an established practice for States submitting an application to the Court to reserve the right to present additional facts and legal considerations. The limit of the freedom to present such facts and considerations is that the result is not to transform the dispute brought before the Court by the application into another dispute which is different in character.[28]

---

the disputed area so as to resolve the dispute between the parties. The answer is simple. The 1962 judgment explicitly precluded that issue and the Court in interpreting that judgment could not and should not have gone beyond what was decided in 1962.

25 *Request for Interpretation of the Judgment of 31 March 2004 in the Case concerning* Avena and Other Mexican Nationals (Mexico *v.* United States of America) (*Mexico* v. *United States of America*), *Judgment, I.C.J. Reports 2009*, p. 10, para. 21.

26 *Certain Phosphate Lands in Nauru* (*Nauru* v. *Australia*), *Preliminary Objections, Judgment, I.C.J. Reports 1992*, pp. 266–267, para. 69; *Case concerning the Temple of Preah Vihear* (*Cambodia* v. *Thailand*), *Merits, Judgment, I.C.J. Reports 1962*, p. 36; *Fisheries Jurisdiction* (*Federal Republic of Germany* v. *Iceland*), *Merits, Judgment, I.C.J. Reports 1974*, p. 203, para. 72.

27 The Court has on a number of occasions emphasized that these requirements are "essential from the point of view of legal security and the good administration of justice." *Fisheries Jurisdiction* (*Spain* v. *Canada*), *Jurisdiction of the Court, Judgment, I.C.J. Reports 1998*, p. 448, para. 29; *Certain Phosphate Lands in Nauru* (*Nauru* v. *Australia*), *Preliminary Objections, Judgment, I.C.J. Reports 1992*, pp. 266–267, para. 69.

28 *Military and Paramilitary Activities in and against Nicaragua* (*Nicaragua* v. *United States of America*), *Jurisdiction and Admissibility, Judgment, I.C.J. Reports 1984*, p. 427, para. 80; *Land*

To ensure procedural justice, admissibility prevents defective claims. Otherwise, one party would be put in a disadvantageous position to defend its case. These grounds are largely governed by the Statute, the Rules of Court, as well as the case law of the Court.

Under general international law, there are certain rules governing international claims. For international litigation, non-observation of such rules may constitute a legal ground for the inadmissibility of a claim. In the field of diplomatic protection, any international claim by a State for its national must observe two rules: the principle of nationality and the rule of exhaustion of local remedies. The principle of nationality means that when a State is exercising its right of diplomatic protection of its national, there must be an effective nationality link between the State and the national concerned at the time when the injurious act happened. Such nationality link must be effective and continuous during the course of the event and till the time when the case is in process.

The rule of exhaustion of local remedies requires the injured person to first seek and exhaust local remedies in the country where the injury occurred. Only when justice is denied to the person, whether natural or legal, may his country bring an international claim on his behalf to the Court. If these conditions or either of them is not satisfied, the case is inadmissible.

The grounds for objecting to the admissibility of an application are rather broad, often mixed with the question of jurisdiction. It is for the Court to determine the limits of its judicial function.

4 Justiciability

Justiciability is a term that appears in scholarly writings rather than in the case law of the Court. Connected with judicial propriety—a concept to be discussed subsequently, justiciability refers to the typology of cases that a judicial organ should, and is competent to, deal with.

Generally speaking, the function of the Court is to settle disputes. Article 36, paragraph 2, of the Statute provides for the kinds of disputes that fall within the competence of the Court. Unless it is ascertained that there exists a dispute between the parties at the time when an application is filed in the Court, the Court is not in a position to consider whether it has jurisdiction in the case. That is to say, the Court's contentious jurisdiction is confined to settling disputes. The Court must exercise its jurisdiction to the fullest extent

and Maritime Boundary between Cameroon and Nigeria (*Cameroon* v. *Nigeria*), *Preliminary Objections, Judgment, I.C.J. Reports 1998*, pp. 318–319, para. 99.

as conferred upon it, but at the same time it must not go beyond that limit. On the conditions for justiciability, the Court would normally consider three aspects. First, the dispute before the Court should be capable of being settled by the application of rules and principles of international law. Second, the Court has jurisdiction to adjudicate it. Finally, the jurisdiction is not fettered by any circumstances rendering the application inadmissible.

With regard to the competence of the Court, the most frequently-asked question is whether a judicial organ should deal with disputes that are primarily of a political nature and proceedings that are apparently driven by political or other non-legal purposes, e.g. as a means to serve some political goals. In other words, this relates to how the Court tackles cases that involve sensitive political aspects in its judicial work.

The General List of the Court reveals that the Court does not shy away from cases simply because they involve complicated political, military and other important aspects. Those aspects do not by themselves render a case unjusticiable. Simultaneous seisin of a case by other major UN organs, particularly the General Assembly and the Security Council, does not necessarily deprive the Court of its competence to hear the case. Notwithstanding this general proposition, it is also true that there are certain judicial limitations that the Court should not step beyond. For domestic lawyers, this is a constitutional issue. For instance, under the U.S. Constitution, by virtue of separation of powers, the judiciary should duly exercise self-restraint by declining to exercise jurisdiction in the event that the subject-matter of a case falls within the domain of the political branch or constitutes an act of the State. This is the so-called "political question doctrine" or "act of State doctrine."[29] In international law, however, there exist no such doctrines based on the separation of powers.

Under the Charter, there are provisions on the relationship between the Security Council and General Assembly in terms of their responsibilities in the maintenance of international peace and security; under Articles 11, 12 and 24 of the Charter, the Security Council bears the primary responsibility for the maintenance of international peace and security, while the General Assembly may discuss and make recommendations with regard to any question relating to peace and security. However, "[w]hile the Security Council is exercising in respect of any dispute or situation the functions assigned to it in the present Charter, the General Assembly shall not make any recommendation with regard to that dispute or situation unless the Security Council so

29 The most cited case is U.S. Supreme Court decision in *Banco Nacional de Cuba v. Sabbatino*, 376 U.S. 398 (1964), pp. 416–439.

requests."[30] With respect to the Court, there is no such provision on its relationship with the other major organs of the Organization.

In the case law of the Court, if a dispute involves political, military or other aspects, or the matter is also being dealt with by the Security Council, that fact alone does not necessarily render the case non-justiciable. The Court, as a matter of fact, is frequently confronted with disputes arising from territorial disputes, use of force, ethnic disputes, military activities and armed conflicts. As is mentioned in the first Chapter, in the *South West Africa* cases related to the Mandate system, all the major organs of the United Nations played a role in bringing an end to the apartheid regime in South West Africa and achieving the ultimate independence of Namibia (the former South West Africa).

The very first case, the *Corfu Channel* case, submitted to the Court in 1947 by the United Kingdom against Albania, involved serious elements of the use of force. On 22 October 1946, a squadron of British Navy ships was passing the international highway of the Corfu Channel that separated Albania from Greece. While sailing through a previously swept minefield on their way, two British warships struck mines, and as a result, were seriously damaged by the explosions, with 44 officers and men on board killed and 42 injured. Later it was found that the mines were "recently laid." In November that year the United Kingdom again conducted mine-sweeping activities in that area. Because the incident took place in the Albanian territorial waters, the British Government held the Albanian Government responsible for the damage. After the failure of diplomatic negotiations between the two countries to settle the problem, the United Kingdom referred the dispute to the Security Council in 1947. During the course of Security Council deliberations, the Soviet Union vetoed one draft resolution.[31]

On 9 April 1947, the Security Council adopted a resolution, which recommended "that the United Kingdom and Albanian Governments should immediately refer the dispute to the International Court of Justice in accordance with the provisions of the Statute of the Court."[32] On 22 May 1947 the United Kingdom filed in the Court an application instituting proceedings against Albania. Albania informed the Court of its view that the British unilateral institution was neither in conformity with the Statute of the Court nor in line with the

30 Article 12 of the Charter of the United Nations.

31 Shabtai Rosenne, *The World Court, What It is and How It Works*, 5th completely revised edition, Martinus Nijhoff Publishers, 1995, pp. 155–158; *Corfu Channel case (United Kingdom of Great Britain and Northern Ireland* v. *Albania), Judgment of April 9th, 1949: I.C.J. Reports 1949, pp. 12–13.*

32 *Corfu Channel case (United Kingdom* v. *Albania), Preliminary Objection, Judgment, I.C.J. Reports 1948*, p. 17.

resolution of the Security Council. According to Albania, the two States should submit their dispute to the ICJ by a Special Agreement. Notwithstanding its position, Albania indicated its readiness to participate in the case. Before the Counter-Memorial was submitted, Albania raised preliminary objections to the jurisdiction of the Court. Proceedings on the merits were suspended.

The Court, in the 25 March 1948 judgment (the first ever made by the Court since its establishment), rejected Albania's preliminary objections. Before that judgment was delivered, the United Kingdom and Albania concluded a Special Agreement.[33] The Court recognized that the Special Agreement constituted the basis for the future conduct of the case. Albania took part in the second phase, but did not appear in the third phase on compensation. Albania was of the opinion that the parties did not ask the Court to rule on the amount of compensation in the Special Agreement, and the Court therefore did not have the jurisdiction over the matter. The Court overruled Albania's objection.[34]

In this case, the Court did not decline to exercise jurisdiction even when the case had political implications involving military action. The Security Council was unable to resolve it due to the opposition between the major powers in the Security Council over the event. After the Security Council referred the matter to the Court for judicial settlement, the Court was able to perform its function in settling the dispute against a very complicated situation. This is the first case in which the Court and the major political organs had managed to work out a way to bring down an international tension.

Likewise, in the case concerning *United States Diplomatic and Consular Staff in Tehran* between the United States and Iran, also called the *Tehran Hostages* case, when the United States requested the Court to indicate provisional measures for protection, Iran contended through a communication with the Court that the hostage issue formed only "'a marginal and secondary aspect of an overall problem' involving the activities of the United States in Iran over a period of more than 25 years,"[35] indicating that the case was not purely a legal matter justiciable by the Court. The Court did not accept that argument, but

33 In the Special Agreement, the two States put two questions for the Court to decide. First, whether Albania was responsible under international law for the explosions and for the damage and loss of human life resulted therefrom. Secondly, whether there was any duty to pay compensation.

34 In its final judgment delivered on 15 December 1949, the Court ordered Albania to pay compensation in the amount of 843,947 pound to the United Kingdom. Albania never paid the reparation. Consequently, the two countries broke their diplomatic relations. They ultimately settled the matter in 1992, when they resumed their diplomatic relations.

35 *United States Diplomatic and Consular Staff in Tehran* (*United States of America* v. *Iran*), *Provisional Measures, Order of 15 December 1979, I.C.J. Reports 1979*, p. 15, para. 22.

held that "no provision of the Statute or Rules contemplates that the Court should decline to take cognizance of one aspect of a dispute merely because that dispute has other aspects, however important."[36]

In the judgment on the merits, the Court further emphasized that,

> legal disputes between sovereign States by their very nature are likely to occur in political context, and often form only one element in a wider and longstanding political dispute between the States concerned. Yet never has the view been put forward before that, because a legal dispute submitted to the Court is only one aspect of a political dispute, the Court should decline to resolve for the parties the legal questions at issue between them.[37]

Indeed, as is observed, should the Court decline to deal with cases with political sensitivities, it would have just virtually emasculated itself.[38]

On the relationship between the Court and the Security Council in dealing with international disputes, the fact that the Security Council is concurrently seized of the matter has never been an obstacle to the jurisdiction of the Court. The adoption by the Council of resolutions on the same matter cannot deprive the Court of its jurisdiction as long as it has been validly seised, as is stated by the Court in the *Lockerbie* cases.[39]

This element was particularly acute and controversial in the case concerning *Military and Paramilitary Activities in and against Nicaragua* in 1984. The issues raised in this case directly involved the use of force and an on-going armed conflict, pertaining to the maintenance of peace and security, for which the primary responsibility is conferred upon the Security Council by the Charter. The Court considered at great length the issue of justiciability in this case. In its Counter-Memorial on jurisdiction and admissibility the United States

---

36 *Ibid.*, p. 15, para. 24.

37 *United States Diplomatic and Consular Staff in Tehran* (*United States of America* v. *Iran*), *Judgment, I.C.J. Reports 1980*, p. 20, para. 37.

38 See Christian Tomuschat, "Article 36," in Andreas Zimmermann, Karin Oellers-Frahm, Christian Tomuschat, and Christian J. Tams (eds.), *The Statute of the International Court of Justice: A Commentary*, 2nd edition, Oxford University Press, 2012, p. 645.

39 See *Questions of Interpretation and Application of the 1971 Montreal Convention arising from the Aerial Incident at Lockerbie* (*Libyan Arab Jamahiriya* v. *United Kingdom*), *Preliminary Objections, Judgment, I.C.J. Reports 1998*, p. 26, para. 44; *Questions of Interpretation and Application of the 1971 Montreal Convention arising from the Aerial Incident at Lockerbie* (*Libyan Arab Jamahiriya* v. *United States of America*), *Preliminary Objections, Judgment, I.C.J. Reports 1998*, pp. 130–131, para. 43.

advanced a number of arguments with regard to why Nicaragua's application should be treated as inadmissible. It contended that a claim relating to unlawful use of armed force was a matter committed by the Charter of the United Nations and by practice to the *exclusive competence* of other organs, in particular the Security Council. The subject-matter of the present dispute concerning an "ongoing armed conflict" and the use of armed force was a matter with which a court could not deal effectively without overstepping proper judicial bounds.[40]

In its judgment of 26 November 1984 on jurisdiction and admissibility, the Court rejected all these arguments advanced by the United States, and stated that "the fact that a matter is before the Security Council should not prevent it being dealt with by the Court and that both proceedings could be pursued *pari passu*."[41] Recalling its previous cases, it added that in dealing with issues of peace,

> [t]he Charter accordingly does not confer *exclusive* responsibility upon the Security Council for the purpose... The Council has functions of a political nature assigned to it, whereas the Court exercises purely judicial functions. Both organs can therefore perform their separate but complementary functions with respect to the same events.[42]

The Court apparently set up a very broad basis for its jurisdiction.[43]

In regard to the political motivation a State may have in instituting proceedings, the Court does not consider that element as a barrier to the jurisdiction of

40 See *Military and Paramilitary Activities in and against Nicaragua (Nicaragua* v. *United States of America), Jurisdiction and Admissibility, Judgment, I.C.J. Reports 1984*, pp. 431–432, paras. 89, 91.

41 *Ibid.*, p. 433, para. 93.

42 *Ibid.*, p. 434, para. 95.

43 On the political implication of the judgment in the *Military and Paramilitary Activities* case, Shabtai Rosenne observes that "[t]his judgment was an impressive achievement for Nicaragua. At the same time it is one of the most significant judgments on ostensibly technical questions of jurisdiction and admissibility to have been rendered by the present Court. What had Nicaragua gained? Nicaragua's forensic triumph had powerful political resonances, largely concealed by the technicalities of this judgment. From the point of view of the Court proceedings, Nicaragua was now assured that its grievances would be fully ventilated in the Court and in that way brought before a wider public. The political objective of the exercise, commencing with the approach to the Security Council, would be met. In litigation terms, the Court had established the broadest possible base for its jurisdiction." Shabtai Rosenne, *op. cit. supra* footnote 31, p. 136.

the Court. In the case concerning *Border and Transborder Armed Actions* (*Nicaragua* v. *Honduras*), a case that Nicaragua instituted against its neighbours right after it won the *Military and Paramilitary Activities* case, the Court, in addressing the justiciability of the application, stated that the Court "cannot concern itself with the political motivation which may lead a State at a particular time or in particular circumstances, to choose judicial settlement."[44]

The Court has taken the same stand when examining its competence in giving advisory opinions. In the case concerning *Legality of the Threat or Use of Nuclear Weapons,* the Court stated that the political character of a question submitted to it did not affect its advisory jurisdiction.[45]

Notwithstanding the established jurisprudence, it is important to emphasize that in principle if the Security Council has adopted a decision under Chapter 7 of the Charter concerning an on-going dispute, under Article 103 of the Charter, obligations under that decision should prevail over any obligations derived from other international agreements. Such situation must be taken into account by the Court when it issues orders, because such orders may not impose on the parties any obligations that contradict the obligations they have undertaken under the decisions of the Security Council.

5 Judicial Propriety

Judicial propriety refers to the situations where the Court finds that it is not appropriate for it to exercise jurisdiction or its judgment may not be of any effect or object even if it were to exercise jurisdiction. Such self-restraint is inherent to its judicial function. Both notions of justiciability and judicial propriety refer to the judicial limits. The Court on more than one occasion stated that even

---

44 *Border and Transborder Armed Actions (Nicaragua* v. *Honduras), Jurisdiction and Admissibility, Judgment, I.C.J. Reports 1988,* p. 91, para. 52.

45 *Legality of the Threat or Use of Nuclear Weapons, Advisory Opinion, I.C.J. Reports 1996,* pp. 233–234, para. 13. On the issue of justiciability, it is also necessary to read the dissenting and separate opinions of individual judges in the relevant cases. See *Military and Paramilitary Activities in and against Nicaragua (Nicaragua* v. *United States of America), Merits, Judgment, I.C.J. Reports 1986,* Separate Opinion of Judge Lachs, pp. 166–170, Dissenting Opinion of Judge Oda, pp. 219–246, Dissenting Opinion of Judge Schwebel, pp. 284–296; *Border and Transborder Armed Actions (Nicaragua* v. *Honduras), Jurisdiction and Admissibility, Judgment, I.C.J. Reports 1988,* Separate Opinion of Judge Shahabuddeen, pp. 144–146; *Legality of the Threat or Use of Nuclear Weapons, Advisory Opinion, I.C.J. Reports 1996,* Dissenting Opinion of Judge Oda, pp. 350, 373, paras. 25, 54, Dissenting Opinion of Judge Weeramantry, p. 550.

if it finds that it has jurisdiction, "the Court is not compelled in every case to exercise that jurisdiction."[46] The Court, as a judicial organ, like all the superior courts in national system, possesses certain judicial discretion as to whether to entertain a case. If it deems it incompatible with its judicial function or its judicial character to decide a case, it may choose not to do so. Under Article 36, paragraph 6, of the Statute, if the parties have a dispute as to whether the Court has jurisdiction, "the matter shall be settled by the decision of the Court." This implies that the Court may decide not to entertain the case. To do so, of course, the Court must give its reasons, which usually are stated in the form of a judgment, as is the case with every decision on the question of jurisdiction.

In the *Northern Cameroons* case the Court gave an elaborated statement on judicial propriety. After the First World War, the League of Nations placed the former German colony of Kamerun partially under the British Mandate and partially under the French Mandate. After WWII, these mandates were transformed into Trusteeship agreements. During the decolonization movement in the 1960s, the situation of the trust territories of Cameroon respectively under the British and French administrations received a lot of attention from the Trusteeship Council and the General Assembly of the United Nations.

After the Republic of Cameroon gained independence on 1 January 1960 and the Federation of Nigeria on 1 October 1960, a plebiscite under the supervision of the United Nations was held in these territories (the territory under the British administration was called the northern Cameroons and the territory under the French administration, the southern Cameroons). The result of the plebiscite showed that part of the population wished to join Cameroon, while the northern Cameroons wished to merge with Nigeria. On 21 April 1961, the General Assembly adopted resolution 1608 (XV), which endorsed the result of the plebiscite. The Republic of Cameroon was dissatisfied with the organization of the plebiscite and the way in which the United Kingdom had administered the northern Cameroons. Its criticism, however, was not accepted by the United Kingdom. The whole question of administrative unions in trust territories was, over many years, the subject of repeated study within the United Nations.

In May 1961 Cameroon proposed a special agreement with the United Kingdom to bring the dispute to the ICJ, which the United Kingdom initially rejected. Later Cameroon filed an application instituting proceedings against the United Kingdom in the Court. Cameroon based the jurisdiction of the Court on the compromissory clause of the Trusteeship Agreement for the Northern

46 *Case concerning the Northern Cameroons (Cameroon* v. *United Kingdom), Preliminary Objections, Judgment of 2 December 1963: I.C.J. Reports 1963*, p. 29; *Frontier Dispute (Burkina Faso/Republic of Mali), Judgment, I.C.J. Reports 1986*, p. 577, para. 45.

Cameroons. The case was filed on 30 May 1961 and that Trusteeship Agreement was to be terminated two days later on 1 June 1961. The United Kingdom raised a series of preliminary objections. In the judgment, the Court considered at some length its role. The following long passage from the judgment is worth citing:

> There are inherent limitations on the exercise of the judicial function which the Court, as a court of justice, can never ignore. There may thus be an incompatibility between the desires of an applicant, or, indeed, of both parties to a case, on the one hand, and on the other hand the duty of the Court to maintain its judicial character. The Court itself, and not the parties, must be the guardian of the Court's judicial integrity.
>
> ... in both situations [contentious and advisory], the Court is exercising a judicial function. That function is circumscribed by inherent limitations which are none the less imperative because they may be difficult to catalogue, and may not frequently present themselves as a conclusive bar to adjudication in a concrete case. Nevertheless, it is always a matter for the determination of the Court whether its judicial functions are involved. This Court, like the Permanent Court of International Justice, has always been guided by the principle which the latter stated in the case concerning the *Status of Eastern Carelia* on 23 July 1923: 'The Court, being a Court of Justice, cannot, even in giving advisory opinions, depart from the essential rules guiding their activity as a Court.' (P.C.I.J., Series B, No. 5, p. 29.)[47]

In the judgment, the Court, after a lengthy deliberation of the applicant's submission, stated that given the fact that all the relevant claims made by Cameroon had become *fait accompli*,[48] it would not be possible for the Court

47 *Case concerning the Northern Cameroons (Cameroon v. United Kingdom), Preliminary Objections, Judgment of 2 December 1963: I.C.J. Reports 1963*, pp. 29–30.

48 The Court stated in that context that "[i]f the Court were to proceed and were to hold that the Applicant's contentions were all sound on the merits, it would still be impossible for the Court to render a judgment capable of effective application. The role of the Court is not the same as that of the General Assembly. The decisions of the General Assembly would not be reversed by the judgment of the Court. The Trusteeship Agreement would not be revived and given new life by the judgment. The former Trust Territory of the Northern Cameroons would not be joined to the Republic of Cameroon. The union of that territory with the Federation of Nigeria would not be invalidated. The United Kingdom would have no right or authority to take any action with a view to satisfying the underlying desires of the Republic of Cameroon in accordance with Article 59 of the Statute, the

to render a judgment capable of effective implementation by the United Kingdom. It considered that even if Cameroon had won the case, the decisions of the General Assembly would not be reversed by the judgment of the Court. The Trusteeship Agreement would not be revived and given new life by the judgment. The United Kingdom would have no right or authority to take any action with a view to implementing the judgment. The Court emphasized,

> [t]he Court's judgment must have some practical consequence in the sense that it can affect existing legal rights or obligations of the parties, thus removing uncertainty from their legal relations. No judgment on the merits in this case could satisfy these essentials of the judicial function.[49]

Ultimately, the Court found that the proper limits of its judicial function did not permit it to entertain the claims submitted by Cameroon. Any judgment which the Court might pronounce would be without object. In this case, judicial propriety was given such predominant consideration that the Court did not even deem necessary to decide the question of jurisdiction, because whatever judgment the Court may pronounce would have no object.

In the *Nuclear Tests* (*Australia* v. *France*) (*New Zealand* v. *France*) cases,[50] Australia and New Zealand respectively filed a legal action in the Court against France for its ongoing and planned atmospheric nuclear tests in the Pacific Ocean. The applicants asked the Court to declare that further atmospheric nuclear tests by France were not in accordance with international law and violated the rights of the two countries. France raised objections to the jurisdiction of the Court. During the proceedings, the French Government made public statements that it would cease atmospheric nuclear tests in the South Pacific Ocean. The Court dismissed the cases on the ground that, since the situation in which the dispute arose disappeared, the claims advanced by Australia and New Zealand no longer had any object.

In the judgment the Court explained its decision on the basis of judicial propriety in the following terms:

> The Court, as a court of law, is called upon to resolve existing disputes between States. Thus the existence of a dispute is the primary condition for the Court to exercise its judicial function… The dispute brought before

judgment would not be binding on Nigeria, or on any other State, or on any organ of the United Nations. These truths are not controverted by the Applicant." *Ibid.*, p. 33.

49 *Ibid.*, p. 34.

50 For the basic facts of the case, see *Nuclear Tests* (*Australia* v. *France*), *Judgment, I.C.J. Reports 1974*, pp. 257–259, paras. 16–20.

> it must therefore continue to exist at the time when the Court makes its decision. It must not fail to take cognizance of a situation in which the dispute has disappeared because the object of the claim has been achieved by other means... It follows that any further finding would have no raison d'être.
>
> ...
>
> The Court therefore sees no reason to allow the continuance of proceedings which it knows are bound to be fruitless. While judicial settlement may provide a path to international harmony in circumstances of conflict, it is none the less true that the needless continuance of litigation is an obstacle to such harmony.[51]

The difference between the *Northern Cameroons* case and the *Nuclear Tests* cases is that, in the former case, the dispute as claimed by Cameroon still existed, but the facts it challenged in the Court could not be changed by virtue of the Court's judgment, even if rendered. Moreover, the Court, as a judicial organ, could not render a judgment that requires a change of the resolutions of the General Assembly, so its judgment would be meaningless. Therefore there was no point for the Court to proceed to the merits. In the latter case, by interpreting the intentions of the French Government, the Court drew the conclusion that the dispute no longer existed. The judicial function of the Court was not called for anymore, so its judgment was unnecessary.

Judicial propriety may apply to but a part of a case; the Court may find that some of the claims submitted are without object or moot. In exercising self-restraint, the Court must ensure that its discretion to refrain from deciding a case is based on persuasive reasoning.[52]

6 Non-appearance

In introducing international adjudication, the concept of non-appearance deserves a special mention. Although default is not unfamiliar in national legal

51 *Ibid.*, pp. 270–271, paras. 55–58.

52 In comparison with its predecessor, the PCIJ, the ICJ is more active in exercising its jurisdiction in matters that the PCIJ might have considered as substantially non-legal in nature. See Christian Tomuschat, "Article 36," in Andreas Zimmermann, Karin Oellers-Frahm, Christian Tomuschat, and Christian J. Tams (eds.), *op. cit. supra* footnote 38, p. 645, citing *Free Zones of Upper Savoy and the District of Gex, Order of 6 December 1930 (second phase), P.C.I.J., Series A, No. 24*, pp. 3, 15; *Judgment of June 7th, 1932, P.C.I.J., Series A/B, No. 46*, pp. 95, 160–163; *Société commerciale de Belgique, Judgment of June 15th, 1939, P.C.I.J., Series A/B, No. 78*, p. 159.

systems, where the respondent, for one reason or another, fails to appear before a court, the notion of non-appearance in international practice is entirely different in nature.[53] While a default judgment rendered by a national court that totally relies on the claims of one party is invariably unfavourable to the non-appearing party, in international adjudication that is not necessarily the case.

In the practice of the ICJ, if a State considers that there does not exist any consensual basis for the jurisdiction of the Court or that it does not accept the jurisdictional basis of an application filed against it by another State, it may choose not to appear before the Court and not appoint an Agent on its behalf. This special practice is unique in international judicial settlement.[54]

Non-appearance in the Court's practice is not rare. So far there have been several such situations. In the first type of cases the respondent fails to appear during the entire course of the proceedings. In legal writings, such States are often referred to as "the named State," "the unwilling party," or "the unwilling respondent."

The first unwilling respondent State was Iceland. In the 1972 *Fisheries Jurisdiction* cases, the United Kingdom and the Federal Republic of Germany each filed an application against Iceland for its unilateral extension of the fishery zone to 50 nautical miles measured from its baselines. Iceland informed the Court that there was no basis for the Court to entertain the case. Given the vital interests of the country involved, Iceland was not willing to confer jurisdiction on the Court in the cases. It would not appoint an Agent to represent its government in the Court.[55] Subsequently Iceland did not appear in either the provisional measures procedure or the merits phase. Notwithstanding, Iceland furnished the Court with documents and statements on its position. The Court stated in the judgment that,

> the Court, in accordance with its Statute and its settled jurisprudence, must examine *proprio motu* the question of its own jurisdiction... in the present case the duty of the Court to make this examination on its own initiative is reinforced by the terms of Article 53 of the Statue of the

53 Preliminary objections procedure may be compared to the special appearance in the common law system.

54 More discussions on the preliminary objections will be given in Chapter VIII.

55 Iceland previously entered into agreement by exchange of notes with these two countries on the fishing arrangement in its adjacent waters. Iceland agreed to postpone the implementation of the 50 miles control. The Notes also stated that in case of dispute, they agreed to submit it to the ICJ. Before the two countries instituted the cases, Iceland notified them to terminate the agreement. When Iceland started to enforce its law on fisheries, the two States filed the cases.

> Court. According to this provision, whenever one of the parties does not appear before the Court, or fails to defend its case, the Court, before finding upon the merits, must satisfy itself that it has jurisdiction.[56]

In the *Nuclear Tests* (*Australia* v. *France*) (*New Zealand* v. *France*) cases, as mentioned above, France was the unwilling respondent. It did not take part at all in the entire course of the proceedings before the Court. It insisted that the Court was "manifestly not competent" in the case; that the French Government could not accept the Court's jurisdiction; and that accordingly it did not intend to appoint an Agent, and requested the Court to remove the case from its list. No Agent was thus appointed by the French Government.

During the course of the legal proceedings, the French Government made a number of public statements, including those issued by its President, Minister of Defence and Minister of Foreign Affairs, to the effect that France would discontinue its nuclear tests in the atmosphere, after the completion of the series of tests planned for the summer of 1974. The atmospheric tests would be replaced by underground tests at France's nuclear testing station in the French Polynesia, approximately 6000 kilometres east of Australia. Based on these public statements, the Court found that the case was moot.[57]

The same situation also happened in the *Tehran Hostages* case, where the respondent State—Iran, did not appear before the Court in either the incidental proceedings or the merits phase.

The second kind of situation is that of the unwilling party appearing in some part of the proceedings, but refusing to participate in the subsequent phase. In the case concerning *Military and Paramilitary Activities in and against Nicaragua* (*Nicaragua* v. *United States of America*), the United States, as the respondent, appeared before the Court during the preliminary objections phase. After the Court delivered its judgment on jurisdiction and admissibility rejecting all the United States' preliminary objections, the United States decided not to participate in further proceedings in the case.[58]

The third one is that of the respondent initially objecting to the jurisdiction of the Court, but deciding to appear after the Court had decided that it had jurisdiction in the case. For example, in the 1951 *Nottebohm* (*Liechtenstein* v. *Guatemala*) case, after Liechtenstein instituted proceedings in the Court, the

---

56 *Fisheries Jurisdiction* (*United Kingdom* v. *Iceland*), *Jurisdiction of the Court, Judgment, I.C.J. Reports 1973*, p.7, para. 12.

57 See *Nuclear Tests* (*Australia* v. *France*), *Judgment, I.C.J. Reports 1974*, pp. 271–272, para. 59, *Nuclear Tests* (*New Zealand* v. *France*), *Judgment, I.C.J. Reports 1974*, p. 477, para. 62.

58 Shabtai Rosenne, *op. cit. supra* footnote 31, p. 136.

Guatemalan Foreign Minister made communications with the Court. In the communication letter, the Minister stated, *inter alia*, that:

> since the jurisdiction of the International Court of Justice in relation to Guatemala has terminated and because it would be contrary to the domestic laws of that country, my Government is unable to appear and to contest the claim which has been made.
>
> That, as a consequence, it cannot, for the time being, appoint an Agent in the case in question.[59]

The Court took the communication as a preliminary objection to its jurisdiction and decided to consider that question first. After the Court founded its jurisdiction, the second phase on the merits resumed. Guatemala took part in the subsequent proceedings.

When a party deliberately fails to appear before the Court on the ground that the Court lacks jurisdiction, it certainly places itself in a disadvantageous position, to say the least, as it will miss the opportunity to defend its case in the Court. However, unlike in some domestic system, where the court would entirely rely on the facts as submitted by the applicant to the prejudice of the default party, the Court is obliged to, first of all, satisfy itself that it has jurisdiction in the case in accordance with Articles 36 and 37 of the Statute and assure that the claim is well-founded in fact and law.[60] In order to do that, the Court in practice accepts the communications from the non-appearing party with the statement of its positions on the dispute, or obtains necessary information and documents to ascertain the facts.

There have been 12 cases in the Court where the unwilling party did not appear before the Court in the proceedings, either in whole or in part. Notwithstanding the various reasons for their non-appearance, it is clear that when matters of national security, territorial sovereignty and vital interests in natural resources are at stake, the consent of *both* parties to resort to third-party dispute settlement is vital. Such consent must be unequivocal, express and specific to the case, a point to be discussed in the following chapters. The Court, by using legal techniques, has successfully managed to deal with some most difficult cases in the absence of the unwilling party. Its caution in handling the communications from the unwilling respondent paved the way for a fair outcome.

---

59 *Nottebohm case (Liechtenstein* v. *Guatemala) (Preliminary Objection), Judgment of November 18th, 1953: I.C.J. Reports 1953*, pp. 115–116.

60 See Article 53 of the Statute.

CHAPTER III

Basic Rules and Principles—Part One

Judicial settlement of international disputes is not a compulsory procedure imposed on States by international law. In other words, States are not required to resort to judicial means to settle their international disputes. Jurisdiction must be conferred upon the Court, specifically and explicitly, by the State parties to a dispute. Such conferral is governed by the provisions of the Charter of the United Nations, the Statute of the Court, the Rules of Court, as well as the relevant resolutions relating to the jurisdiction of the Court adopted by the General Assembly and the Security Council. To reflect this consensual basis, there are certain basic rules and principles governing the question of jurisdiction.

1 The Importance of the Principle of Consent

The first principle that underpins the jurisdiction of the Court is the principle of consent. It underscores that the jurisdiction of the Court must be conferred by the parties on the Court in each and every case. It is considered by some scholars as a "truism" that international judicial jurisdiction is based on and derives from the consent of States.[1] This is because, in accordance with the principle of sovereignty, no State is obliged to accept the jurisdiction of a third party. The authority of a third party, unless conferred upon by a State, has no legal basis in international law. It is not an overstatement to say that the entire clause of Article 36 of the Statute on the jurisdictional bases of the Court reflects the principle of consent. It permeates each and every aspect of jurisdiction, from mainline proceedings to all the incidental procedures.

The Court has invariably upheld the principle of consent in its jurisprudence.[2] Derived from the principle of sovereignty, as stated previously, free choice of means of settlement of international disputes is a long established principle of international law. So long as a peaceful means of settlement is resorted to, States are not obliged to use judicial means for the settlement of

1 Hugh Thirlway, "The Law and Procedure of the International Court of Justice 1960–1989: Part Nine," *British Yearbook of International Law*, Vol. 69, 1998, p. 4.

2 See Christian Tomuschat, "Article 36," in Andreas Zimmermann, Karin Oellers-Frahm, Christian Tomuschat and Christian J. Tams (eds.), *The Statute of the International Court of Justice: A Commentary*, 2nd edition, Oxford University Press, 2012, p. 647.

 | DOI 10.1163/9789004342767_004

international disputes. On a general basis, no priority or superiority is attached to the various means of settlement, as enumerated in Article 33, paragraph 1, of the Charter of the United Nations. This free choice in no way weakens or otherwise strengthens the judicial settlement. As the Court pointed out in the case concerning *Passage through the Great Belt*,

> the judicial settlement of international disputes, with a view of which the Court has been established, is simply an alternative to the direct and friendly settlement of such disputes between the Parties; consequently it is for the Court to facilitate, so far as is compatible with its Statute, such direct and friendly settlement.... [A]ny negotiation between the parties with a view to achieving a direct and friendly settlement is to be welcomed.[3]

The idea to impose compulsory jurisdiction of judicial settlement on States was advocated and promoted by European scholars long before WWI, but with little effect among States. When the PCIJ was founded, the idea remerged, but still without any success. It was revived at the San Francisco Conference when the Charter of the United Nations was being adopted. Various proposals were made to the effect that the membership of States to the Organization should be linked with the jurisdiction of the International Court of Justice. Since the Statute of the ICJ was made an integral part of the Charter, it was suggested that if a State wished to become a member of the United Nations, it must accept the compulsory jurisdiction of the ICJ for certain types of legal disputes. This is apparently a very high criterion for the membership, too restrictive for many States to accept. Unsurprisingly, none of these proposals received much support from States at the San Francisco Conference. Article 33, paragraph 1, of the Charter instead explicitly provides that the parties to a dispute have the right to resort to methods of settlement of "their own choice." This term "own choice" implies that no State can be subjected to the compulsory jurisdiction of the Court; the principle of consent prevails.

The principle of consent dictates that the decision to have recourse to the Court, in all cases, is a deliberate political choice of a State. That is to say, the question of whether to submit a dispute to the judicial settlement of the Court is not governed by legal rules, but determined by the State concerned upon the consideration of various factors that are generally involved in the political process of decision-making; factors such as domestic politics (upcoming

3 *Passage through the Great Belt (Finland* v. *Denmark), Provisional Measures, Order of 29 July 1991, I.C.J. Reports 1991*, p. 20, para. 35.

parliamentary elections, internal oppositions), diplomatic relations with the disputant party, trade and economic sanctions that might be imposed, can all in one way or another affect such decision-making. Once a dispute is submitted to the Court, however, the extent of that consent will be placed under the judicial examination of the Court.

2 Modes of Expression of Consent

According to the principle of consent, consent must be given expressly and unequivocally. That does not mean that, each time when a case is to be submitted to the Court, the parties have to express their consent to the jurisdiction of the Court. Under Articles 36 and 37 of the Statute and Article 38, paragraph 5, of the Rules of Court, there are several ways by which a State may express its consent to the jurisdiction of the Court in advance. So in practice, when the Court is deciding on the question of jurisdiction in a case, it will not consider the consent of the parties as such, but the scope and content of the terms under which the parties have accepted the Court's jurisdiction. Each of such modalities will be discussed in turn.

a *Consent Granted by Agreements*

1 A Special Agreement—A *Compromis*

The first, and often-used, means to accept the Court's jurisdiction is the conclusion of a special agreement between the disputant States to submit a specific legal dispute with a defined mandate and object to the Court for settlement. Such special agreement is also called "*compromis*." Article 36, paragraph 1, of the Statute reads:

> The jurisdiction of the Court comprises all cases which the parties refer to it and all matters specifically provided for in the Charter of the United Nations or in treaties and conventions in force.

This provision nowhere refers to special agreements, but the term "the parties refer to it" implies that the parties may do so by agreement. This is the most direct and specific means to express the consent of the parties to confer jurisdiction on the Court, so it gives rise to the least controversy on the question of jurisdiction.

The parties should in the *compromis* specify the legal issues to be resolved, the applicable law for the Court to decide the case, and the object to achieve. Unlike the traditional agreement for arbitration, the *compromis* thus envisaged tends to be quite succinct and straightforward; it does not have to contain clauses on the composition of the tribunal and procedural rules. For the Court, such matters are institutionally ready; the members of the Court are permanent and the procedural rules and the applicable law are provided for by the Statute and the Rules of Court. In this aspect, judicial procedure is much more formal and predictable than arbitration.

There are a few merits to confer jurisdiction on the Court by a special agreement. First of all, it is up to the parties to decide to what extent they wish the Court to exercise its jurisdiction. The parties may choose to submit their entire dispute to the Court for final settlement, submit a portion of their dispute to the Court for adjudication, or simply ask the Court to pronounce on the applicable principles and rules for them to apply. This selective submission does not mean that the parties do not have full trust in the Court. It shows that the parties are in the best position to assess at which point of time and to what extent that judicial resource is most desirable for the settlement of their disputes. The Court gives full deference to the wish of the States.

In the *North Sea Continental Shelf* cases (*Federal Republic of Germany/Denmark; Federal Republic of Germany/Netherlands*), for instance, the parties only requested the Court to lay down and define in a final and binding decision the applicable legal principles and rules for the delimitation of continental shelf, leaving the parties subsequently to negotiate their maritime boundaries in pursuance of these principles and rules.[4] Article 1 of the Special Agreement between Germany and Netherlands states:

> Article 1
>
> (1) The International Court of Justice is requested to decide the following question:
> What principles and rules of international law are applicable to the delimitation as between the Parties of the areas of the continental shelf in the North Sea which appertain to each of them beyond the partial boundary determined by the above-mentioned Convention of 1 December 1964?
>
> (2) The Governments of the Federal Republic of Germany and of the Kingdom of the Netherlands shall delimit the continental shelf in the North Sea as between their countries by agreement in pursuance of the decision requested from the International Court of Justice.

4 Special Agreement of 20 February 1967, *North Sea Continental Shelf* (*Federal Republic of Germany/Denmark; Federal Republic of Germany/Netherlands*), *Pleadings, Oral Arguments, Documents, Vol. I, 1968*, pp. 6–10.

In 1998 Indonesia and Malaysia reached an agreement to submit their territorial dispute over two islands—*Pulau Ligitan* and *Pulau Sipadan*—to the Court. Article 2 of the Special Agreement provides that,

> the Court is requested to determine on the basis of the treaties, agreements and any other evidence furnished by the Parties, whether sovereignty over Pulau Ligitan and Pulau Sipadan belongs to the Republic of Indonesia or to Malaysia.[5]

Technically the subject-matter submitted to the Court seems a bit too restrictive for the settlement of the dispute, but given the potential stakes for the future maritime delimitation, it is not incomprehensible that the parties only agreed to submit the sovereignty over two islands rather than the whole issue of maritime delimitation to the Court for settlement. The principle of consent ensures that the parties have ample room to take their political decision to go to the Court.

It should be pointed out that to reach a special agreement by itself often requires intensive negotiations between the parties and their good will and cooperation to settle disputes. For peaceful settlement of international disputes, that part of negotiations often proves to be a crucial stage for the subsequent process of settlement.

The *Pedra Branca* case serves as a good example. Singapore and Malaysia had territorial disputes over some small islands—*Pedra Branca, Middle Rocks and South Ledge*—for over 30 years. After 14 years of diplomatic negotiations between the two countries after the dispute arose, they ultimately agreed to submit it to the ICJ for settlement. Then they started the negotiation to draft the terms of the Special Agreement. It took them four years (1995–1998) and three rounds of negotiation to work out the Special Agreement.[6] On the terms of the Agreement, the parties had three major differences. First, how to list *"Pedra Branca"* or *"Pulau Batu Puteh,"* the island in dispute, when describing the subject-matter of the litigation. The former was used by Singapore while the latter by Malaysia. As the parties seized the Court by a special agreement, they had to agree between themselves which name should be put first. Ultimately they agreed to adopt the conventional alphabetical sequence. The second issue was whether to include *Middle Rocks* and *South Ledge* in the subject-matter.

5 *Sovereignty over Pulau Ligitan and Pulau Sipadan (Indonesia/Malaysia), Judgment, I.C.J. Reports 2002*, p. 630, para. 2.

6 S. Jayakumar and Tommy Koh, *Pedra Branca: The Road to the World Court*, NUS Press, 2009, pp. 35–41.

This was the most contentious issue, because Pedra Branca was the central issue in dispute. To include other islands into the Agreement would expand the scope of the Court's jurisdiction and the stake in losing the case would be higher for either of the governments. The third was whether to accept Malaysia's proposal to include a provision in the Agreement to the effect that, if one side was adjudged to have sovereignty over *Pedra Branca*, the ICJ should also be asked to determine the rights or interests of the other party. The objective of this proposal was to ensure that both parties would gain something from the decision of the Court. Malaysia eventually did not insist on the proposal. After the conclusion of the Special Agreement, it took the two States another five years (1998–2003) to ratify it. This is partly because there were other more urgent matters between the two countries for settlement. Moreover, Malaysia had another ongoing case concerning *Sipadan* and *Ligitan* with Indonesia in the Court. It may have wished to see the result of that case first.[7]

The Court delivered its judgment on 23 May 2008. The whole process of the settlement is recorded by the chief negotiators of Singapore in a book entitled "*Pedra Branca: the Road to the World Court*," which vividly tells what factors can truly drive the parties to finally accept judicial settlement.[8]

Since 1946 there have been 18 cases filed by a special agreement of the parties.

2 A Compromissory Clause

The second way to submit a case to the Court is by a final clause of a treaty, which normally provides that, in case of dispute arising from the interpretation and application of the treaty, the dispute may be, at the request of a party, referred to the Court for settlement. Such clause is called "compromissory clause." It can be contained in a treaty provision or a separate instrument, for instance, the Optional Protocol concerning the Compulsory Settlement of Disputes to the Vienna Convention on Diplomatic Relations. Treaties and conventions that contain such a clause, in most cases, would also allow the State parties to make reservations to the clause. Each State party can decide, when it signs and ratifies the treaty, whether to accept the jurisdiction of the Court for the settlement of disputes arising from the interpretation and application of

---

7 *Ibid.*, p. 42.

8 *Ibid.* The book gives a very detailed account of each phase of the process, illustrating the policy consideration, interests at stake and strategy for the successful settlement of the dispute with the neighbouring country. It is a rare record of an ICJ case by a State party. It explains why and how States submit their disputes to the Court, but it also offers some thought as to why States do not resort to third-party dispute settlement.

the treaty. If a State party does not make any reservation to the compromissory clause or joins the Optional Protocol, it means that that State has accepted the jurisdiction of the Court.

There are numerous international treaties and conventions which contain such compromissory clauses. They serve as the jurisdictional bases for a major bulk of business of the Court. It is said that, in the last decade, about half of the cases instituted in the Court were filed on the basis of such clauses.[9] A compromissory clause provides the possibility for a State to unilaterally institute a case in the Court. Albeit abiding by treaty terms, the applicant may nevertheless take the respondent State by surprise in practice.

As the compromissory clause is treaty-based, the jurisdictional scope of the Court is therefore confined to the interpretation and application of the treaty concerned. For example, in the case concerning *Application of the Convention on the Prevention and Punishment of the Crime of Genocide* (*Croatia* v. *Serbia*), Croatia instituted proceedings against Serbia (the Federal Republic of Yugoslavia then) in respect of a dispute concerning alleged acts of genocide, war crimes, and crimes against humanity.[10] The application only invoked Article IX of the Genocide Convention as the basis of the jurisdiction of the Court. The Court, therefore, had to confine its jurisdiction to the question of genocide. The other alleged acts of war crimes or crimes against humanity presented by Croatia fell outside the scope of the Court's jurisdiction.

b Consent Conferred by a Declaration of Acceptance of Compulsory Jurisdiction

1 Article 36, Paragraph 2, of the Statute of the ICJ

The third way to confer jurisdiction on the Court is by unilateral declaration. A State may at any time make a declaration accepting the compulsory jurisdiction of the Court in accordance with Article 36, paragraph 2, of the Statute. Article 36, paragraph 2, reads:

> The States parties to the present Statute may at any time declare that they recognize as compulsory *ipso facto* and without special agreement, in relation to any other state accepting the same obligation, the jurisdiction of the Court in all legal disputes concerning:

9 Christian Tomuschat, "Article 36," in Andreas Zimmermann, Karin Oellers-Frahm, Christian Tomuschat and Christian J. Tams (eds.), *op. cit. supra* footnote 2, p. 657.

10 *Application of the Convention on the Prevention and Punishment of the Crime of Genocide* (*Croatia* v. *Serbia*), *Preliminary Objections, Judgment, I.C.J. Reports 2008*, p. 412.

a. the interpretation of a treaty;
b. any question of international law;
c. the existence of any fact which, if established, would constitute a breach of an international obligation;
d. the nature or extent of the reparation to be made for the breach of an international obligation.

The notification of the declaration shall be deposited with the Secretary-General of the United Nations. The list of declarations can be found on the website of the Court. So far there are 72 States that have made such declarations recognizing the compulsory jurisdiction of the Court.

A State may accept the compulsory jurisdiction unconditionally or conditionally. Apart from the standard terms of Article 36, paragraph 2, of the Statute with regard to the reciprocal obligations of other States, a State may lay down certain conditions or set specific terms for its acceptance. Reservations or exclusions may be attached to a declaration.[11]

Among the States who have made unilateral declarations recognizing as compulsory the jurisdiction of the Court, only a few of them have accepted the terms of Article 36, paragraph 2, without attaching any conditions. Most of the States have made reservations and exclusions. On the whole, such reservations and exclusions fall into several categories. First, they retain the general right of the declarant State to resort to other peaceful means of its own choice for the settlement of disputes. Secondly, they exclude certain types of disputes from the scope of the Court's jurisdiction, including disputes that essentially fall within domestic jurisdiction, territorial and boundary disputes, disputes concerning armed conflicts and hostilities, maritime delimitation disputes, or disputes of particular concern.[12] Thirdly, they limit the time frame for the effect of the declarations.

Pursuant to Article 36, paragraph 5, of the Statute, declarations made during the time of the PCIJ may continue to be valid unless lapsed or withdrawn. To date, there are still six such declarations in existence.[13] Interesting to note,

11 Article 36, paragraph 3, provides that, "[t]he declarations referred to above may be made unconditionally or on condition of reciprocity on the part of several or certain States, or for a certain time."

12 For instance, Ireland excludes disputes with the United Kingdom with regard to Northern Ireland. Australia and New Zealand exclude disputes concerning maritime delimitation and exploitation of resources in the area pending such delimitation.

13 These six States are the Dominican Republic (30 September 1924); Haiti (4 October 1921); Nicaragua (24 September 1929); Panama (25 October 1921); Uruguay (28 January 1921); and Luxembourg (15 September 1930).

five out of these six States are from Latin-America, with Luxembourg as the only exception. Their declarations unconditionally recognized the Court's jurisdiction as compulsory. This gives an idea of how States initially perceived compulsory jurisdiction. Needless to mention that the composition of the international community of States at that time was much different from today.

Under the specific terms of Article 36, paragraph 2, reciprocity is inherent to the system. If States attach different reservations to their declarations, jurisdictional basis between them can be founded only to the extent that they coincide in scope. In the *Anglo-Iranian Oil Co.* case, the Court stated that,

> [i]n the present case the jurisdiction of the Court depends on the Declarations made by the Parties under Article 36, paragraph 2, on condition of reciprocity, which were, in the case of the United Kingdom, signed on February 28th, 1940, and, in the case of Iran, signed on October 2, 1930, and ratified on September 8, 1932. By these Declarations, jurisdiction is conferred on the Court only to the extent to which the two Declarations coincide in conferring it. As the Iranian Declaration is more limited in scope than the United Kingdom Declaration, it is the Iranian Declaration on which the Court must base itself. This is common ground between the Parties.[14]

In practice, it is the terms of these reservations and conditions that often give rise to disputes between the parties on the title of jurisdiction of the Court. In the *Whaling* case, one of Japan's arguments regarding the jurisdictional basis of the Court was that, in its declaration made under Article 36, paragraph 2, of the Statute, Australia excluded any dispute relating to the exploitation of the disputed area from the jurisdiction of the Court. As the present case concerned the exploitation of whaling resources in the relevant area, the subject-matter, in Japan's view, therefore, fell outside of the scope of the Court's jurisdiction.[15] Australia, of course, did not agree with that interpretation.

During the drafting process of the PCIJ Statute, two schools of thought emerged in the Committee of Jurists responsible for the drafting work. One

14 *Anglo-Iranian Oil Co. case (United Kingdom* v. *Iran), jurisdiction, Judgment of July 22, 1952: I.C.J. Reports 1952*, p. 103.

15 Australia's reservation excludes "any dispute concerning or relating to the delimitation of maritime zones, including the territorial sea, the exclusive economic zone and the continental shelf, or arising out of, concerning, or relating to the exploitation of any disputed area of or adjacent to any such maritime zone pending its delimitation." International Court of Justice, *Yearbook 2006–2007*, No. 61, p. 123.

school proposed to impose general compulsory jurisdiction for all legal disputes,[16] while the other insisted on the exclusively consensual basis of the jurisdiction.[17] Unilateral declarations came out as a compromise between these two schools. In the early years of the PCIJ, the Optional Clause was not popular among States, and was in particular not accepted by the major European powers. Only from 1929 did they accept the Optional Clause, but their reservations and safeguards attached thereto were so extensive that they cast doubt on the sincerity of these States in making such declarations. By 1934, 42 States had made such declarations. Out of 11 cases instituted in the Court on the basis of unilateral declarations, 10 were submitted after 1930.

Compared with its predecessor, the ICJ's experience was less encouraging at its initial stage. The number of States that accepted the Optional Clause remained rather low for many years. By 1993, out of 186 State parties to the Statute, 55 States, less than one third, had accepted compulsory jurisdiction under Article 36, paragraph 2. Two permanent members, France and the United States withdrew their declarations after the *Nuclear Tests* cases and the *Military and Paramilitary Activities* case, respectively. Currently among the five permanent members, only the United Kingdom still accepts such compulsory jurisdiction.[18] The situation has improved in recent years. To date, 72 States, out of 192 State parties to the Statute, have accepted the compulsory jurisdiction of the Court.[19]

2 Declarations Based on Treaties Concluded Prior to 1946

The fourth way to confer jurisdiction on the Court is provided in Article 36, paragraph 5, and Article 37 of the Statute. Article 36, paragraph 5, reads:

> Declarations made under Article 36 of the Statute of the Permanent Court of International Justice and which are still in force shall be deemed, as between the parties to the present Statute, to be acceptance of the compulsory jurisdiction of the International Court of Justice for the period which they still have to run and in accordance with their terms.

16 Such legal disputes are enumerated in Article 13 of the Covenant of the League of Nations, which was later copied in Article 36, paragraph 2, of the Statute of the ICJ.

17 Shabtai Rosenne, *The World Court, What It Is and How It Works,* 5th completely revised edition, Martinus Nijhoff Publishers, 1995, p. 90.

18 It has recently revised its declaration to exclude certain situations from the scope of the Court's jurisdiction.

19 6 Asian States have made Declarations under Article 36, paragraph 2, of the ICJ Statute accepting the compulsory jurisdiction of the Court: Cambodia(19 September 1957); India(18 September 1974); Pakistan (13 September 1960); Philippines (18 January 1972); Japan (6 October 2015); Timor-Leste(21 September 2012).

Article 37 states that:

> Whenever a treaty or convention in force provides for reference of a matter to a tribunal to have been instituted by the League of Nations, or to the Permanent Court of Justice, the matter shall, as between the parties to the present Statute, be referred to the International Court of Justice.

Both of these articles are meant to be a transitional arrangement between the PCIJ and the ICJ. The former provision is intended to ensure that declarations made under the PCIJ Statute be maintained so as to retain the continuity of the two Courts. Given the almost identical terms of the relevant provisions of the two Courts' Statutes on jurisdiction, it is logical that unilateral declarations made under the PCIJ Statute should be preserved under their original terms, so far as the State parties wish to maintain them. As is mentioned above, six such declarations remain effective under Article 36, paragraph 5, of the Statute.

Article 37 mainly deals with old treaties concluded before 1946. Theoretically, today, many of those treaties are still in force, some of which conferred jurisdiction on the Permanent Court, e.g. the 1928 General Act for the Pacific Settlement of International Disputes. There are at least six cases in which the applicant States invoked Article 17 of the 1928 General Act as one of the jurisdictional bases of the Court.[20] In two cases, the Court directly discussed the 1928 General Act.

In the *Aegean Sea Continental Shelf* case, for example, Greece instituted proceedings against Turkey on the issue of the continental shelf.[21] One of its jurisdictional grounds was the 1928 General Act, to which both Greece and Turkey were parties. Turkey took the view that the Court had no jurisdiction to entertain the case and did not take part in the proceedings. The Court examined the jurisdictional issue *proprio motu*. The Court ultimately avoided any ruling on the status of the 1928 General Act, for fear that it might have legal effect on State parties other than Greece and Turkey. Instead it examined the effect of the reservation attached by Greece at its accession to the Act. The Court found that the subject-matter of the present case fell within the meaning of the reservation, and therefore, it had no jurisdiction on the basis of Article 17 of the 1928 General Act.

---

20 See cases concerning the *Temple of Preah Vihear, Trial of Pakistani Prisoners of War, Nuclear Tests, Aegean Sea Continental Shelf,* and *Aerial Incident of 1999*. Article 17 of the General Act is a compromissory clause, providing resort to the Permanent Court of International Justice.

21 *Aegean Sea Continental Shelf, Judgment, I.C.J. Reports, 1978,* p. 3.

Statistics are not available as to how many such treaties still exist and which of them contain clauses that confer jurisdiction on the Court. Article 37 of the Statute, however, remains pertinent whenever such treaty is invoked by the parties.

Article 37 has been invoked 16 times in the Court. The jurisprudence of the Court on this Article provides some important principles governing successive and conflicting acceptances of the Court's jurisdiction. According to the case law of the Court, if the applicant relies on several grounds, i.e. a declaration recognizing the compulsory jurisdiction of the Court, a compromissory clause of a treaty concluded after the declaration, and a declaration made before 1946, the Court would rely on the most relevant basis.[22] Therefore old treaties are less used as a ground of jurisdiction.

3 Declarations Based on Regional Treaties

Compulsory jurisdiction can also be accepted through bilateral and regional treaties. The most-cited example is the American Treaty on Pacific Settlement signed on 30 April 1948, officially designated, according to Article LX thereof, as the "Pact of Bogotá."[23] So far 14 American States are parties to the Pact.[24] Article XXXI of the Pact of Bogotá provides that:

> In conformity with Article 36, paragraph 2, of the Statute of the International Court of Justice, the High Contracting Parties declare that they recognize, in relation to any other American State, the jurisdiction of the Court as compulsory *ipso facto*, without the necessity of any special agreement so long as the present Treaty is in force, in all disputes of a juridical nature that arise among them concerning:
> (a) The interpretation of a treaty;
> (b) Any question of international law;
> (c) The existence of any fact which, if established, would constitute the breach of an international obligation; or
> (d) The nature or extent of the reparation to be made for the breach of an international obligation.

22 See, for example, *Case concerning the Temple of Preah Vihear (Cambodia* v. *Thailand), Preliminary Objections, Judgment of 26 May 1961: I.C.J. Reports 1961*, p. 17; case of *Certain Norwegian Loans (France* v. *Norway), Judgment of July 6th, 1957: I.C.J. Reports 1957*, p. 9.

23 American Treaty on Pacific Settlement, 30 *UNTS* 55.

24 After the Court delivered its Judgment of 19 November 2012 in the case concerning *Territorial and Maritime Dispute (Nicaragua* v. *Colombia)*, Colombia denunciated its acceptance of the compulsory jurisdiction of the ICJ by withdrawing from the Pact of Bogotá.

This collectively made declaration by virtue of the Pact of Bogotá has the same effect as any other unilateral declaration. Since the cases concerning *Border and Transborder Armed Actions* (*Nicaragua* v. *Costa Rica*) (*Nicaragua* v. *Honduras*), where Nicaragua invoked Article XXXI of the Pact of Bogotá as one of its grounds to found the jurisdiction of the Court, this Pact has been frequently invoked by the American States before the Court in recent cases.

Another regional treaty for the acceptance of the compulsory jurisdiction of the Court is the European Convention for the Peaceful Settlement of Disputes. The *Certain Property* case between Liechtenstein and Germany was instituted on that basis.[25]

c *Consent Based on* Forum Prorogatum

The fifth way to express consent to the jurisdiction of the Court is by the conduct of the respondent party. This is called *forum prorogatum*. It is provided in Article 38, paragraph 5, of the Rules of Court. The practice is derived from the principle that a party is not permitted to benefit from its own inconsistencies (*allegans contraria non audiendus est*), similar to the notion of *estoppel* in common law. The doctrine denotes the situation where, if a party, by its own words or conducts, indicates that it accepts the Court's jurisdiction on the merits of a case, it cannot subsequently claim that the Court is not competent to adjudicate.

The institution of *forum prorogatum* originally was not regulated by the Statute and the Rules of Court, but evolved from the practice of the PCIJ. In interpreting Article 36, paragraph 1, of the Statute, the Permanent Court, in a number of cases, deduced the parties' consent to the jurisdiction of the Court from certain acts.[26] For instance, the respondent State, without raising any objection to the jurisdiction of the Court, directly appeared in the Court and pleaded on the merits of the case. The Court could, upon those acts, found its jurisdiction.[27]

This judicial practice gave rise to two questions among the judges of the Permanent Court. First, under the Rules of Court, whether it was a prerequisite for the applicant State to spell out the jurisdictional basis of its application. Following from that, secondly, should the application necessarily indicate

---

25 *Certain Property* (*Liechtenstein* v. *Germany*), *Preliminary Objections, Judgment, I.C.J. Reports 2005*, p. 6.

26 See *Mavrommatis Palestine Concessions, Judgment No. 2, 1924, P.C.I.J., Series A, No. 2*, and *Rights of Minorities in Upper Silesia* (*Minority Schools*), *Judgment No. 12, 1928, P.C.I.J., Series A, No. 15*.

27 *Rights of Minorities in Upper Silesia* (*Minority Schools*), *Judgment No. 12, 1928, P.C.I.J., Series A, No. 15*, p. 24.

whether the respondent State had given its consent to the jurisdiction of the Court. Judges, in their individual opinions, held different views on these issues, revealing two approaches to the principle of consent; one is a strict approach, insisting on express consent while the other prefers to leave open the possibility of *forum prorogatum*, being more inclined to unilateral submission of disputes to the Court. The ensuing practice shows that the latter approach gradually prevailed, expanding the scope of the Court's jurisdiction.[28] In instituting proceedings, the applicant State is only required to specify in its application "as far as possible the legal grounds upon which the jurisdiction of the Court is said to be based."[29] This is a less strict requirement.

In the *Anglo-Iranian Oil Co.* case, the Court states that "the principle of *forum prorogatum*, if it could be applied to the present case, would have to be based on some conduct or statement of the Government of Iran which involves an element of consent regarding the jurisdiction of the Court."[30]

Forum prorogatum was added to the Rules of Court in 1978 as Article 38, paragraph 5, stipulating under what circumstances *ad hoc* jurisdictional basis is permitted in the Court. The Article reads:

> When the applicant State proposes to found the jurisdiction of the Court upon a consent thereto yet to be given or manifested by the State against which such application is made, the application shall be transmitted to that State. It shall not however be entered in the General List, nor any action be taken in the proceedings, unless and until the State against which such application is made consents to the Court's jurisdiction for the purposes of the case.

In simple terms, this clause means that in the absence of any of the jurisdictional bases between the parties to a dispute, one of the parties may nevertheless unilaterally submit an application to the Court, virtually inviting the other

28 In analysing this phenomenon, Shabtai Rosenne observes three deliberate omissions in the Statute and the Rules of Court. Namely, first, the applicant in instituting a case is not required to transmit the consent of the respondent. Secondly, there is no provision on the specific manner in which the consent of the respondent should be expressed. Thirdly, there is no requirement as to when proceedings should be instituted by special agreement and when by unilateral application. All these considerations are left to practice with Article 53 to deal with each specific case. Shabtai Rosenne, *The Law and Practice of the International Court, 1920–2005, Vol. II, Jurisdiction,* 4th edition, Martinus Nijhoff Publishers, 2006, p. 675.

29 Article 38, paragraph 2, of the Rules of Court.

30 *Anglo-Iranian Oil Co. case (jurisdiction), Judgment of July 22nd, 1952: I.C.J. Reports 1952,* p. 114.

party to give consent to the jurisdiction of the Court to entertain the application. If the invited State accepts the invitation, the Court's jurisdiction is thus founded and the case enters the General List.[31] Unless and until that State notifies the Court or the applicant State of its consent, the Court is not regarded as seised and the case will not enter the docket of the Court and, therefore, no proceedings will take their course. On this amendment, the Court observed that,

> [t]he purpose of this amendment was to allow a State which proposes to found the jurisdiction of the Court to entertain a case upon a consent thereto yet to be given or manifested by another State to file an application setting out its claims and inviting the latter to consent to the Court dealing with them, without prejudice to the rules governing the sound administration of justice.[32]

Some scholars compare the institution as a "summons" as is used in domestic law, but Judge Winiarski criticized such a comparison on the ground that a summons is issued in the name of the sovereign, and therefore the concept of summons is not appropriate for describing relations with States.[33] The respondent State is not obliged to accept the jurisdiction.

Of course, the respondent State may consent to the jurisdiction of the Court to entertain the application as is submitted, or use the offer to enter into a special agreement with the applicant State so as to ascertain the scope of the Court's jurisdiction and the terms of the settlement.

In the *Corfu Channel* case,[34] after the Security Council resolution recommended the United Kingdom and Albania to "immediately" refer the case to

---

31 Before 1978, in case of application on the basis of *forum prorogatum*, the case would first enter the list. If the respondent explicitly rejected the jurisdiction of the Court, the Court would issue an order to remove it from the list. The current procedure is not only simpler, but also renders the legal status of the named State certain. Under the current provision, the named State would not be regarded as an unwilling respondent, or a non-appearing State party.

32 *Certain Questions of Mutual Assistance in Criminal Matters (Djibouti* v. *France), Judgment, I.C.J. Reports 2008*, p. 204, para. 63.

33 Shabtai Rosenne, *op. cit. supra* footnote 28, *Vol. II, Jurisdiction,* p. 673, citing Bohdan Winiarski, "Quelques réflexions sur le soi-disant forum prorogatum en droit international," *Festschrift für Jean Spiropoulos* 445 (1957).

34 Normally the respondent State's reaction to the application should be made before the date for the filing of its counter-memorial or preliminary objection. In the *Corfu Channel* case, the special agreement was made immediately before the reading of the Judgment

the ICJ, the United Kingdom unilaterally instituted the proceedings in the Court. The Court founded its jurisdiction on the basis of *forum prorogatum,* because Albania indicated its willingness to go to the Court. Normally, a special agreement should be reached, at the latest, before the date of filing the counter-memorial, but the United Kingdom and Albania reached a special agreement right before the Court delivered its judgment on jurisdiction. The Court, none the less, gave sufficient consideration to the wishes of the parties and applied the agreement in the subsequent proceedings. This kind of procedural flexibility exercised by the Court shows that the Court, in the administration of justice, takes full account the agreement of the parties.

In the 1950s, there had been a number of cases concerning prorogated jurisdiction, for instance, *Treatment in Hungary of Aircraft and Crew of United States of America* (*United States of America* v. *Hungary*)(*United States of America v. Union of Soviet Socialist Republics*), and *Aerial Incident of 27 July 1955* (*Israel* v. *Bulgaria*) (*United States of America v. Bulgaria*) and (*United Kingdom v. Bulgaria*). In these cases the applicant invoked *forum prorogatum* as the ground for jurisdiction, but in none of them, the named States gave their consent to the jurisdiction of the Court. Consequently, the cases were removed from the General List of the Court.

The first instance where jurisdiction was founded on *forum prorogatum* pursuant to Article 38, paragraph 5, of the Rules of Court is the case filed by the Republic of the Congo against France in 2003, i.e., *Certain Criminal Proceedings in France.*[35] France gave its consent to the jurisdiction of the Court pursuant to Article 38, paragraph 5, of the Rules of Court. The case was thus placed on the General List.[36]

When a State gives its consent to the jurisdiction of the Court to entertain an application filed on the basis of *forum prorogatum*, the case will directly enter the merits phase; there will not be any preliminary proceedings on the question of jurisdiction, as the jurisdictional basis is founded on Article 38, paragraph 5, of the Rules of Court. However, that does not mean that the

---

on jurisdiction. That actually changed the jurisdictional basis of the case. The special agreement governed the proceedings afterwards.

35 *Certain Criminal Proceedings in France* (*Republic of the Congo* v. *France*), *Provisional Measures, Order of 17 June 2003, I.C.J. Reports 2003,* p. 102.

36 This case lasted for a long time in the Court. Having had provisional measures and finished the two rounds of written pleadings, the parties eventually agreed to discontinue the proceedings and remove it from the General List of the Court. See *Certain Criminal Proceedings in France* (*Republic of the Congo* v. *France*), *Order of 16 November 2010, I.C.J. Reports 2010,* p. 635.

parties would not have any contention over the scope of the Court's jurisdiction. That dispute on the jurisdiction will first be dealt with by the Court during the merits phase.

In the case concerning *Certain Questions of Mutual Assistance in Criminal Matters* (*Djibouti* v. *France*), the Court analysed the principle of consent in the context of *forum prorogatum*. It stated that "for the Court to exercise jurisdiction on the basis of *forum prorogatum*, the element of consent must be either explicit or clearly to be deduced from the relevant conduct of a State."[37] As the respondent State is invited to accept the Court's jurisdiction, it "is completely free to respond as it sees fit; if it consents to the Court's jurisdiction, it is for it to specify, if necessary, the aspects of the dispute which it agrees to submit to the judgment of the Court."[38]

The practice of *forum prorogatum* seems to be on the rise in recent years. In 2014 the Marshall Islands instituted proceedings against nine nuclear power States, namely five permanent members of the UN Security Council and 4 other States possessing nuclear weapons.[39] To those that do not accept the Court's jurisdiction, either in general or for such subject-matter, the Marshall Islands invoked Article 38, paragraph 5, of the Rules of Court as the basis of the Court's jurisdiction.[40] China and Israel duly notified the Court that they did not consent to the jurisdiction of the Court to entertain the cases, while the other four States did not reply, presumably not accepting the invitation of the Marshall Islands.[41]

---

37 *Certain Questions of Mutual Assistance in Criminal Matters* (*Djibouti* v. *France*), *Judgment, I.C.J. Reports 2008,* p. 204, para. 62.

38 *Ibid.*, p. 205, para. 63.

39 These States are India, Pakistan, Israel and North Korea.

40 Cases concerning *Obligations concerning Negotiations relating to Cessation of the Nuclear Arms Race and to Nuclear Disarmament* against India, Pakistan and the United Kingdom. Subsequent to the filing of the case, the United Kingdom notified the Secretary-General of its amendment to its declaration under the Optional Clause of the Statute. See Chapter 1, Section 4, "Declarations recognizing as compulsory the jurisdiction of the International Court of Justice under Article 36, paragraph 2, of the Statute of the Court," United Kingdom of Great Britain and Northern Ireland, 31 December 2014, *Multilateral Treaties Deposited with the Secretary-General,* United Nations, New York (ST/LEG/SER.E), https://treaties.un.org/Pages/ParticipationStatus.aspx, 14 April 2016. Pakistan has also modified the terms of its Optional Clause on 29 March 2017.

41 A judgment on jurisdiction and admissibility was rendered in each of the three cases against India, Pakistan and the United Kingdom; on 5 October 2016, the Court found that no dispute existed between the parties at the date of the filing of the applications.

d *Consent Derived from Other Sources*

The last type of jurisdictional ground is based on agreements concluded between the parties. Such agreements do not formally constitute a special agreement as provided for by Article 36, paragraph 1, of the Statute, but contain express provisions for the recourse to the Court for settlement of disputes under given circumstances. The Court has dealt with three such cases.[42] In each of them, the respondent State objected to the jurisdictional ground, contending the validity of the agreements. The Court none the less founded its jurisdiction through treaty interpretation.

These are the basic modes by which a State may give its consent to accept the jurisdiction of the Court.

3 Mutuality and Reciprocity

As is stated above, according to Article 36, paragraph 2, of the Statute, acceptance of the compulsory jurisdiction of the Court is based on mutuality and reciprocity, *ratione personae, ratione materiae* and *ratione temporis*. These conditions are inherent in the special agreements and compromissory clauses. In case of jurisdiction accepted by unilateral declarations, one State's conditions and reservations apply reciprocally to other States. Judge Jiménez de Aréchaga attributed that condition to the credit of Sr. Raoul Fernandes of Brazil, one of the architects of the Optional Clause. Sr. Raoul Fernandes expressed his opinion during the deliberation of the Assembly of the League of Nations on the text of what became Article 36 that "it was inadmissible for a State to accept the principle of compulsory jurisdiction without knowing exactly towards whom it accepted such an obligation." In light of this discussion, in addition to paragraph 2 of Article 36, paragraph 3 provides that reciprocity may be required on the part of certain States.[43]

To establish the jurisdiction of the Court, a State must demonstrate to the Court that the parties to a dispute have not only *both* accepted the

42 Cases concerning *Fisheries Jurisdiction* (*United Kingdom* v. *Iceland*) (*Federal Republic of Germany* v. *Iceland*); case concerning *Maritime Delimitation and Territorial Questions between Qatar and Bahrain* (*Qatar* v. *Bahrain*).

43 The Pact of Bogotá, nevertheless, falls under paragraph 1 of Article 36 as a treaty in force rather than declarations of the State parties to the Pact. See Eduardo Jiménez de Aréchaga, "The Compulsory Jurisdiction of the International Court of Justice under the Pact of Bogotá and the Optional Clause," Yoran Dinstein (ed.), *International Law at a Time of Perplexity: Essays in Honour of Shabtai Rosenne*, Kluwer Academic Publishers, 1989, p. 356.

jurisdiction of the Court in general terms by acceding to the Charter and the Statute, but also conferred jurisdiction on the Court on the basis of reciprocity; they have not only *both* accepted the jurisdiction of the Court for the settlement of disputes by any of the means mentioned above, but also *specifically* conferred jurisdiction on the Court for the particular subject-matter of the application.

Among the various means of acceptance of the Court's jurisdiction, the obligation thus undertaken is always mutual and reciprocal, with *forum prorogatum* as an exception. As the Court pointed out in the case concerning the *Right of passage* (*Portugal* v. *India*):

> The principle of reciprocity forms part of the system of the Optional Clause by virtue of the express terms both of Article 36 of the Statute and of most Declarations of Acceptance...However, it is clear that the notions of reciprocity and equality are not abstract conceptions. They must be related to some provision of the Statute or of the Declarations.[44]

More specifically, mutuality and reciprocity determine the scope of consent and the limits of such consent.

a Scope of Consent

First of all, by the term of Article 36, paragraph 2, of the Statute, when a State declares to recognize as compulsory *ipso facto* and without special agreement the jurisdiction of the Court in all legal disputes, such commitment is not absolute, but conditional. Its effect is only limited to another State who has accepted the same obligation, no more, no less. It does not have the effect of general application to all States.[45]

In the case of a multilateral convention, this condition is also implicit in the terms of the compromissory clause. The dispute must be confined to the interpretation and application of the convention, and limited to the subject-matter it governs. Even when the applicant claims the interests on behalf of the international community, such interests must fall within the scope

44 Case concerning *Right of Passage over Indian Territory* (*Portugal* v. *India*), *Preliminary Objections, Judgment of November 26th, 1957: I.C.J. Reports 1957*, p. 145.

45 Article 36, paragraph 2, reads: "[t]he States parties to the present Statute may at any time declare that they recognize as compulsory *ipso facto* and without special agreement, *in relation to any other State accepting the same obligation*, the jurisdiction of the Court in all legal disputes..." (emphasis added).

of the convention.[46] If a State party to a convention makes a reservation to the compromissory clause with regard to the jurisdiction of the ICJ, no other State party may bring a legal action against it in the Court for the settlement of a dispute concerning the interpretation or application of the convention, nor can it do the same to any other State party which has accepted the compromissory clause.

In the case of a treaty that contains a clause identical to Article 36, paragraph 2, of the Statute, the contracting parties undertake the obligation to accept the compulsory jurisdiction of the Court in their mutual relations. Although the treaty is a multilateral instrument, the obligation thus assumed remains mutual and reciprocal. For instance, under the Pact of Bogotá, a State party may institute an application in the Court against another State party to the Pact. Each State knows that such action may be taken against it by any of the State parties. Such commitment is made among these States collectively and reciprocally.

b *Reservations and Conditions Attached to the Consent*

More relevant to the elements of mutuality and reciprocity in practice is the reservations attached to the declarations accepting the compulsory jurisdiction of the Court, which either exclude certain disputes from the jurisdiction of the Court, or attach certain conditions to the acceptance. It is these reservations that often give rise to contestations between the parties on the question of jurisdiction.

In addition to the reaffirmation of the terms of Article 36, paragraph 2, several States in their declarations attach two additional conditions to ensure reciprocity. First, they require that if any State wishes to institute a legal action in the Court, the period between that State's acceptance of the compulsory jurisdiction of the Court under Article 36, paragraph 2, and the filing of its application in the Court must be no shorter than twelve months.[47] Secondly, such declaration should not be made only for the purpose of filing a particular case.[48] These conditions are meant to leave no room for any other State to misuse or abuse their declaration, rendering the obligation non-reciprocal.

In practice, limited by the requirement of mutuality, a legal action in the Court cannot be instituted against a group of States, even if several States are allegedly in breach of their international obligation against one single State.

---

46 See, for example, *Questions relating to the Obligation to Prosecute or Extradite* (*Belgium* v. *Senegal*), *Judgment, I.C.J. Reports 2012*, pp. 445–446, 450, paras. 54, 69.

47 See, for example, the declarations of Germany and United Kingdom.

48 See, for example, the declarations of Bulgaria, Cyprus, India.

Should that be the case, that State has to institute proceedings against each of them in separate applications. This is because the jurisdictional basis between that State and each of the respondent States must be specifically and bilaterally established. Moreover, the procedural rules of the Court are designed in such a way that the principle of equality is supposedly to maintain fairness between two States, e.g. appointment of judges *ad hoc*.

In the cases concerning *Legality of Use of Force*, Serbia and Montenegro filed a series of applications against ten NATO member States for breach of their obligation not to use force under international law.[49] Except for the applications against the United States and Spain, eight cases entered the General List, with Serbia and Montenegro against each of the eight States. In the case against the United States, Serbia and Montenegro's application was based on *forum prorogatum*. The United States did not give its consent to the jurisdiction of the Court. With regard to Spain, Serbia and Montenegro's acceptance of the Court's compulsory jurisdiction was made at the time when it filed its application, which did not meet the condition attached by Spain to its own declaration. Spain's acceptance of the compulsory jurisdiction of the Court does not apply to those declarations made less than 12 months prior to the filing of the application. The Court therefore had no jurisdiction with regard to the applications against the United States and Spain.[50]

The same situation happened in the recent cases instituted by the Marshall Islands against nine nuclear weapon States. Five cases were brought up on the basis of Article 38, paragraph 5, of the Rules of Court, *forum prorogatum*. Two of the named States gave express refusal, while the other three did not respond at all. The Court deemed them not accepting the Court's jurisdiction. As a result, only three cases entered the General List of the Court; all of them are based on the declarations made under Article 36, paragraph 2, of the Statute. Even so, the parties held different positions on the question of jurisdiction regarding the scope of the reservations and conditions they attached to the declarations. The respondent States contended against the jurisdiction of the Court not only on the basis of their reservations, but also on the conditions attached to the applicant's declaration.

49 The ten countries are the United States, the United Kingdom, France, the Netherlands, Germany, Italy, Portugal, Belgium, Canada, and Spain.

50 *Legality of Use of Force* (*Yugoslavia* v. *Spain*), *Provisional Measures, Order of 2 June 1999, I.C.J. Reports 1999*, p. 761; *Legality of Use of Force* (*Yugoslavia* v. *United States of America*), *Provisional Measures, Order of 2 June 1999*, p. 916.

In some cases, there are more than one State instituting proceedings against one single State for the same claims. Likewise, they are regarded as separate cases; each of the applicant States has to establish the jurisdictional basis for its application against the respondent State.[51] Once their jurisdictional grounds are founded, the Court may consider whether it is appropriate to join them. In the *South West Africa* cases, the Court decided to join the two cases instituted by Liberia and Ethiopia respectively. But in the *Legality of Use of Force* cases, the Court did not consider it appropriate to join the cases filed by Serbia and Montenegro.[52]

4 Withdrawal of Consent

It goes without saying that if a State is free to give consent to the jurisdiction of the Court, it certainly has the freedom to decide to withdraw its consent. In regard to declarations made under Article 36, paragraph 2, of the Statute, a State may amend, revise its conditions and reservations, and even denounce its acceptance, in part or in whole. With respect to optional protocols or special treaties conferring jurisdiction on the ICJ, the condition for denunciation is normally governed by the provisions of the relevant treaties.

In practice, a State often proceeds to withdraw or modify its consent accepting the compulsory jurisdiction of the Court right before or after another State institutes proceedings against it in the Court. The purpose of its withdrawal or modification is mainly to stop the proceedings and avoid such legal actions in

51 For example, the *Fisheries Jurisdiction* cases (*United Kingdom* v. *Iceland*) (*Federal Republic of Germany* v. *Iceland*); the *North Sea Continental Shelf* cases (*Federal Republic of Germany/Denmark; Federal Republic of Germany/Netherlands*). In the *Fisheries Jurisdiction* cases, although the UK and Germany filed separate applications, their claims and the respondent party were the same. The Court, instead of joining the two cases, ensured in the two cases that the right of the respondent, Iceland, was guaranteed. In the case with Germany, the Court considered that since Germany had similar interests with the United Kingdom it was not appropriate to allow Germany to appoint a judge *ad hoc* to the case.

52 *Legality of Use of Force* (*Serbia and Montenegro* v. *United Kingdom*), *Preliminary Objections, Judgment, I.C.J. Reports 2004*, p. 1314, para. 16. In the *North Sea Continental Shelf* cases (*Federal Republic of Germany/Denmark; Federal Republic of Germany/Netherlands*), together with the two special agreements, the three countries, Federal Republic of Germany, Denmark and the Netherlands, submitted a protocol concluded among them to the Court. Under the protocol the three States asked the Court to join the two cases. They also agreed that for the purpose of appointing a judge *ad hoc*, Denmark and the Netherlands should be considered parties in the same interest within the meaning of Article 31, paragraph 5, of the Statute of the Court and thereby chose one judge *ad hoc*. The Court joined the proceedings of the two cases.

the future. With respect to a pending case, the Court has consistently upheld the principle it enunciated in the *Nottebohm* case that once the Court is validly seised, subsequent lapses or termination of a treaty shall not affect the pending case;[53] the respondent State's unilateral denunciation of its acceptance of the Court's compulsory jurisdiction shall produce no effect on the pending case. This equally applies to amendments or modifications to the declaration.

In the *Anglo-Iranian Oil Co.* case,[54] due to the rising tension between the two countries over the affairs of the Anglo-Iranian Oil Company and the possible nationalization of oil industry by Iran, the United Kingdom filed a case against Iran on the basis of the acceptance by both parties of the compulsory jurisdiction of the Court under Article 36, paragraph 2, of the Statute. After the United Kingdom requested the indication of provisional measures of protection, Iran notified the Court that it did not consider that the Court had jurisdiction in the case and the United Kingdom's request should therefore be rejected. It thus did neither appear before the Court during the oral hearings for provisional measures, nor did it exercise its right to appoint a judge *ad hoc*. The Court, however, ruled that it had the jurisdiction *prima facie* to indicate measures of protection without prejudice to its subsequent decision on the question of jurisdiction.[55] After that, Iran withdrew its acceptance of the compulsory jurisdiction of the Court.[56] The Court nevertheless proceeded to consider the question of jurisdiction. Only by interpreting the terms of the reservation attached to Iran's declaration,[57] did the Court decide that it had no jurisdiction in the case. With that decision, its Order on provisional measures ceased to operate.

In the case concerning *Right of Passage over Indian Territory*, the Court made it clear that:

> It is a rule of law generally accepted, as well as one acted upon in the past by the Court that, once the Court has been validly seised of a dispute, unilateral action by the respondent State in terminating its Declaration, in

---

53 This is called the principle of the perpetual forum or *perpetuatio fori. Nottebohm case (Liechtenstein* v. *Guatemala) (Preliminary Objection), Judgment, I.C.J. Reports 1953*, p. 123.

54 *Anglo-Iranian Oil Co. case (United Kingdom* v. *Iran), jurisdiction, Judgment of July 22nd, 1952: I.C.J. Reports 1952*, p. 93.

55 *Anglo-Iranian Oil Co. case (United Kingdom* v. *Iran), Order of July 5th, 1951: I.C.J. Reports 1951*, p. 89.

56 *Anglo-Iranian Oil Co. case (United Kingdom* v. *Iran), Pleadings, Part IV, Correspondence*, pp. 718–722 (in French).

57 The Court concluded that "[Iran's] Declaration is limited to disputes relating to the application of treaties or conventions accepted by Iran after the ratification of the Declaration." *Anglo-Iranian Oil Co. case (United Kingdom* v. *Iran), jurisdiction, Judgment of July 22nd, 1952: I.C.J. Reports 1952*, p. 107.

> whole or in part, cannot divest the Court of jurisdiction. In the *Nottebohm* case the Court gave expression to that principle in the following words:
>
> 'An extrinsic fact such as the subsequent lapse of the Declaration, by reason of the expiry of the period or by denunciation, cannot deprive the Court of the jurisdiction already established.' (I.C.J. Reports 1953, p. 123.)
>
> That statement by the Court must be deemed to apply both to total denunciation, and to partial denunciation...[58]

The timing of denunciation and modification was one of the crucial issues on jurisdiction in the *Military and Paramilitary Activities* case. After Nicaragua filed its application, the United States terminated the Treaty of Friendship, Commerce and Navigation between the two countries,[59] which was one of the jurisdictional bases upon which Nicaragua relied to file its application. The Court nevertheless upheld its jurisdiction by stating that

> [t]hese circumstances do not however affect the jurisdiction of the Court under Article 36, paragraph 2, of the Statute, or its jurisdiction under Article XXIV, paragraph 2, of the Treaty to determine 'any dispute between the Parties as to the interpretation or application' of the Treaty.[60]

The withdrawal of consent during the course of proceedings does not affect the jurisdiction of the Court, once it is duly established. This restriction in the application of the principle of consent ensures stability in the recourse to judicial process. To allow a State to apply the principle of consent to the extent it wishes, regardless of the reliance of other States on such commitment, would certainly tilt the reciprocal relationship between the parties.

When a State withdraws from a treaty which confers jurisdiction on the ICJ, the matter often falls on treaty interpretation. In the two recent cases between Nicaragua and Colombia,[61] Nicaragua sought to found the jurisdiction of the

58 *Case concerning right of Passage over Indian Territory* (*Portugal* v. *India*) (*Preliminary Objections*), *Judgment of November 26th, 1957: I.C.J. Reports 1957*, p. 142.

59 It gave written notice to the Government of Nicaragua to terminate the Treaty on 1 May 1985; the treaty thus expired on 1 May 1986.

60 *Military and Paramilitary Activities in and against Nicaragua* (*Nicaragua* v. *United States of America*), *Merits, Judgment, I.C.J. Reports 1986*, p. 28, para 36.

61 *Question of the Delimitation of the Continental Shelf between Nicaragua and Colombia beyond 200 nautical miles from the Nicaraguan Coast* (*Nicaragua* v. *Colombia*), which was filed on 16 September 2013; *Alleged Violations of Sovereign Rights and Maritime Spaces in the Caribbean Sea* (*Nicaragua* v. *Colombia*), which was filed on 26 November 2013.

Court on Article XXXI of the Pact of Bogotá, but Colombia raised a number of preliminary objections to the jurisdiction of the Court.

Article XXXI of the Pact contains similar terms to Article 36, paragraph 2, of the Statute with regard to compulsory jurisdiction of the Court. Article LVI provides that the treaty shall cease to be in force between a denouncing State and the other State parties one year after the denouncing State transmits its notification of denunciation. It further provides that the denunciation shall have no effect with respect to pending procedures initiated prior to the transmission of the particular notification. Colombia gave its notification of denunciation of the Pact on 27 November 2012. Nicaragua filed its application in the Court in both cases within a one year period from that date. In its first preliminary objection, Colombia contended that, in its notification, it specified that the denunciation had an immediate effect upon the jurisdiction of the Court under Article XXXI. Moreover, it argued that, by virtue of general rules of treaty interpretation, proceedings initiated after the transmission of a notification of denunciation are affected by the denunciation. Colombia therefore considered that the Court had no jurisdiction in the present cases.

With regard to Colombia's contentions, the Court recalled its established jurisprudence in the following terms:

> 'the removal, after an application has been filed, of an element on which the Court's jurisdiction is dependent does not and cannot have any retroactive effect.' (*Application of the Convention on the Prevention and Punishment of the Crime of Genocide* (*Croatia* v. *Serbia*), *Preliminary Objections, Judgment, I.C.J. Reports 2008*, p. 438, para. 80). Thus, even if the treaty provision by which jurisdiction is conferred on the Court ceases to be in force between the applicant and the respondent, or either party's declaration under Article 36, paragraph 2, of the Statute of the Court expires or is withdrawn, after the application has been filed, that fact does not deprive the Court of jurisdiction.[62]

The Court did not accept Colombia's argument that its intention stated in the notification of denunciation could override the explicit terms of Article LVI, which provides that the treaty would remain in force between the denouncing party and the other parties for a period of one year following the transmission

62 *Alleged Violations of Sovereign Rights and Maritime Spaces in the Caribbean Sea* (*Nicaragua* v. *Colombia*), *Preliminary Objections, Judgment*, para. 33; *Question of the Delimitation of the Continental Shelf between Nicaragua and Colombia beyond 200 nautical miles from the Nicaraguan Coast* (*Nicaragua* v. *Colombia*), *Preliminary Objections, Judgment*, para. 31.

of the notification. So long as the treaty remained in force, the State parties could refer their dispute to the Court for settlement. In accordance with the object and purpose of the Pact, legal actions initiated after the transmission of the notification but before the one-year period had lapsed should not be affected by the denunciation. Consequently, the Court rejected Colombia's first preliminary objection.

In short, the principle of consent, "retains its dominant position as the ultimate foundation of the Court's mainline jurisdiction to decide the merits of any particular case."[63]

63 Shabtai Rosenne, *op. cit. supra* footnote 28, *Vol. II, Jurisdiction,* p. 570.

CHAPTER IV

Basic Rules and Principles—Part Two

Apart from the principle of consent, there are some other basic rules and principles relating to the question of jurisdiction of the Court. The principle of finality, *res judicata*, and the *res inter alios acta* rule govern the effect of a judgment rendered by the Court and the extent of such effect as a result of its exercise of jurisdiction. The *Monetary Gold* rule sets the limits of the Court's jurisdiction. The *non ultra petita* rule requires that while the Court exercises its jurisdiction to the fullest extent, it does not go beyond the limits of the *petitum* of the parties. This chapter will discuss each of these rules and principles.

1 The Principle of Finality, *res judicata*

The World Court is the first and last instance of judicial proceedings. Article 60 of the Statute of the Court provides that "[t]he judgment is final and without appeal." Article 94, paragraph 2, of the Rules of Court states: "The judgment shall be read at a public sitting of the Court and shall become binding on the parties on the day of the reading." By accepting the jurisdiction of the Court, a State undertakes to comply with its judgment in any case to which it is a party. This voluntary compliance constitutes a unique attribute of international judicial practice, demonstrating the characteristics of the State system.

According to the Charter of the United Nations and the Statute, the judgment of the Court is final and binding on the State parties in respect of that particular case. The principle of finality means that the decision of the Court, once delivered, has binding force on the parties and that "the matter is finally disposed of for good."[1] The parties can neither appeal to challenge the legality and effect of the decision, nor can they reopen the issue upon which the Court has rendered its decision with binding force. In other words, the Court's decision has the formal value of *res judicata*.

1 *Barcelona Traction, Light and Power Company, Limited (New Application: 1962) (Belgium* v. *Spain), Preliminary Objections, Judgment, I.C.J. Reports 1964*, p.20.

 | DOI 10.1163/9789004342767_005

a *The Concept of* res judicata

The principle of *res judicata* is rooted in all legal systems.[2] For civil lawsuits, it serves both the general interest of society as well as the individual interests of the parties concerned. This double function of *res judicata* is based on two Latin maxims, namely, "*interest rei publicae sit finis litium*," (it is in the public interest that lawsuits have an end) and "*nemo debet bis vexari pro una et eadem causa*" (nobody may be twice disturbed for one and the same matter).[3]

In international judicial practice, *res judicata* was accepted as a general principle of law with little question. As the *Trail Smelter* Arbitral Tribunal stated in its final award:

> That the sanctity of res judicata attaches to a final decision of an international tribunal is an essential and settled rule of international law.
>
> If it is true that international relations based on law and justice require arbitral or judicial adjudication of international disputes, it is equally true that such adjudication must, in principle, remain unchallenged, if it is to be effective to that end.[4]

On the meaning of *res judicata*, the Permanent Court in the *Société commerciale de Belgique* case stated the following:

> Recognition of an award as *res judicata* means nothing else than recognition of the fact that the terms of that award are definitive and obligatory.[5]

The principle of *res judicata* is provided for in Articles 59 and 60 of the Statute of both the PCIJ and the ICJ, under which the decision of the Court has no binding force except between the parties and in respect of that particular case. In the event of a dispute as to the meaning or scope of the judgment, the Court shall construe it upon the request of either party. As the Court underlined in

---

2 *Interpretation of Judgments Nos. 7 and 8 (Factory at Chorzów), Judgment No. 11, 1927, P.C.I.J., Series A, No. 13*, Dissenting Opinion by Judge Anzilotti, p. 27; for different interpretations of the doctrine, see Albrecht Zeuner and Harald Koch, "Effects of Judgments (*Res Judicata*)," in M. Cappelletti (chief ed.), *Volume XVI Civil Procedure, International Encyclopedia of Comparative Law*, 2012, pp. 3–84.

3 *Cf.* Halsbury XII (Zuckerman, Civil Procedure) no. 1518, cited in Albrecht Zeuner and Harald Koch, *ibid.*, p. 4.

4 *United Nations Reports of International Arbitral Awards*, Vol. III, pp. 1950–1951; see also Bin Cheng, *General Principles of Law as Applied by International Courts and Tribunals*, Cambridge University Press, 1953, p. 336.

5 *Société Commerciale de Belgique, Judgment of June 15th, 1939, P.C.I.J., Series A/B, No. 78*, p. 175.

its judgment on the preliminary objections in the case concerning *Request for Interpretation of the Judgment of 11 June 1998 in the Case concerning the* Land and Maritime Boundary between Cameroon and Nigeria (Cameroon *v.* Nigeria) (*Nigeria* v. *Cameroon*), "[t]he language and structure of Article 60 reflect the primacy of the principle of *res judicata*."[6] Further developed through the jurisprudence of the Court,[7] *res judicata* is now considered "an essential and settled rule of international law."[8]

On the rationale of the principle, the Court gave an elaborated statement in the *Bosnian Genocide* case:

> Two purposes, one general, the other specific, underlie the principle of *res judicata*, internationally as nationally. First, the stability of legal relations requires that litigation come to an end. The Court's function, according to Article 38 of its Statute, is to 'decide,' that is, to bring to an end 'such disputes as are submitted to it.' Secondly, it is in the interest of each party that an issue which has already been adjudicated in favour of that party be not argued again. Article 60 of the Statute articulates this finality of judgments. Depriving a litigant of the benefit of a judgment it has already obtained must in general be seen as a breach of the principles governing the legal settlement of disputes.[9]

By confining what is determined by the Court and what is not in the legal relations of the parties, *res judicata* ensures judicial justice as well as judicial economy, a policy that every legal system pursues. In a way it can be said that *res judicata* is a corollary of the principle of consent; every State has the right to decide whether or not to give its consent to the jurisdiction of the Court. Once jurisdiction is conferred on the Court, the State undertakes to comply with the judgment of the Court, which is definitive and obligatory.

---

6 *Request for Interpretation of the Judgment of 11 June 1998 in the Case concerning the* Land and Maritime Boundary between Cameroon and Nigeria (Cameroon *v.* Nigeria), Preliminary Objections (*Nigeria* v. *Cameroon*), *Judgment, I.C.J. Reports, 1999*, p. 36, para. 12.

7 The principle was discussed in the cases concerning, among others, *Request for Interpretation of the Judgment of 11 June 1998 in the Case concerning the* Land and Maritime Boundary between Cameroon and Nigeria (Cameroon *v.* Nigeria), Preliminary Objections (*Nigeria* v. *Cameroon*) and *Application of the Convention on the Prevention and Punishment of the Crime of Genocide* (*Bosnia and Herzegovina* v. *Serbia and Montenegro*).

8 *United Nations Reports of International Arbitral Awards*, Vol. III, p. 1950.

9 *Application of the Convention on the Prevention and Punishment of the Crime of Genocide* (*Bosnia and Herzegovina* v. *Serbia and Montenegro*), *Judgment, I.C.J. Reports 2007* (*I*), pp. 90–91, para. 116.

b *What Constitutes* res judicata

As aforementioned, the principle of finality does not mean that a judgment, once delivered, is untouchable. If the parties have disputes with regard to the meaning or scope of a judgment, they may, under Article 60, request the Court to interpret and construe the meaning of the terms of the judgment and clarify the scope of what has been definitively decided and what has not.

Regarding the scope of *res judicata*, traditionally three elements are underscored: the parties (*persona*), the object (*petitum*), and the cause (*causa petendi*).[10] They are regarded as the "material limits" of *res judicata*.[11] This means that the judgment only applies to the parties. It has no binding force on third States.[12] It does not apply to any matters between the parties other than the particular case. The effect of the judgment only goes to the extent as determined by the Court.

There is little controversy with the first limit: a judgment is binding only on the States in a case to which they are the parties. The other two limits, the object and the legal ground of a judgment, however, often give rise to controversy and debate.[13] In other words, what has been decided by the Court and what

10 Arbitral Tribunal (Great Britain-United States) constituted under the Special Agreement of August 18, 1910, *Newchwang* case, 9 December 1921, *United Nations Reports of International Arbitral Awards*, Vol. VI, p. 64; *Interpretation of Judgments Nos. 7 and 8 (Factory at Chorzów), Judgment No. 11, 1927, P.C.I.J., Series A, No. 13*, Dissenting Opinion by Judge Anzilotti, p. 27.

11 Bin Cheng, *op. cit. supra* footnote 4, p. 340.

12 The principle of *res judicata* should be distinguished from the institution of binding judicial precedents as practised in Anglo-Saxon legal systems. Independently of the Statute of the Court, a system of binding judicial precedents does not exist in international law. While Article 59 expressly prevents legal principles accepted by the Court in a particular case from being binding upon other States in other disputes, the Court is free to recall its previous decisions between other parties on particular points of law whenever the same question arose. Reliance on judicial precedents, established either by themselves or by other tribunals, is a frequent practice of both national and international tribunals. Precedents are concerned with questions of law *in abstracto*, but *res judicata* is essentially the solution of a concrete dispute over the respective rights and obligations of the parties. The requirement of the identity of the parties for the application of the *excetio rei judicatae* has the effect of preventing the rights of third parties from being conclusively settled without their direct involvement in submitting their own disputes, even concerning the same points of law, or the same subject-matter, to fresh judicial consideration. See Bin Cheng, *ibid.*, p. 341, footnote 22.

13 In domestic practice, different approaches are taken with regard to the scope of *res judicata*. In Greek legal practice, for instance, it is held that even preliminary issues are covered by *res judicata*, if the decision was essential for the ruling on the main claim,

constitute the legal and factual grounds for the decision may be subject to different interpretations.

On the scope of a Court's decision, it is a general rule that only the operative part of a judgment, the *dispositif*, has binding force.[14] In the Advisory Opinion concerning *Polish Postal Service in Danzig*, the PCIJ stated that "reasons contained in a decision, at least in so far as they go beyond the scope of the operative part, have no binding force as between the Parties concerned."[15] In his dissenting opinion in the *Factory at Chorzów* (*interpretation*) case, Judge Anzilotti elaborated on this point. He said:

> It appears to me to be clear that a binding interpretation of a judgment can only have reference to the binding portion of the judgment construed.
>
> When I say that only the terms of a judgment are binding, I do not mean that only what is actually written in the operative part constitutes the Court's decision. On the contrary, it is certain that it is almost always necessary to refer to the statement of reasons to understand clearly the operative part and above all to ascertain the *causa petendi*. But, at all events, it is the operative part which contains the Court's binding decision and which, consequently, may form the subject of a request for an interpretation.
>
> It is, moreover, clear that, under a generally accepted rule which is derived from the very conception of *res judicata*, decisions on incidental or preliminary questions which have been rendered with the sole object of adjudicating upon the Parties' claims (*incidenter tantum*) are not binding in another case.[16]

provided that the Court involved had subject-matter jurisdiction for ruling on such issues. Under German and English laws, *res judicata* is limited only to the essential object of the litigation in question. Coupled with those approaches is the further question whether the conclusive and preclusive effects of a judgment are limited to those rights and claims that have actually been asserted in the lawsuit and have been the object of the judgment. See Albrecht Zeuner and Harald Koch, *op. cit. supra* footnote 2, pp. 23–41.

14 The Court has stated in its decisions that "the operative part of a judgment of the Court possesses the force of *res judicata*." *Application of the Convention on the Prevention and Punishment of the Crime of Genocide* (*Bosnia and Herzegovina* v. *Serbia and Montenegro*), *Judgement, I.C.J. Reports 2007* (*I*), p. 94, para. 123.

15 *Polish Postal Service in Danzig, Advisory Opinion of May 16th, 1925, P.C.I.J., Series B, No. 11*, pp. 29–30.

16 *Interpretation of Judgments Nos. 7 and 8* (*Factory at Chorzów*), *Judgment No. 11, 1927, P.C.I.J., Series A, No. 13*, Dissenting Opinion by Judge Anzilotti, pp. 23–26.

It is certain that *obiter dicta*, subsidiary matters in a judgment, should have no binding force.[17] Decisions on incidental and preliminary matters are of binding effect only to the extent of that procedure.[18] No force of *res judicata* is attached to such decisions.

If the parties have any doubt about the meaning of a judgment, either of them may submit a request to the Court for interpretation. In the *Asylum* case between Colombia and Peru, on the very day the Court delivered its judgment, Colombia requested the Court to interpret the judgment on a number of points. It considered that there were "gaps" existing in the decision and wished the Court to clarify them. The Court in its Interpretation Judgment made clear at the outset that, in the case of a request for interpretation of a judgment,

> one must bear in mind the principle that it is the duty of the Court not only to reply to the questions as stated in the final submissions of the parties, but also to abstain from deciding points not included in those submissions.[19]

The Court did not agree that there were such "gaps" as claimed by Colombia in the judgment. In its view, they were in reality new questions, which the Court considered could not be decided by means of interpretation. It held that "interpretation can in no way go beyond the limits of the Judgment, fixed in advance by the Parties themselves in their submissions."[20] It therefore declared that the request for interpretation was inadmissible.

After the Court rendered its decision, Colombia filed a new application in the Court, requesting the Court to determine the manner in which effect should be given to the judgment of November 20th, 1950 and whether Colombia was, or was not, bound to deliver to Peru Mr. Víctor Raúl Haya de la Torre, a refugee in the Colombian Embassy at Lima.[21] The latter question was raised

17 *Application of the Convention on the Prevention and Punishment of the Crime of Genocide (Bosnia and Herzegovina* v. *Serbia and Montenegro), Judgment, I.C.J. Reports 2007 (I)*, p. 95, para. 126; see also *Factory at Chorzów, Merits, Judgment No. 13, 1928, P.C.I.J., Series A, No. 17*, Dissenting Opinion of Judge Ehrlich, p. 76.

18 Chester Brown, "Article 59," in Andreas Zimmermann, Karin Oellers-Frahm, Christian Tomuschat, and Christian J. Tams (eds.), *The Statute of the International Court of Justice: A Commentary*, 2nd edition, Oxford University Press, 2012, p. 1429, para. 33, citing *South West Africa (Ethiopia* v. *South Africa), Second Phase, Judgment, I.C.J. Reports 1966*, pp. 36–37, para. 59.

19 *Request for interpretation of the Judgment of November 20th, 1950, in the asylum case (Colombia/Peru), Judgment, Judgment of November 27th, 1950: I.C.J. Reports 1950*, p. 402.

20 *Ibid.*, p. 403.

21 *Haya de la Torre case (Colombia* v. *Peru), Judgment of June 13th, 1951: I.C.J. Reports 1951*, p. 71.

by Colombia in the *Asylum* case (interpretation), but rejected by the Court as it considered that the matter fell outside the scope of interpretation. In the judgment in the *Haya de la Torre* case, the Court stated that, in the two previous judgments in the *Asylum* case, Peru did not demand the surrender of the refugee. The question was not submitted to the Court and consequently was not decided by it. It considered that that question was new, and consequently there was no *res judicata* upon the question of surrender.[22]

There is no doubt that in determining the meaning of a judgment, the force of *res judicata* is attached to the operative part. It is also agreed that "all the parts of a judgment concerning the points in dispute explain and complete each other and are to be taken into account in order to determine the precise meaning and scope of the operative portion."[23] Nevertheless, not every reason in a judgment constitutes a decision. Reasons that do not necessarily lead to the decision on the question at issue are not *res judicata*.

In 2011, Cambodia instituted proceedings against Thailand in the Court with a request for interpretation of the 1962 Judgment in the case concerning the *Temple of Preah Vihear*.[24] It asked the Court to clarify the meaning of the operative paragraphs of the judgment, in particular to determine whether the Court in 1962 ruled on the issue of territorial sovereignty of the Temple. In that regard, it especially requested the Court to declare that the Annex I map indicated the boundary between the parties in the Temple area.

The question of the Annex I map concerned the reasoning of the judgment. Although the Court definitively decided in its 1962 judgment that the Temple was situated in the territory of Cambodia, it did not rule on the legal status of the Annex I map.[25] It expressly stated in the judgment that,

> Cambodia's first and second Submissions, calling for pronouncements on the legal status of the Annex I map and on the frontier line in the disputed region, can be entertained only to the extent that they give expression to grounds, and not as claims to be dealt with in the operative provisions of the Judgment.[26]

---

22 *Ibid.*, p. 80.

23 *Polish Postal Service in Danzig, Advisory Opinion of May 16th, 1925, P.C.I.J., Series B, No. 11*, pp. 29–30.

24 *Request for Interpretation of the Judgment of 15 June 1962 in the Case concerning the* Temple of Preah Vihear (Cambodia *v.* Thailand) (*Cambodia* v. *Thailand*), *Judgment, I.C.J. Reports 2013*, p. 281.

25 *Case concerning the Temple of Preah Vihear* (*Cambodia* v. *Thailand*), *Merits, Judgment of 15 June 1962: I.C.J. Reports 1962*, pp. 36–37.

26 *Ibid.*, p. 36.

Although the Court, in 1962, relied to a large extent on the Annex I map to determine the territorial area on which the Temple was situated, it purposely pronounced that such reference to the Annex I map did not constitute part of the decision, thus precluding any effect of *res judicata* to the Annex I map.

The finality of a judgment may be reconsidered if one of the parties requests the revision of the judgment because new facts are discovered. According to Article 61 of the Statute, the new fact must be of such a nature as to be of a decisive factor. It should be unknown both to the Court and the party claiming revision when the judgment was given. Such ignorance should not be due to the negligence on the part of the claimant party. It is up to the Court to decide whether such new fact indeed exists and whether it has the character required to lay the case open to revision.

The question of *res judicata* was raised in the recent case concerning *Question of the Delimitation of the Continental Shelf between Nicaragua and Colombia beyond 200 nautical miles from the Nicaraguan Coast*; however, it is neither a case for interpretation nor a case for revision. In this case, Columbia argues in its third preliminary objection that Nicaragua's claim is in essence a resubmission of its claim presented in the *Territorial and Maritime Dispute* case between the parties. As the Court already adjudicated in subparagraph 3 of the operative clause of the 2012 judgment that Nicaragua's submission could not be upheld, the principle of *res judicata* bars the Court from examining Nicaragua's requests again in the present case.

In deciding to what extent the principle of *res judicata* should apply in this case, the Court states that:

> It is not sufficient, for the application of *res judicata*, to identify the case at issue, characterized by the same parties, object and legal ground; it is also necessary to ascertain the content of the decision, the finality of which is to be guaranteed. The Court cannot be satisfied merely by an identity between requests successively submitted to it by the same Parties; it must determine whether and to what extent the first claim has already been definitively settled.[27]

On the content of subparagraph 3 of the operative clause over which the parties disagrees, the Court, while acknowledging that this is not a case for interpretation, takes the view that "the requirement that the meaning of the operative

27 *Question of the Delimitation of the Continental Shelf between Nicaragua and Colombia beyond 200 nautical miles from the Nicaraguan Coast* (*Nicaragua* v. *Colombia*), *Preliminary Objections, Judgment*, para. 59.

part of a judgment be ascertained through an examination of the reasoning on which the operative part is based is of more general application."[28] The Court recalls that in the 2012 judgment it did not examine the evidence in substance about Nicaragua's claim to the extended continental shelf which purportedly overlapped with Colombia's continental shelf measured from its mainland coast. As Nicaragua had only handed in Preliminary Information to the Commission on the Outer Limits of the Continental Shelf (CLCS), the Court in 2012 found that "Nicaragua, in the present proceedings, has not established that it has a continental margin that extends far enough to overlap with Colombia's 200-nautical-mile entitlement to the continental shelf, measured from Colombia's mainland coast."[29] The Court thus states that it did not rule on the substance of Nicaragua's claim. It dismissed Nicaragua's claim in 2012 because Nicaragua had not yet fulfilled its obligation under Article 76, paragraph 8, of UNCLOS. As now Nicaragua has submitted the information to the CLCS, the case is not barred by *res judicata*.

The Court is heavily divided over the extent of effect of its decision in the *Territorial and Maritime Dispute* (*Nicaragua* v. *Colombia*) case. In the joint dissenting opinion, seven judges disagree with the conclusion of the judgment. In their view, the Court in its 2012 judgment rejected Nicaragua's claim because it failed to prove the existence of an extended continental shelf overlapping with Colombia's continental shelf. The majority's interpretation of the obligation under Article 76, paragraph 8, of UNCLOS is inconsistent with its previous judgment. Procedurally, the recommendation from the CLCS is also required. Nicaragua actually brings the same claim, for the same object and with the same party again in a new case. On the principle of *res judicata*, they emphasize that according to the case law of the Court,

> *res judicata* may attach to the reasons of a judgment of the Court if those reasons are 'inseparable' from the operative clause of a judgment (*Request for Interpretation of the Judgment of 11 June 1998 in the Case concerning the* Land and Maritime Boundary between Cameroon and Nigeria (Cameroon *v.* Nigeria), Preliminary Objections (*Nigeria* v. *Cameroon*), *Judgment, I.C.J. Reports 1999* (*I*), p. 35, para. 10) or if they constitute a 'condition essential to the Court's decision' (*Request for Interpretation of the Judgment of 15 June 1962 in the Case concerning the* Temple of Preah Vihear (Cambodia *v.* Thailand) (*Cambodia* v. *Thailand*), *Judgment, I.C.J. Reports*

28 *Ibid.*, para. 75.

29 *Ibid.*, para. 82.

2013, p. 296, para. 34; *Interpretation of Judgments Nos. 7 and 8 (Factory at Chorzów), Judgment No. 11, 1927, P.C.I.J. Series A, No. 13*, p. 20).[30]

It is apparent that to what extent the principle *res judicata* should apply is not always a clear-cut issue in practice.[31]

The finality of a judgment, however, does not prevent the parties from reaching an agreement on the modification of the terms of the judgment. For example, in the *Jan Mayen* (*Denmark* v. *Norway*) case,[32] after the Court rendered its judgment on the maritime delimitation, the parties further negotiated to finalize the maritime boundary. There is no rule either in the Statute or in the case law that prohibits the parties from doing so, because, after all, the parties as sovereign States have the ultimate right to determine their affairs, so long as they do so by agreement.

2 Article 59 of the Statute—The *res inter alios acta* Rule

Directly connected with the principle of *res judicata* is the rule of *res inter alios acta*, namely, what is binding and obligatory on the parties to a case does not have that effect on a third State.

a *The Scope of* res inter alios acta

Res inter alio acta means that the Court's judgment does not have binding effects on a third State or in other circumstances than the case at hand. It is a long-standing rule established by arbitral and judicial practice. The negative term of Article 59 in a way speaks of the two sides of the same coin. On the one hand, the judgment of the Court binds on the parties to the case only. On the

30 *Question of the Delimitation of the Continental Shelf between Nicaragua and Colombia beyond 200 nautical miles from the Nicaraguan Coast* (*Nicaragua* v. *Colombia*), *Preliminary Objections, Judgment*, joint dissenting opinion of Vice-President Yusuf, Judges Cançado Trindade, Xue, Gaja, Bhandari, Robinson and Judge *ad hoc* Brower, para. 6.

31 It is interesting to note that several judges in their dissenting or separate opinions have different views on the scope of *res judicata* in this case. Judge Donoghue is of the view that "[i]n Nicaragua v. Colombia I (the 2012 case—the author), Nicaragua made full use of the opportunity to prove its claim that its continental shelf entitlement extended far enough to overlap with Colombia's mainland entitlement. It failed to do so. This is precisely the sort of situation in which, for reasons of procedural fairness, the doctrine of *res judicata* applies." See also separate opinion of Judge Owada.

32 *Maritime Delimitation in the Area between Greenland and Jan Mayen* (*Denmark* v. *Norway*), *Judgment, I.C.J. Reports 1993*, p. 38.

other hand, such judgment has no binding effects on any other State. Article 59 provides what it governs, and also clarifies what it does not.

By virtue of *res judicata*, the binding effect and the extent of such effect are confined to the parties and to the case. *Res inter alios acta* further ensures that such decision should not affect the right or interest of a third State. From a jurisdictional point of view, the rule of *res inter alios acta* restricts the scope of the Court's competence. If the Court acts outside its jurisdiction, ruling on the right of a third State, *res judicata* would not attach to such decision; the decision in that respect would be null and void.[33]

It should be noted that, as is the case with the principle of *res judicata*, *res inter alios acta* should also be distinguished from the practice of binding precedents. While Article 59 expressly prevents legal principles accepted by the Court in a particular case from being binding upon other States in other disputes, the Court is free to recall its previous decisions between other parties on particular points of law whenever the same question arises. However, such precedents are concerned with questions of law *in abstracto*, not particularly relating to the solution of the concrete dispute over the respective rights and obligations of the parties. Reliance on judicial precedents does not contradict the *res inter alios acta* rule; third parties may submit their own disputes, even on the same question at issue and involving the same points of law.

Another aspect of the *res inter alios acta* rule is that because the decision of the Court binds only the parties to the case, a third State cannot request interpretation or revision of a judgment in a case to which it is not a party.[34]

b *Protection of the Interest of the Third Party*

In practice, the meaning of Article 59 is three-fold. First of all, it provides to what extent a judgment has binding force: it only concerns the parties before the Court and the particular case that it deals with. Principles and rules used to resolve the dispute in one case, for instance, may not automatically be used in another case. In other words, a State cannot use a judgment of the Court in a case to which it is a party against a third State, even if its dispute with that third State involves the same question at issue. What the Court has decided is

33 Bin Cheng, *op. cit. supra* footnote 4, p. 357.

34 In the *Société Française de Banque et de Dépôts* case, the Franco-German Mixed Arbitral Tribunal stated that "[t]he request for revision presented to the Tribunal has been submitted by a person not directly involved in the suit leading to the impugned decision; this fact alone suffices to reject as inadmissible this request for revision filed by a party which is, in truth, a third party." See Bin Cheng, *op. cit. supra* footnote 4, p. 371.

confined to the parties to the case and to the particular subject-matter that is settled in the case.

Secondly, by virtue of Article 59, the Court, in adjudicating a dispute, cannot prejudice the rights and interests of a third State. This point is particularly sensitive in territorial and maritime delimitation cases where overlapping claims of the parties often involve the rights and interests of a third State. Under such circumstances, even if the third State does not exercise its right under Article 62 to request for permission to intervene, it is still incumbent upon the Court to ensure that the third State's right and legal interest will not be adversely affected by its judgment. In several maritime delimitation cases, the boundary line drawn up by the Court stops short of where the rights or interests of a third State might be affected.[35] Citing the Permanent Court, the Court in the *Continental Shelf* (*Libyan Arab Jamahiriya/Malta*) case (intervention) emphasized that, "the object of Article 59 is simply to prevent legal principles accepted by the Court in a particular case from being binding upon other States or in other disputes."[36]

In the case concerning *Land and Maritime Boundary between Cameroon and Nigeria*, the boundary between the parties extended to Lake Chad. According to Nigeria, this boundary contained the tripoint in that lake, where the frontiers of Cameroon, Chad and Nigeria met and the fixing of the tripoint would directly affect Chad. Nigeria contended that since Chad was a third party absent from the proceedings, the jurisdiction of the Court was therefore barred by Article 59. The Court, however, did not accept Nigeria's argument. Referring to its settled jurisprudence, it took the view that the Court

> is not necessarily prevented from adjudicating when the judgment it is asked to give might affect the legal interests of a State which is not a party to the case; and the Court has only declined to exercise jurisdiction when the interests of the third State 'constitute the *very subject-matter of the judgment* to be rendered on the merits' (*Certain Phosphate Lands in Nauru* (*Nauru* v. *Australia*), *Preliminary Objections, Judgment, I.C.J. Reports 1992*, p. 261, para. 55; *East Timor* (*Portugal* v. *Australia*), *Judgment, I.C.J. Reports 1995*, pp. 104–105, para. 34).[37]

35 *Continental Shelf* (*Libyan Arab Jamahiriya/Malta*), *Application for Permission to Intervene, Judgment, I.C.J. Reports 1984*, pp. 26–27, para. 43.

36 *Ibid.*, p. 26; see also *Interpretation of Judgments Nos. 7 and 8* (*Factory at Chorzów*), *Judgment No. 11, 1927, P.C.I.J., Series A, No. 13*, pp. 10–11; *Certain German Interests in Polish Upper Silesia, Judgment No. 7, 1926, P.C.I.J., Series A, No. 7*, p. 19.

37 *Land and Maritime Boundary between Cameroon and Nigeria* (*Cameroon* v. *Nigeria*), *Preliminary Objections, Judgment, I.C.J. Reports 1998*, p. 312, para. 79 (emphasis added).

In the merits phase, in order to avoid affecting Chad's rights, the Court decided, as was agreed by the parties, to leave the tripoint open without taking any decision on it.[38]

In that case, the respondent State also referred to some other third States whose interests, in its view, might be affected by the decision of the Court, should it decide that it had jurisdiction. The Court examined the area and the extent to which the interests of the third States might be involved. The Court observed:

> The jurisdiction of the Court is founded on the consent of the parties. The Court cannot therefore decide upon legal rights of third States not parties to the proceedings. In the present case there are States other than the parties to these proceedings whose rights might be affected, namely Equatorial Guinea and Sao Tome and Principe. Those rights cannot be determined by decision of the Court unless Equatorial Guinea and Sao Tome and Principe have become parties to the proceedings… It follows that, in fixing the maritime boundary between Cameroon and Nigeria, the Court must ensure that it does not adopt any position which might affect the rights of Equatorial Guinea and Sao Tome and Principe.[39]

Equatorial Guinea was granted permission to intervene as a non-party under Article 62 of the Statute, while Sao Tome and Principe did not make such request to intervene. In drawing up the maritime boundary between the parties, the Court drew the line which stopped short of where Equatorial Guinea's rights might be affected. The Court stated that "it must remain mindful, as always in situations of this kind, of the limitations on its jurisdiction that such presence imposes."[40]

The third aspect of the *res inter alios acta* rule is that, if the legal interests of the third State form the very subject-matter of the dispute, the Court, by virtue of Article 59, should decline to adjudicate a case. This is because in the absence of the third State's consent, the Court does not have the necessary jurisdiction in the case. In the Court's jurisprudence, a separate rule applies to this kind of circumstances—the *Monetary Gold* rule—which will be discussed in the next section.

38 *Land and Maritime Boundary between Cameroon and Nigeria* (*Cameroon* v. *Nigeria: Equatorial Guinea intervening*), *Judgment, I.C.J. Reports 2002*, p. 421, para. 238.

39 *Ibid.*

40 *Ibid.*

In the application of Article 59, the Court is fully aware that, oftentimes, particularly in the case of delimitation of boundaries where several States are involved, the protection afforded by the *res inter alios acta* rule may not always be sufficient. Even if the Court is mindful of the legal rights of third States, the result may nevertheless produce certain effects on them.[41]

In the *Aegean Sea Continental Shelf* case between Greece and Turkey, the Court addressed this issue. Regarding the interpretation of the 1928 General Act, the Court observed that,

> [a]lthough under Article 59 of the Statute 'the decision of the Court has no binding force except between the parties and in respect of that particular case,' it is evident that any pronouncement of the Court as to the status of the 1928 Act, whether it were found to be a convention in force or to be no longer in force, may have implications in the relations between States other than Greece and Turkey.[42]

Notwithstanding, the principle enshrined in Article 59 is not straightforward in its application. In the case concerning *Land and Maritime Boundary between Cameroon and Nigeria*, Nigeria contested Cameroon's invocation of the Court's rule in *Right of Passage* case about the way in which an Article 36, paragraph 2 declaration should take effect. Nigeria claimed that, in accordance with Article 59 of the Statute, judgments given earlier had no direct compelling effect in

---

41 For the Court's practice on the third party intervention, see the dissenting opinion of Judge Oda in the case concerning *Sovereignty over Pulau Ligitan and Pulau Sipadan (Indonesia/Malaysia), Judgment of 23 October 2001*, pp. 610–612, paras. 4–7. The *Nuclear Tests* cases were the first occasion where a third State (Fiji) requested for permission to intervene under Article 62. In the *Continental Shelf (Tunisia/Libyan Arab Jamahiriya)* case in 1981 was the second case where a third State (Malta) requested for permission to intervene under Article 62. In the *Continental Shelf (Libyan Arab Jamahiriya/Malta)* case in 1984, for the third time, Italy requested for permission to intervene under Article 62. In 1990, in the *Land, Island and Maritime Frontier Dispute* under the chamber procedure, Nicaragua's request for intervention was granted for the first time. It entered the case as a non-party. No jurisdictional link with the parties in the principal case was required. In the case concerning *Land and Maritime Boundary between Cameroon and Nigeria*, the Court, in its Order of 21 October 1999, unanimously granted Equatorial Guinea permission to intervene (*Application by Equatorial Guinea for permission to intervene, I.C.J. Reports 1999 (II)*, p. 1029). Equatorial Guinea then pleaded as a non-party. All these three cases relate to maritime delimitation or status of maritime areas.

42 *Aegean Sea Continental Shelf (Greece* v. *Turkey), Judgment, I.C.J. Reports 1978*, pp. 16–17, para. 39.

the present case.[43] The Court did not accept Nigeria's argument. It noted that the judgment on this point in the *Right of Passage* case had been reaffirmed in several subsequent cases.[44] The Court held that,

> It is true that, in accordance with Article 59, the Court's judgments bind only the parties to and in respect of a particular case. There can be no question of holding Nigeria to decisions reached by the Court in previous cases. The real question is whether, in this case, there is cause not to follow the reasoning and conclusions of earlier cases.[45]

In his dissenting opinion to the judgment, Judge Koroma disapproved of this method of judicial accretion adopted by the Court. He did not agree that such precedents should have a controlling effect on the present case. Moreover, he pointed out that, in international law, there was no system of binding precedents. It was an important principle of the Court that it did not recognize the principle of *stare decisis*. He underscored that:

> It is also part of the Court's jurisprudence that even when legal principles are accepted by the Court in a particular case, they are not regarded as binding upon other States or in other disputes. The Court has the power and the duty to depart from previous decisions when this is necessary and in the interests of justice.[46]

For those who are familiar with the common law practice, Article 59 and the rule of *res inter alios acta* are certainly distinctive and unique to international adjudication.

---

43 *Land and Maritime Boundary between Cameroon and Nigeria* (*Cameroon* v. *Nigeria*), *Preliminary Objections, Judgment, I.C.J. Reports 1998*, p. 292, para. 28.

44 The point in question was reaffirmed in the *Case concerning the Temple of Preah Vihear* (*Cambodia* v. *Thailand*), *Preliminary Objections, Judgment of 26 May 1961: I.C.J. Reports 1961*, p. 31, and in the case concerning *Military and Paramilitary Activities in and against Nicaragua* (*Nicaragua* v. *United States of America*), *Jurisdiction and Admissibility, Judgment, I.C.J. Reports 1984*, p. 412, para. 45.

45 *Land and Maritime Boundary between Cameroon and Nigeria* (*Cameroon* v. *Nigeria*), *Preliminary Objections, Judgment, I.C.J. Reports 1998*, p. 292, para. 28.

46 *Land and Maritime Boundary between Cameroon and Nigeria* (*Cameroon* v. *Nigeria*), *Preliminary Objections, Judgment, I.C.J. Reports 1998*, dissenting opinion of Judge Koroma, p. 380.

3 The *Monetary Gold* Rule

The *Monetary Gold* rule is taken from the ruling in the case of the *Monetary Gold Removed from Rome in 1943*. It became an established precedent in the case law of the Court. It means that, in accordance with the established principle of international law embodied in the Court's Statute, the Court can only exercise jurisdiction over a State with its consent; when the legal interests of the third State would form the very subject-matter of the Court's decision, the Court could not take a decision in the absence of the consent of the third State.

The *Monetary Gold* case derived from the events that happened during WWII. In September 1943, the Nazi Germans looted from a bank in Rome nearly 2340 kilograms of monetary gold, which allegedly belonged to the National Bank of Albania, and transferred it to Germany. The Paris Act on Reparation from Germany of 4 January 1946 provided that monetary gold found in Germany by the Allied forces should be pooled for distributing proportionately as restitution among the countries which had lost gold because of Germany's looting during the War. Both Italy and Albania were parties to the Paris Act. Under Part III of the Act, a Tripartite Commission, consisting of the United States, France and the United Kingdom, was established to assist the distribution of the gold from the pool.

Both Italy and Albania had claims over the monetary gold removed from the bank in Rome. Since the Tripartite Commission was unable to resolve the question, the three powers decided to submit it to arbitration. Before that, the three powers reached an agreement that, in the event that the arbitration decided that the gold was Albanian, the gold would be given to the United Kingdom for the partial satisfaction of the unpaid compensation awarded to the United Kingdom by the ICJ in the *Corfu Channel* case, unless, within a period of 90 days, either Albania or Italy instituted proceedings against any of the three powers in the ICJ for the determination of the right to the gold. For that purpose, the three powers agreed to accept the Court's jurisdiction in advance.

On 20 February 1953 the arbitrator rendered the award, deciding that the gold belonged to Albania in 1943 within the meaning of the Paris Act. As a result, a month later Italy filed the case in the Court against three powers. Albania refused either to institute a case of its own or to intervene in Italy's case. Before filing the Memorial, Italy asked the Court to decide the preliminary question, namely, whether under such circumstances the Court could exercise jurisdiction.[47]

47 Shabtai Rosenne, *The World Court, What It Is and How It Works*, 5th completely revised edition, Martinus Nijhoff Publishers, 1995, pp. 181–182.

In its application, Italy made two submissions to the Court:

> (1) that the Governments of the French Republic, Great Britain and Northern Ireland and the United States of America should deliver to Italy any share of the monetary gold that might be due to Albania under Part III of the Paris Act of January 14 1946, in partial satisfaction for the damage caused to Italy by the Albanian law of January 13th 1945;
> (2) that Italy's right to receive the said share of monetary gold must have priority over the claim of the United Kingdom to receive the gold in partial satisfaction of the Judgment in the *Corfu Channel* case.[48]

The Court examined the admissibility of these two submissions. On the first question, the Court considered that, in order to determine the existence of the international wrongfulness by Albania against Italy and reparation for the wrongful act, the Court had to first determine whether or not the relevant Albanian Law of 1945 was contrary to international law. However, it stated that,

> [t]o adjudicate upon the international responsibility of Albania without her consent would run counter to a well-established principle of international law embodied in the Court's Statute, namely, that the Court can only exercise jurisdiction over a State with its consent.[49]

It further stated that,

> [i]n the present case, Albania's legal interests would not only be affected by a decision, but would form the very subject-matter of the decision. In such a case, the Statute cannot be regarded, by implication, as authorizing proceedings to be continued in the absence of Albania.[50]

On the second question, the Court equally decided that, in the absence of Albania, it could not possibly decide whether the gold belonged to Italy or to Albania, therefore not being able to address the question submitted by Italy.[51] The Court thus dismissed the case.

48 *Case of the monetary gold removed from Rome in 1943 (Preliminary Question), Judgment of June 15th, 1954: I.C.J. Reports 1954*, p. 22.

49 *Ibid.*, p. 32.

50 *Ibid.*, p. 32.

51 *Ibid.*, pp. 33–34. The gold remained in a vault in London in the name of the Tripartite Commission until it was restored to Albania on 8 May 1992, when Albania and the United

In the subsequent cases concerning the absent third party, the meaning and scope of the *Monetary Gold* rule were further developed.

In the case concerning *Military and Paramilitary Activities in and against Nicaragua*, with regard to the United States' assertion that the decision would inevitably pronounce on the rights and obligations of the indispensable third parties, Costa Rica and El Salvador, the Court observed that the rule of "indispensable parties," as claimed by the United States in this case, could not be found in the Statute and the case law of the Court. The relevant third parties could either file a request for permission to intervene under Article 62 or institute separate proceedings. They were not to be bound by the decision of the Court under Article 59 in any event. It stated that:

> The circumstances of the *Monetary Gold* case probably represent the limit of the power of the Court to refuse to exercise its jurisdiction; and none of the States referred to [in this case] can be regarded as in the same position as Albania in that case, so as to be truly indispensable to the pursuance of the proceedings.[52]

The Court reaffirmed that, for the *Monetary Gold* rule to apply, the legal interest of a State not a party to the proceedings should not only be affected by the decision, but should form the very subject-matter of the decision.

In the case concerning *Certain Phosphate Lands in Nauru*, Australia raised objections to the jurisdiction of the Court.[53] It contended that, since New Zealand and the United Kingdom made up the Administering Authority together with Australia, any decision of the Court as to the alleged breach by Australia of its obligations under the Trusteeship Agreement would necessarily involve a finding as to the discharge by those two other States of their obligations in that respect, which would be contrary to the fundamental principle that the jurisdiction of the Court derives solely from the consent of States.

The Court observed that, under national legal systems, courts often have the necessary power to order *proprio motu* the joinder of the third parties who might be affected by the decision to be rendered. That solution makes

---

Kingdom normalized their diplomatic relations and the judgment debt in the *Corfu Channel* case was discharged by Albania. See Shabtai Rosenne, *op. cit. supra* footnote 47, p. 182.

52 *Military and Paramilitary Activities in and against Nicaragua* (*Nicaragua* v. *United States of America*), *Jurisdiction and Admissibility, Judgment, I.C.J. Reports 1984*, p. 431, para. 88.

53 *Certain Phosphate Lands in Nauru* (*Nauru* v. *Australia*), *Preliminary Objections, Judgment, I.C.J. Reports 1992*, p. 240.

it possible to settle a dispute in the presence of all the parties concerned. On the international plane, however, the Court cannot compel a State to appear before it; notwithstanding that limitation, the fact that such States do not wish to come forward to intervene, does not preclude the Court from adjudicating the claims submitted to it, provided that the legal interests of the third party do not form the very subject-matter of the decision to be rendered.[54]

The Court reiterated the ruling in the *Monetary Gold* case and emphasized that, "[i]n the present case, the determination of the responsibility of New Zealand or the United Kingdom is not *a prerequisite* for the determination of the responsibility of Australia."[55] It went on to say that,

> In the present case, a finding by the Court regarding the existence or the content of the responsibility attributed to Australia by Nauru might well have implications for the legal situation of the two other States concerned, but no finding in respect of that legal situation will be needed *as a basis* for the Court's decision on Nauru's claims against Australia. Accordingly, the Court cannot decline to exercise its jurisdiction.[56]

By this ruling, the criterion for the application of the *Monetary Gold* rule is supplemented by an additional element: the determination of the legal situation of the third party should be a prerequisite, or a basis, for the determination of the rights and obligations of the parties to the principal case.

In the individual opinions, President Jennings dissented from the majority. In his view, that the legal interests of New Zealand and the United Kingdom will form the very subject-matter of any decision in Nauru's case against Australia was surely manifest. This was especially true at the merits phase, should the Court have found that reparation must be made to Nauru, the matter would certainly have borne jointly on the three States. Therefore, Jennings considered that the *Monetary Gold* rule should apply in this case.[57]

In the *East Timor* (*Portugal* v. *Australia*) case, Portugal asked the Court to rule that Australia had violated the obligation to respect Portugal's status as the administering Power and East Timor's right as a non-self-governing territory by concluding with Indonesia the 1989 Treaty concerning the "Timor Gap" for the joint exploration and exploitation of the resources of the area. On the

54 *Ibid.*, pp. 260–261, paras. 53–54.
55 *Ibid.*, p. 261, para. 55 (emphasis added).
56 *Ibid.*, pp. 261–262, para. 55 (emphasis added).
57 *Ibid.*, Dissenting Opinion of President Jennings, p. 301.

basis of the *Monetary Gold* rule, Australia raised preliminary objections to the jurisdiction of the Court.[58]

After examining the evidence submitted by Portugal with respect to its status in East Timor and the situation in the Territory, the Court came to the conclusion that,

> in this case, the effects of the judgment requested by Portugal would amount to a determination that Indonesia's entry into and continued presence in East Timor are unlawful and that, as a consequence, it does not have the treaty-making power in matters relating to the continental shelf resources of East Timor. Indonesia's rights and obligations would thus constitute the very subject-matter of such a judgment made in the absence of that State's consent. Such a judgment would run directly counter to the 'well-established principle of international law embodied in the Court's Statute, namely, that the Court can only exercise jurisdiction over a State with its consent' (*Case of the monetary gold removed from Rome in 1943* (*Italy v. France, United Kingdom and United States of America*), *Judgment, I.C.J. Reports 1954*, p. 32).[59]

In the recent case concerning *Application of the Convention on the Prevention and Punishment of the Crime of Genocide* (*Croatia* v. *Serbia*), the *Monetary Gold* rule was invoked by the respondent in an entirely different context. In that case, Croatia claimed that by the rules of State succession, Serbia was responsible for the alleged genocidal acts committed by the Socialist Federal Republic of Yugoslavia (the "SFRY"). To determine whether Serbia was or was not responsible, the Court had to examine the alleged acts of the SFRY. The Respondent contended that in the absence of the SFRY, the Court should decline to exercise jurisdiction over those acts by virtue of the *Monetary Gold* rule. The Court did not accept that argument, but took the view that:

> In both *Monetary Gold* and *East Timor*, the Court declined to exercise its jurisdiction to adjudicate upon the application, because it considered that to do so would have been contrary to the right of a State not party to the proceedings not to have the Court rule upon its conduct without its consent. That rationale has no application to a State which no longer exists, as is the case with the SFRY, since such a State no longer possesses any rights and is incapable of giving or withholding consent to the

58 *East Timor* (*Portugal* v. *Australia*), *Judgment, I.C.J. Reports 1995*, p. 90.

59 *Ibid.*, p. 105, para. 34.

jurisdiction of the Court. So far as concerns the position of the other successor States to the SFRY, it is not necessary for the Court to rule on the legal situation of those States as a prerequisite for the determination of the present claim. The principle discussed by the Court in the *Monetary Gold* case is therefore inapplicable (cf. *Certain Phosphate Lands in Nauru (Nauru* v. *Australia), Preliminary Objections, Judgment, I.C.J. Reports 1992*, pp. 261–262, para. 55).[60]

4 The *non ultra petita* Rule

The last rule to be discussed in this section is the *non ultra petita* rule, which means that the Court is under a duty to abstain from deciding points not included in the submissions of the parties. In international adjudication, the *non ultra petita* rule has been well established, especially in the jurisprudence of the Court.[61]

Non ultra petita bears on the jurisdiction of the Court. As the judicial function of the Court is to settle disputes submitted by the parties to the Court, the terms of their submissions dictate the exact scope of the Court's jurisdiction. They in a way confine the power of the Court to render its decision within the limits of the jurisdiction conferred upon it by the parties through their submissions.

Initially, the Court applied the rule in a narrow sense. In the first case it ever dealt with, the *Corfu Channel* case, with regard to the amount of compensation, the United Kingdom claimed 843,947 pounds for the damage to the warships and the casualties, while the experts' estimation of the compensation was 716,780 pounds. The Court took the view that "it cannot award more than the amount claimed in the submissions of the United Kingdom Government."[62]

---

60 *Application of the Convention on the Prevention and Punishment of the Crime of Genocide (Croatia* v. *Serbia), Merits, Judgment*, para. 116. The essential question on this point is not the effect of the decision on the legal right of a third party, but to what extent the rules of State responsibility could apply to the case of State succession with regard to treaties. See also the individual opinion of Judge Xue Hanqin in the judgment.

61 See *Request for interpretation of the Judgment of November 20th, 1950, in the asylum case (Colombia/Peru), Judgment of November 27th, 1950: I.C.J. Reports 1950*, p. 402; *Arrest Warrant of 11 April 2000 (Democratic Republic of the Congo* v. *Belgium), Judgment, I.C.J. Reports 2002*, pp. 18–19, para. 43.

62 *Corfu Channel case (United Kingdom* v. *Albania), Judgment of December 15th, 1949: I.C.J. Reports 1949*, p. 249. The Court's decision was criticized by Judge *ad hoc* Ečer, partly on the ground that the *non ultra petita* rule was one of procedure, having the effect of limiting

The rule was broadened in the subsequent practice of the Court, particularly in the interpretation cases. In the *Asylum* (*Colombia* v. *Peru*) case (interpretation), after the Court delivered its judgment in the *Asylum* case, Colombia submitted a request for the interpretation of the judgment. In considering its admissibility, the Court laid down two conditions for the interpretation:

> (1) The real purpose of the request must be to obtain an interpretation of the judgment. This signifies that its object must be solely to obtain clarification of the meaning and the scope of what the Court has decided with binding force, and not to obtain an answer to questions not so decided. Any other construction of Article 60 of the Statute would nullify the provision of the article that the judgment is final and without appeal. (2) In addition, it is necessary that there should exist a dispute as to the meaning or scope of the judgment.[63]

The Court went on to say that to determine the first question, "one must bear in mind the principle that it is the duty of the Court not only to reply to the questions as stated in the final submissions of the parties, but also to abstain from deciding points not included in those submissions."[64]

According to the Court's jurisprudence, a request for interpretation "cannot concern the reasons for the judgment except in so far as these are inseparable from the operative clause."[65] In the Joint Declaration by Judges Owada, Bennouna and Gaja in the *Temple* case (interpretation), they drew a distinction between the notions of "inseparable reasons" and "essential reasons," a term used by the Court in the judgment.[66] In their view, reasons are "inseparable" when the operative part of the judgment is not self-standing and contains an express or implicit reference to these reasons. They are different from "essential

---

the actual award made by the Court, but not one of substance, to affect the basis of its calculation. See Shabtai Rosenne, *The Law and Practice of the International Court, 1920–2005, Vol. II, Jurisdiction*, 4th edition, Martinus Nijhoff Publishers, 2006, p. 577.

63 *Request for interpretation of the Judgment of November 20th, 1950, in the asylum case (Colombia/Peru), Judgment of November 27th, 1950: I.C.J. Reports 1950*, p. 402

64 *Ibid.* See also *Request for Interpretation of the Judgment of 11 June 1998 in the Case concerning the* Land and Maritime Boundary between Cameroon and Nigeria (Cameroon *v.* Nigeria), Preliminary Objections (*Nigeria* v. *Cameroon*), *Judgment, I.C.J. Reports 1999*, pp. 36–37, para. 12.

65 *Request for Interpretation of the Judgment of 15 June 1962 in the Case concerning the* Temple of Preah Vihear (Cambodia *v.* Thailand) (*Cambodia* v. *Thailand*), *Judgment, I.C.J. Reports 2013*, p. 296, para. 34.

66 *Ibid.*, Joint Declaration by Judges Owada, Bennouna and Gaja, p. 320, paras. 1–2

reasons." To assimilate the term "essential reasons" to "inseparable reasons" actually lowers the criterion for the determination of *res judicata*. This could imply that State parties to a case may find themselves bound by pronouncements on matters that were not submitted to the Court or that were even beyond the Court's jurisdiction.

Although the reasoning itself cannot be the object for interpretation, in order to clarify the meaning and scope of the decision, the Court may have to resort to the reasoning far enough to obtain the full meaning of the operative part. This is particularly true when a judgment was rendered a long time ago and none of the judges sitting in that case is present.

In the *Temple* case (interpretation), Cambodia asked the Court to clarify the meaning of the first two operative paragraphs of the 1962 judgment.[67] It particularly underlined that

> on account of the terms used and given the context (specifically, the Court's decision concerning the legal status of the Annex I map as representing the frontier between the two States), the first paragraph of the *dispositif* must be understood as determining, with binding force, that all of the disputed area that lies on the Cambodian side of the line on the Annex I map—including, therefore, the Temple of Preah Vihear itself—is to be regarded as falling under Cambodian sovereignty.[68]

67 *Request for Interpretation of the Judgment of 15 June 1962 in the Case concerning the* Temple of Preah Vihear (Cambodia *v.* Thailand) (*Cambodia* v. *Thailand*), *Judgment, I.C.J. Reports 2013*, p. 287, para. 11.

68 *Ibid.*, p. 288, para. 12. In 1904, France (as the protecting power of Indo-China) concluded a boundary treaty with Siam (Thailand), which specified that the frontier in the Dangrek sector was to follow the watershed line "between the basins of the Nam Sen and the Mekong, on the one hand, and the Nam Moun, on the other hand." The 1904 Treaty provided for the establishment of Mixed Commissions composed of officers appointed by the two parties which were responsible for delimiting the frontier between Siam and French Indo-China (of which Cambodia formed part). The final stage of the operation of delimitation was to be the preparation and publication of maps, a task assigned to a team of four French officers, three of whom had been members of the Mixed Commission. In 1907, that team prepared a series of 11 maps covering a large part of the frontiers between Siam and French Indo-China. In particular, it drew up a map entitled "Dangrek—Commission of Delimitation between Indo-China and Siam," on which the frontier passed to the north of Preah Vihear, thus leaving the Temple in Cambodia. Those maps were duly communicated to the Siamese Government in 1908, but were never approved by the Mixed Commission which had ceased to function some months before the production of the map. The Annex I map depicted the Temple area. See *Case concerning*

Through this request, Cambodia apparently wished the Court to confirm the legal status of the Annex I map as the boundary map, and that the line on the map constituted the boundary line.

Thailand, for its part, argued that

> the dispute which was before the Court in 1962 concerned territorial sovereignty, not delimitation of a frontier, and that the 1962 Judgment decided only that the Temple fell under the sovereignty of Cambodia. The Annex I map was significant only as evidence of whether the Temple lay in Cambodian territory and did not serve the purpose of defining the boundary…it would have been contrary to the principle *non ultra petita* for the Court to have ruled upon the boundary line, since Cambodia had not included any request for a ruling on the map in its original submissions and the Court had declined to entertain the new submissions which Cambodia had advanced at the end of the oral proceedings.[69]

In Thailand's view, the Court in the 1962 judgment had not ruled on the legal status of the Annex I map.

Based on its jurisprudence laid down in the *Asylum* case, the Court reiterated that it "must keep strictly within the limits of the original judgment and cannot question matters that were settled therein with binding force, nor can it provide answers to questions the Court did not decide in the original judgment."[70] Regarding the *non ultra petita* rule, it took the view that "[t]he Court in 1962 necessarily made an assessment of the scope of the *petitum* before it; Article 60 of the Statute does not give the Court the power today to substitute a different assessment for that made at the time of the Judgment."[71] As the parties did not ask the Court to decide on the legal status of the Annex I map, by virtue of the *non ultra petita* rule, in the present case for the interpretation of the 1962 judgment, the Court could not go beyond the *petita* submitted to the Court then.

---

the Temple of Preah Vihear (*Cambodia* v. *Thailand*), *Merits, Judgment of 15 June 1962: I.C.J. Reports 1962*, pp. 16–24.

69 *Request for Interpretation of the Judgment of 15 June 1962 in the Case concerning the* Temple of Preah Vihear (Cambodia *v.* Thailand) (*Cambodia* v. *Thailand*), *Judgment, I.C.J. Reports 2013*, p. 305, para. 61.

70 *Ibid.*, p. 306, para. 66.

71 *Ibid.*, p. 307, para. 71.

CHAPTER V

Preconditions for the Exercise of Jurisdiction

Unilateral institution of proceedings in the Court often leaves certain issues that have to be first disposed of by the Court. These issues are characterized as the "preconditions" to the jurisdiction of the Court. In practice, the respondent may raise them as part of its objections to the jurisdiction of the Court or the admissibility of the application. Unless these preconditions are satisfied, the Court has no jurisdiction in the case. As these preconditions directly relate to the competence and jurisdiction of the Court, the Court has to examine them *in limine litis*. Therefore, these preconditions are considered as pre-preliminary matters.

1 Existence of a Dispute

The purpose of litigation is to settle a dispute. Under Article 38, the function of the Court is to decide in accordance with international law disputes that States submit to it. Therefore, "[t]he existence of a dispute between the parties is a condition of the Court's jurisdiction."[1] The existence of a dispute, however, is not always self-evident in practice. It cannot be self-claimed by the applicant State; the respondent State may contend that there existed no dispute between the parties or that the essence of the subject-matter of the dispute is not as described by the applicant.

The need to determine the existence of a dispute is not merely for the purpose of its settlement.[2] It is the first condition for the seisin of the Court. It is the very existence of such a dispute that may place every aspect of the judicial process into meaningful perspective. It concerns both law and fact.

---

1 *Alleged Violations of Sovereign Rights and Maritime Spaces in the Caribbean Sea* (*Nicaragua* v. *Colombia*), *Preliminary Objections, Judgment*, para. 50.

2 In the early days the role of an arbitrator or a judge was only to give a ruling to resolve a dispute. By its very nature, such role was limited to the concrete resolution of disputes according to law. He was not supposed to seek fairest solutions by looking beyond the law. Nor was he to make law. By acting impartially and objectively, he made the ruling on the case. As is described by a metaphor, "the sword must decide the dispute," cutting the Gordian knot. See Robert Kolb, *The International Court of Justice*, Hart Publishing, 2013, pp. 300–301.

 | DOI 10.1163/9789004342767_006

a The Notion of a Dispute

What constitutes a "dispute" which falls within the meaning of Articles 36 and 37 of the Statute is a question that has given rise to an incredible amount of jurisprudence of the Court, especially in the recent years.

According to Article 38, paragraph 1, of the Statute, the function of the Court is to settle "*disputes.*" Article 36, paragraph 1, uses the term "legal dispute." For the purpose of the judicial function of the Court, these two terms should be considered as synonyms. That is to say, a dispute before the Court must be of a legal nature. The Statute and the Rules of Court do not provide any definition to the term "dispute." The issue of the existence of a dispute was first raised in the *Mavrommatis Palestine Concessions* case, where the PCIJ stated: "A dispute is a disagreement on a point of law or fact, a conflict of legal views or of interests between two persons."[3] This formulation has been repeatedly cited in the Court's jurisprudence till today.

The existence of a dispute, however, was not a particular point of concern for the Court until the late 1950s. It was in the cases concerning *Right of Passage over Indian Territory*, *South West Africa* and *Northern Cameroons* that the existence of a dispute gradually became one of the central issues for the Court's consideration of its jurisdiction and the admissibility of an application.[4]

In the *South West Africa* cases, the Court raised this issue, *proprio motu*, as a preliminary question. It stated that,

> the Court finds it necessary to decide a preliminary question relating to the existence of the dispute which is the subject of the Applications. The view has been advanced that if no dispute within the purview of Article 7 of the Mandate and Articles 36 and 37 of the Statute of the Court exists in fact, a conclusion of incompetence or *fin de non-recevoir* must follow.[5]

Apparently, Ethiopia and Liberia filed the cases on behalf of the South West African people. South Africa's non-compliance with its obligations under the Mandate and its practice of *apartheid* were not directed at these two States.

---

3 *Mavrommatis Palestine Concessions, Judgment No. 2, 1924, P.C.I.J., Series A, No. 2*, p. 11.

4 See *Case concerning right of Passage over Indian Territory* (*Portugal* v. *India*) (*Preliminary Objections*), *Judgment of November 26th, 1957: I.C.J. Reports 1957*, pp. 148–149; *South West Africa* cases (*Ethiopia* v. *South Africa; Liberia* v. *South Africa*), *Preliminary Objections, Judgment of 21 December 1962, I.C.J. Report: 1962*, p. 328; *Case concerning the Northern Cameroons* (*Cameroon* v. *United Kingdom*), *Preliminary Objections, Judgment of 2 December 1963: I.C.J. Reports 1963*, p. 27.

5 *South West Africa cases* (*Ethiopia* v. *South Africa; Liberia* v. *South Africa*), *Preliminary Objections, Judgment of 21 December 1962, I.C.J. Report: 1962*, p. 328.

As the Court found that the complaints contained in the applications filed by Ethiopia and Liberia did not constitute a dispute respectively between Ethiopia and South Africa and between Liberia and South Africa, such dispute could not fall within the meaning of Articles 36 and 37 of the Statute, and the Court had no case to adjudicate. Therefore, this was a crucial and preliminary issue that had to be first determined by the Court.

Since then, the question of the existence of a dispute has been brought up regularly by the parties in various cases as a preliminary issue for the consideration of the Court's jurisdiction.[6] Consequently, there is an impressive accretion of judicial practice and jurisprudence on this issue.

In ascertaining the existence of a dispute, the Court in the *South West Africa* cases enunciated that "[i]t must be shown that the claim of one party is positively opposed by the other."[7] According to the Court, such opposition of views of the parties does not require any specific order for raising legal claims. It is

---

6 See *Alleged Violations of Sovereign Rights and Maritime Spaces in the Caribbean Sea (Nicaragua* v. *Colombia), Judgment, Preliminary Objections,* para. 50; see also *Nuclear Tests (Australia* v. *France), Judgment, I.C.J. Reports 1974*, pp. 270–271, para. 55; *Nuclear Tests (New Zealand* v. *France), Judgment, I.C.J. Reports 1974*, p. 476, para. 58. The cases in which parties argued upon this question or the Court discussed it *proprio motu* include: *Interpretation of Peace Treaties with Bulgaria, Hungary and Romania; Case concerning right of passage over Indian territory (Portugal* v. *India); South West Africa cases(Ethiopia* v. *South Africa; Liberia* v. *South Africa); Case concerning the Northern Cameroons (Cameroon* v. *United Kingdom); Nuclear Tests (Australia* v. *France) (New Zealand* v. *France); Aegean Sea Continental Shelf (Greece* v. *Turkey); Applicability of the Obligation to Arbitrate under Section 21 of the United Nations Headquarters Agreement of 26 June 1947; East Timor (Portugal* v. *Australia); Application of the Convention on the Prevention and Punishment of the Crime of Genocide (Bosnia and Herzegovina* v. *Serbia and Montenegro); Questions of Interpretation and Application of the 1971 Montreal Convention arising from the Aerial Incident at Lockerbie (Libyan Arab Jamahiriya* v. *United Kingdom) (Libyan Arab Jamahiriya* v. *United States of America); Land and Maritime Boundary between Cameroon and Nigeria (Cameroon* v. *Nigeria); Arrest Warrant of 11 April 2000 (Democratic Republic of the Congo* v. *Belgium); Certain Property (Liechtenstein* v. *Germany); Territorial and Maritime Dispute; Armed Activities on the Territory of the Congo (New Application: 2002) (Democratic Republic of the Congo* v. *Rwanda); Application of the International Convention on the Elimination of All Forms of Racial Discrimination (Georgia* v. *Russian Federation); Questions relating to the Obligation to Prosecute or Extradite (Belgium* v. *Senegal); Question of the Delimitation of the Continental Shelf between Nicaragua and Colombia beyond 200 nautical miles from the Nicaraguan Coast (Nicaragua* v. *Colombia); Alleged Violations of Sovereign Rights and Maritime Spaces in the Caribbean Sea (Nicaragua* v. *Colombia) ; Obligations concerning Negotiations relating to Cessation of the Nuclear Arms Race and to Nuclear Disarmament (Marshall Islands* v. *India) (Marshall Islands* v. *Pakistan) (Marshall Islands* v. *United Kingdom).*

7 *South West Africa cases (Ethiopia* v. *South Africa; Liberia* v. *South Africa), Preliminary Objections, Judgment of 21 December 1962, I.C.J. Report: 1962*, p. 328.

not necessary that the applicant State raised its claims first, which was then positively opposed by the respondent State. So long as there is an opposition of views and positions taken by the parties, there exists a dispute between them. This issue was considered in the case concerning *Alleged Violations of Sovereign Rights and Maritime Spaces in the Caribbean Sea* (*Nicaragua* v. *Colombia*). Nicaragua did not expressly raise its claims against Colombia's conduct in the maritime areas adjudicated to Nicaragua by the Court's 2012 judgment. It was Colombia, the respondent, who, after the delivery of the said judgment, enacted a Presidential Proclamation establishing a contiguous zone that Nicaragua considered infringed on its maritime sovereign rights. The parties evidently held opposite positions on such conduct. In that regard, the Court considered that,

> It does not matter which one of them advances a claim and which one opposes it. What matters is that the two sides hold clearly opposite views concerning the question of the performance or non-performance of certain international obligations.[8]

b Determination of the Existence of a Dispute

1 Who is to Determine the Existence of a Dispute

When the parties contest whether there existed a dispute between them at the time when the application was filed, it is for the Court to decide on the matter. As the Court has expressed on a number of occasions, that is "a matter for objective determination by the Court."[9] It points out that,

> it is not sufficient for one party to a contentious case to assert that a dispute exists with the other party. A mere assertion is not sufficient to prove the existence of a dispute any more than a mere denial of the existence of the dispute proves its nonexistence.[10]

8 *Alleged Violations of Sovereign Rights and Maritime Spaces in the Caribbean Sea* (*Nicaragua* v. *Colombia*), *Preliminary Objections, Judgment*, para. 50.

9 *Ibid.*; see also *Application of the International Convention on the Elimination of All Forms of Racial Discrimination* (*Georgia* v. *Russian Federation*), *Preliminary Objections, Judgment, I.C.J. Reports 2011*, p. 84, para. 30; *Nuclear Tests* (*Australia* v. *France*), *Judgment, I.C.J. Reports 1974*, p. 271, para. 55; *Nuclear Tests* (*New Zealand* v. *France*), *Judgment, I.C.J. Reports 1974*, p. 476, para. 58.

10 *Territorial and Maritime Dispute* (*Nicaragua* v. *Colombia*), *Preliminary Objections, Judgment, I.C.J. Reports 2007*, p. 874, para. 138; see also *Applicability of the Obligation to Arbitrate under Section 21 of the United Nations Headquarters Agreement of 26 June 1947, Advisory Opinion, I.C.J. Reports 1988*, p. 27, para. 35; *South West Africa cases* (*Ethiopia* v.

This determination, in the Court's words, "is an integral part of the Court's judicial function."[11] In the jurisprudence of the Court, the reference is often made to the "objective determination" without including the phrase "by the Court." That omission in no way implies that the matter could fall outside of the domain of the judicial function.[12]

2 How to Determine the Existence of a Dispute

Normally, the question of the existence of a dispute does not arise when the parties submit their case by a special agreement, because they specify in the agreement the exact content of their dispute and what they wish the Court to settle.[13]

South Africa; Liberia v. *South Africa*), *Preliminary Objections, Judgment of 21 December 1962, I.C.J. Report: 1962*, p. 328. See further *Interpretation of Peace Treaties, Advisory Opinion, I.C.J. Reports 1950*, p. 74, where the Court maintained a similar line that "[t]he mere denial of the existence of a dispute does not prove its non-existence."

11 *Territorial and Maritime Dispute* (*Nicaragua* v. *Colombia*), *Preliminary Objections, Judgment, I.C.J. Reports 2007*, p. 874, para. 138.

12 See *ibid.*; *Armed Activities on the Territory of the Congo* (*New Application: 2002*) (*Democratic Republic of the Congo* v. *Rwanda*), *Jurisdiction and Admissibility, Judgment, I.C.J. Reports 2006*, p. 40, para. 90; *Land and Maritime Boundary between Cameroon and Nigeria* (*Cameroon* v. *Nigeria*), *Preliminary Objections, Judgment, I.C.J. Reports 1998*, p. 315, para. 87; *Questions of Interpretation and Application of the 1971 Montreal Convention arising from the Aerial Incident at Lockerbie* (*Libyan Arab Jamahiriya* v. *United Kingdom*), *Preliminary Objections, Judgment, I.C.J. Reports 1998*, p. 17, para. 22; *Questions of Interpretation and Application of the 1971 Montreal Convention arising from the Aerial Incident at Lockerbie* (*Libyan Arab Jamahiriya* v. *United States of America*), *Preliminary Objections, Judgment, I.C.J. Reports 1998*, p. 123, para. 21; *East Timor* (*Portugal* v. *Australia*), *Judgment, I.C.J. Reports 1995*, p. 100, para. 22; *Applicability of the Obligation to Arbitrate under Section 21 of the United Nations Headquarters Agreement of 26 June 1947, Advisory Opinion, I.C.J. Reports 1988*, p. 27, para. 35; *Interpretation of Peace Treaties with Bulgaria, Hungary and Romania, Advisory Opinion, I.C.J. Reports 1950*, p. 74.

13 In practice, the parties may disagree on what they have agreed in the special agreement. That kind of disagreement between the parties may not constitute, in the strict sense of the term, part of the dispute, but the Court still has to decide whether to include the matter concerned in the judgment. For example, in *Frontier Dispute* (*Burkina Faso/Niger*), although the two parties submitted their dispute to the Court through a special agreement, they still disagreed as to whether the Court could include in the operative part of its judgment the agreed coordinates of the two sectors of their common boundary so as to give them binding force. See *Frontier Dispute* (*Burkina Faso/Niger*), *Judgment, I.C.J. Reports 2013*, pp. 66–73, paras. 35–59. In the *Corfu Channel* case, the parties contested the Court's jurisdiction under the special agreement to assess the amount of compensation. See *Corfu Channel case* (*United Kingdom* v. *Albania*), *Judgment of April 9th, 1949: I.C.J.*

When proceedings are unilaterally instituted, the situation is much more complicated.[14] Under Article 40 of the Statute and Article 38 of the Rules, the applicant is obliged to indicate in its application against whom the case is filed and the subject-matter of the dispute. Therefore, the subject-matter of the dispute is initially defined by the applicant.

The formulation of the subject-matter of a dispute entails a comprehensive understanding of the Court's procedural rules as well as its case law on jurisdiction and admissibility. In formulating the subject-matter of the dispute, the applicant State has to consider and assess the following factors: the reaction of the respondent State to the case so as to predict the direction of the proceedings; the soundness of the jurisdictional basis of its claim; the applicable law between the parties; and the remedies it wishes to obtain from the Court. Not surprisingly, as is often done in a domestic litigation, the formulation of a dispute in an adversarial process may be used, and indeed, has been used in practice as one of the litigating tactics in order to win the case. The respondent State, on the other hand, would, also first assess the dispute as is presented to the Court and evaluate the prospects of the litigation. If it decides to raise objections to the jurisdiction of the Court and the admissibility of the application, it may wish to have the proceedings bifurcated so as to defend its position on the procedural front first. In that regard, the issue of non-existence of a dispute could serve as the first ground of objection to the jurisdiction of the Court.

In order to make an objective determination, the Court has to examine the evidence so as to ascertain the views and positions of the parties to see whether there indeed existed or did not exist a legal dispute. In its often-cited jargon, "The matter is one of substance, not of form."[15]

Reports 1949, pp. 23–26. In both of the *Continental Shelf* cases involving Libya (*Tunisia/Libyan Arab Jamahiriya, Libyan Arab Jamahiriya/Malta*), the parties argued upon the extent to which the Court may indicate how the principles and rules of international law can be applied by the two parties in their delimitation of the continental shelf, as prescribed in the special agreement. See *Continental Shelf (Tunisia/Libyan Arab Jamahiriya), Judgment, I.C.J. Reports 1982*, pp. 38–40, paras. 35–40; *Continental Shelf (Libyan Arab Jamahiriya/ Malta), Judgment, I.C.J. Reports 1985*, pp. 22–24, paras. 18–19.

14 So far there have been 137 contentious cases before the Court, of which 18 were filed by a special agreement and 119 were unilaterally instituted. *See* Mariko Kawano, "The Role of Judicial Procedures in the Process of the Pacific Settlement of International Disputes," *Recueil des cours*, Vol. 346, 2009, pp. 453–462, Tables 2 and 3.

15 *Alleged Violations of Sovereign Rights and Maritime Spaces in the Caribbean Sea (Nicaragua v. Colombia), Judgment, Preliminary Objections*, para. 50; see also *Application of the*

In the case concerning *Applicability of the Obligation to Arbitrate*, the United States had never expressly contradicted the view expressed by the Secretary-General or by the General Assembly with respect to the interpretation of the Headquarters Agreement between the United Nations and the United States. It had nevertheless enacted the Anti-Terrorism Act and, pursuant to that Act, taken measures against the PLO Mission to the United Nations. The Secretary-General, on the other hand, has consistently challenged the decisions taken by the United States Congress and the Administration, and contested the conformity of the Act with the Headquarters Agreement. In the opinion of the Court, these circumstances were sufficient to demonstrate the opposing attitudes of the United Nations and the United States, thus demonstrating the existence of a dispute.[16] In its Advisory Opinion, the Court pointed out that,

> where one party to a treaty protests against the behaviour or a decision of another party, and claims that such behaviour or decision constitutes a breach of the treaty, the mere fact that the party accused does not advance any argument to justify its conduct under international law does not prevent the opposing attitudes of the parties from giving rise to a dispute concerning the interpretation or application of the treaty.[17]

On the opposite positions and conduct of the parties, Judge Morelli in his dissenting opinion in the *South West Africa* cases made the following observation:

> a dispute consists ... in a contrast between the respective attitudes of the parties in relation to a certain conflict of interests ... But it may also be that one of the opposing attitudes of the parties consists, not of a manifestation of the will, but rather of a course of conduct by means of which the party pursuing that course directly achieves its own interest. This is the case of a claim which is followed not by the contesting of the claim but by the adoption of a course of conduct by the other party inconsistent with the claim. And this is the case too where there is in the first

International Convention on the Elimination of All Forms of Racial Discrimination (*Georgia* v. *Russian Federation*), *Preliminary Objections, Judgment, I.C.J. Reports 2011*, p. 84, para. 30.

16 See *Applicability of the Obligation to Arbitrate under Section 21 of the United Nations Headquarters Agreement of 26 June 1947, Advisory Opinion, I.C.J. Reports 1988*, pp. 27–30, paras. 36–43.

17 *Ibid.*, p. 28, para. 38.

> place a course of conduct by one of the parties to achieve its own interest, which the other party meets by a protest.[18]

In examining the positions and conduct of the parties, the Court may also draw inference from such evidence. As the Court elucidated in the case concerning *Land and Maritime Boundary between Cameroon and Nigeria*,

> a disagreement on a point of law or fact, a conflict of legal views or interests, or the positive opposition of the claim of one party by the other need not necessarily be stated *expressis verbis*. In the determination of the existence of a dispute, as in other matters, the position or the attitude of a party can be established by inference, whatever the professed view of that party.[19]

The Court further elaborated on this point in the case concerning *Application of the International Convention on the Elimination of All Forms of Racial Discrimination*, where it stated that, "the existence of a dispute may be inferred from the failure of a State to respond to a claim in circumstances where a response is called for."[20] This condition of necessary response apparently is still subject to demonstration by evidence.

3 Prior Notice and the Existence of a Dispute

In international relations, it is a normal practice that if one State has a claim against another State, it would lodge a complaint with that State through normal diplomatic channels. The parties may argue over the matter or try to negotiate it before seising the Court. If such information is available, it is quite sufficient for the applicant to prove to the Court that the dispute existed between the parties before the filing of the application. That kind of situation is self-explanatory and the Court can reach its conclusion without any difficulty.[21]

---

18 *South West Africa cases* (*Ethiopia* v. *South Africa; Liberia* v. *South Africa*), *Preliminary Objections, Judgment of 21 December 1962: I.C.J. Reports 1962*, Dissenting Opinion of Judge Morelli, p. 567.

19 *Land and Maritime Boundary between Cameroon and Nigeria* (*Cameroon* v. *Nigeria*), *Preliminary Objections, Judgment, I.C.J. Reports 1998*, p. 315, para. 89.

20 *Application of the International Convention on the Elimination of All Forms of Racial Discrimination* (*Georgia* v. *Russian Federation*), *Preliminary Objections, Judgment, I.C.J. Reports 2011*, p. 84, para. 30.

21 See *Questions relating to the Obligation to Prosecute or Extradite* (*Belgium* v. *Senegal*), *Judgment, I.C.J. Reports 2012*, pp. 441–445, paras. 44–55; *Aegean Sea Continental Shelf* (*Greece* v. *Turkey*), *Judgment, I.C.J. Reports 1978*, pp. 12–13, paras. 30–31; *Case concerning right of*

More difficult is the situation where the applicant State, for one reason or another, has neither made its representations in any form with the respondent State, nor had it conducted any negotiation with the respondent before instituting proceedings in the Court. As a defence, the respondent could argue that non-communication, absence of exchange of diplomatic Notes, or lack of prior notice demonstrates that there existed no dispute between the parties.

According to the jurisprudence of the Court, such prior notice is not considered by the Court as a necessary condition for the existence of a dispute. Such notice may be helpful for one party to know the claim of the other party, but it is not a condition. In the Court's view, such prior notice is a matter of form. What the Court should determine is whether the parties in substance held opposite claims against each other.

In the case concerning *Alleged Violations* (*Nicaragua* v. *Colombia*), Nicaragua raised two claims, one relating to Colombia's alleged violations of its maritime rights, the other concerning the threat or use of force under Article 2, paragraph 4, of the Charter and customary international law. Colombia argued that never before the filing of the application had Nicaragua made any complaint to Colombia. Moreover, relations between the parties remained stable and cooperative throughout the relevant period.[22]

On the point of lack of communication, the Court stated that "although a formal diplomatic protest may be an important step to bring a claim of one party to the attention of the other, such a formal protest is not a necessary condition."[23] The Court, having examined the statements made by the highest representatives of the parties, the positions of the parties with regard to Colombia's new Presidential proclamation of an "Integral Contiguous Zone," and the parties' conduct at sea, came to the view that,

> although Nicaragua did not send its formal diplomatic Note to Colombia in protest at the latter's alleged violations of its maritime rights at sea until 13 September 2014, almost ten months after the filing of the Application, in the specific circumstances of the present case, the evidence clearly indicates that, at the time when the Application was filed, Colombia was aware that its enactment of Decree 1946 and its conduct in

passage over Indian territory (*Portugal* v. *India*) (*Preliminary Objections*), *Judgment of November 26th, 1957: I.C.J. Reports 1957*, pp. 148–149; *Interpretation of Peace Treaties with Bulgaria, Hungary and Romania, Advisory Opinion: I.C.J. Reports 1950*, p. 74.

22 *Alleged Violations of Sovereign Rights and Maritime Spaces in the Caribbean Sea* (*Nicaragua* v. *Colombia*), *Preliminary Objections, Judgment*, para. 76.

23 *Ibid.*, para. 72.

> the maritime areas declared by the 2012 Judgment to belong to Nicaragua were positively opposed by Nicaragua. Given the public statements made by the highest representatives of the Parties, such as those referred to in paragraph 69, Colombia could not have misunderstood the position of Nicaragua over such differences.[24]

Based on that determination, the Court drew the conclusion that at the date on which the application was filed, there existed a dispute between the parties over alleged violations by Colombia of Nicaragua's sovereign rights and maritime spaces. Apparently, Colombia's awareness of the situation is not purely a subjective element, nor is it a subjective assessment by the Court. Rather, it is an objective determination of the Court on the basis of the evidence submitted by the parties. Without such evidence, the Court would not have been able to draw its conclusion.

4 Prior Negotiation and the Existence of a Dispute

According to the case law of the Court, prior negotiation is not taken as a necessary condition for the existence of a dispute, either. While the Court has in some cases established the existence of a dispute based on the evidence of prior negotiations and diplomatic consultations,[25] unless otherwise provided, it does not consider such negotiation as a condition for the existence of a dispute.

Because acceptance of the jurisdiction of the Court is always made specifically by a State, whether a precondition of negotiation is attached to the consent of that State has to be ascertained in each specific case. There is no general rule governing the issue. The Court made it clear in the *Land and Maritime Boundary* (*Cameroon* v. *Nigeria*) case that:

> Neither in the Charter nor otherwise in international law is any general rule to be found to the effect that the exhaustion of diplomatic negotiations constitutes a precondition for a matter to be referred to the Court. No such precondition was embodied in the Statute of the Permanent Court of International Justice, contrary to a proposal by the

24 *Ibid.*, para. 73.

25 See *Certain Property* (*Liechtenstein* v. *Germany*), *Preliminary Objections, Judgment, I.C.J. Reports 2005*, pp. 18–19, para. 25; *South West Africa cases* (*Ethiopia* v. *South Africa; Liberia* v. *South Africa*), *Preliminary Objections, Judgment of 21 December 1962: I.C.J. Reports 1962*, pp. 342–346; *Case concerning right of passage over Indian territory* (*Portugal* v. *India*) (*Preliminary Objections*), *Judgment of November 26th, 1957: I.C.J. Reports 1957*, pp. 148–149.

> Advisory Committee of Jurists in 1920 (*Advisory Committee of Jurists, Procès-verbaux of the Proceedings of the Committee (16 June-24 July 1920) with Annexes, pp. 679, 725-726*). Nor is it to be found in Article 36 of the Statute of this Court.[26]

The Court gave the above statement in the particular context of that case where the parties both had made declarations under Article 36, paragraph 2, of the Statute.

In the *Right of Passage* case, for example, India asserted that "unless negotiations had taken place which had resulted in a definition of the dispute between the Parties as a legal dispute, there was no dispute in the sense of Article 36 (2) of the Statute."[27] The Court, in entertaining this question, did not accept India's assertion.[28] In the *Aegean Sea Continental Shelf* case, the Court also gave no credit to the point made by Turkey that "there is no dispute between the parties while negotiations continue."[29] The question of prior negotiation for the existence of a dispute should not be confused with the precondition provided for in a compromissory clause for the seisin of the Court, an issue to be discussed subsequently.

Although a formal diplomatic Note and prior negotiation are not necessary for the existence of a dispute, diplomatic exchanges and negotiations prior to the filing of the application "may help demonstrate the existence of the dispute and delineate its subject-matter,"[30] as the Court suggested in the case concerning *Application of the International Convention on the Elimination of All Forms of Racial Discrimination*. In that case, by examining the exchanges between the Georgian and Russian representatives in the Security Council, among other materials, the Court found that the subject-matter of the dispute between Georgia and Russia was the latter's compliance with its obligations under the Convention.[31] In a similar vein, in the case concerning *Obligation to Prosecute or Extradite*, after a review of the diplomatic exchanges between

---

26 *Land and Maritime Boundary between Cameroon and Nigeria* (*Cameroon* v. *Nigeria*), *Preliminary Objections, Judgment, I.C.J. Reports 1998*, p. 303, para. 56.

27 *Case concerning right of passage over Indian territory* (*Portugal* v. *India*) (*Preliminary Objections*), *Judgment of November 26th, 1957: I.C.J. Reports 1957*, p. 148.

28 See *ibid.*, pp. 148–149.

29 *Aegean Sea Continental Shelf* (*Greece* v. *Turkey*), *Judgment, I.C.J. Reports 1978*, pp. 12–13, paras. 30–31.

30 *Application of the International Convention on the Elimination of All Forms of Racial Discrimination* (*Georgia* v. *Russian Federation*), *Preliminary Objections, Judgment, I.C.J. Reports 2011*, p. 84, para. 30.

31 See *ibid.*, p. 120, para. 113.

Belgium and Senegal, the Court concluded that the dispute between the parties was about the interpretation and application of Article 6, paragraph 2, and Article 7, paragraph 1, of the Convention against Torture and did not relate to alleged breaches of obligations under customary international law.[32]

c *The Relevant Date and the Existence of a Dispute*

According to the Statute and the case law of the Court, a dispute must in principle exist at the time an application is submitted to the Court.[33] This is because the questions of jurisdiction of the Court and the admissibility of the application must be assessed on the date at which the application was instituted.[34]

The question of the relevant date for the existence of a dispute finds its origin in the case concerning *Electricity Company of Sofia and Bulgaria* before the PCIJ, where Bulgaria raised an objection to the admissibility of Belgium's claim on the ground that its claim did not form the subject of a dispute between the two Governments prior to the filing of the Belgian application. The PCIJ upheld this objection and stated that Belgium should prove that "before the filing of the Application, a dispute had arisen."[35] This pronouncement was reaffirmed in the subsequent cases.[36]

---

32 See *Questions relating to the Obligation to Prosecute or Extradite (Belgium* v. *Senegal), Judgment, I.C.J. Reports 2012*, pp. 442–445, paras. 47–55.

33 *Application of the International Convention on the Elimination of All Forms of Racial Discrimination (Georgia* v. *Russian Federation), Preliminary Objections, Judgment, I.C.J. Reports 2011*, p. 85, para. 30; *Questions relating to the Obligation to Prosecute or Extradite (Belgium* v. *Senegal), Judgment, I.C.J. Reports 2012*, p. 442, para. 46.

34 *Application of the Convention on the Prevention and Punishment of the Crime of Genocide (Croatia* v. *Serbia), Preliminary Objections, Judgment, I.C.J. Reports 2008*, p. 438, para. 79; *Application of the Convention on the Prevention and Punishment of the Crime of Genocide (Bosnia and Herzegovina* v. *Yugoslavia), Preliminary Objections, Judgment, I.C.J. Reports 1996 (II)*, p. 613, para. 26. See *Questions of Interpretation and Application of the 1971 Montreal Convention arising from the Aerial Incident at Lockerbie (Libyan Arab Jamahiriya* v. *United Kingdom), Preliminary Objections, Judgment, I.C.J. Reports 1998*, pp. 25–26, paras. 42–44; *Questions of Interpretation and Application of the 1971 Montreal Convention arising from the Aerial Incident at Lockerbie (Libyan Arab Jamahiriya* v. *United States of America), Preliminary Objections, Judgment, I.C.J. Reports 1998*, pp. 130–131, paras. 42–44; *Border and Transborder Armed Actions (Nicaragua* v. *Honduras), Jurisdiction and Admissibility, Judgment, I.C.J. Reports 1988*, p. 95, para. 66.

35 *Electricity Company of Sofia and Bulgaria, Judgment of April 4, 1939, P.C.I.J., Series A/B, No. 77*, p. 83.

36 See *Questions of Interpretation and Application of the 1971 Montreal Convention arising from the Aerial Incident at Lockerbie (Libyan Arab Jamahiriya* v. *United Kingdom), Preliminary Objections, Judgment, I.C.J. Reports 1998*, pp. 25–26, paras. 42–44; *Questions of*

Substantively, the very function of the Court as a judicial organ is to settle disputes between States. If a dispute ceased to exist or became moot after the filing of an application, there would be no point for the Court in continuing the judicial proceedings or rendering a judgment. In the case concerning *Obligation to Prosecute or Extradite*, the Court found that it lacked jurisdiction to decide on Belgium's claim relating to the obligation under Article 5, paragraph 2, of the Convention against Torture, because, by the time the case was filed in the Court, Senegal had already adopted national laws and legislative measures for the fulfilment of Article 5, paragraph 2. The parties no longer held any dispute on that point.[37] This is in line with the Court's statement in the *Northern Cameroons* case that "it may pronounce judgment only in connection with concrete cases where there exists at the time of the adjudication of an actual controversy involving a conflict of legal interests between the parties."[38]

In another situation, where subsequent events remove the very object of a dispute and consequently the case becomes moot, the Court would likewise decline to exercise its jurisdiction. In the *Nuclear Tests* cases, after the French Government announced its policy not to continue nuclear tests in the relevant area of the Pacific Ocean, the Court stated that, for the purpose of exercising its judicial function,

> the dispute brought before it must therefore continue to exist at the time when the Court makes its decision. It must not fail to take cognizance of a situation in which the dispute has disappeared because the

Interpretation and Application of the 1971 Montreal Convention arising from the Aerial Incident at Lockerbie (Libyan Arab Jamahiriya v. *United States of America), Preliminary Objections, Judgment, I.C.J. Reports 1998*, pp. 130–131, paras. 42–44; *Border and Transborder Armed Actions (Nicaragua* v. *Honduras), Jurisdiction and Admissibility, Judgment, I.C.J. Reports 1988*, p. 95, para. 66.

37 See *Questions relating to the Obligation to Prosecute or Extradite (Belgium* v. *Senegal), Judgment, I.C.J. Reports 2012*, pp. 442–443, paras. 47–48.

38 *Case concerning the Northern Cameroons (Cameroon* v. *United Kingdom), Preliminary Objections, Judgment, I.C.J. Reports 1963*, pp. 33–34; see also *Question of the Delimitation of the Continental Shelf between Nicaragua and Colombia beyond 200 nautical miles from the Nicaraguan Coast (Nicaragua* v. *Colombia), Judgment, Preliminary Objections*, para. 123. See further *Application of the International Convention on the Elimination of All Forms of Racial Discrimination (Georgia* v. *Russian Federation), Preliminary Objections, Judgment, I.C.J. Reports 2011*, Separate Opinion of Judge Abraham, p. 229, para. 16: "It is necessary and sufficient if the dispute exists when the Court is seised (which can be shown by subsequently occurring facts) and subsists on the date on which the Court determines whether the conditions for the exercise of its jurisdiction have been met."

> final objective which the Applicant has maintained throughout has been achieved by other means.[39]

Such subsequent event takes away the necessary condition for the Court to exercise its jurisdiction.[40]

In determining whether there existed a dispute at the date of the filing of an application, the Court examines the facts that took place prior to the date when the application was filed.[41] It may, however, also take into consideration the evidence subsequent to that critical date, but just for the purpose of determining with certainty the situation at the relevant time so as to confirm whether such a dispute existed or not on that critical date.[42] Subsequent events and the pleadings of the parties are not by themselves sufficient to demonstrate that there existed a dispute between the parties at the relevant date.

On this issue, the jurisprudence of the Court has however exhibited certain nuance. In the *Genocide Convention* (*Croatia* v. *Serbia*) case,[43] the Court, referring to its own precedents and to those of the PCIJ, observed that the Court

---

39 *Nuclear Tests (Australia* v. *France), Judgment, I.C.J. Reports 1974*, pp. 270–271, para. 55; *Nuclear Tests (New Zealand* v. *France), Judgment, I.C.J. Reports 1974*, p. 476, para. 58.

40 *Questions of Interpretation and Application of the 1971 Montreal Convention arising from the Aerial Incident at Lockerbie (Libyan Arab Jamahiriya* v. *United Kingdom), Preliminary Objections, Judgment, I.C.J. Reports 1998*, p. 26, para. 46; *Questions of Interpretation and Application of the 1971 Montreal Convention arising from the Aerial Incident at Lockerbie (Libyan Arab Jamahiriya* v. *United States of America), Preliminary Objections, Judgment, I.C.J. Reports 1998*, p. 131, para. 45; see also *Border and Transborder Armed Actions (Nicaragua* v. *Honduras), Jurisdiction and Admissibility, Judgment, I.C.J. Reports 1988*, p. 95, para. 66.

41 See *Application of the International Convention on the Elimination of All Forms of Racial Discrimination (Georgia* v. *Russian Federation), Preliminary Objections, Judgment, I.C.J. Reports 2011*, pp. 85–120, paras. 31-113; *Questions relating to the Obligation to Prosecute or Extradite (Belgium* v. *Senegal), Judgment, I.C.J. Reports 2012*, pp. 443–444, paras. 49–52.

42 See *East Timor (Portugal* v. *Australia), Judgment, I.C.J. Reports 1995*, p. 100, para. 22; *Application of the Convention on the Prevention and Punishment of the Crime of Genocide (Bosnia and Herzegovina* v. *Yugoslavia), Preliminary Objections, Judgment, I.C.J. Reports 1996 (II)*, pp. 614–616, paras. 27–33; *Certain Property (Liechtenstein* v. *Germany), Preliminary Objections, Judgment, I.C.J. Reports 2005*, pp. 18–19, para. 25.

43 See *Application of the Convention on the Prevention and Punishment of the Crime of Genocide (Croatia* v. *Serbia), Preliminary Objections, Judgment, I.C.J. Reports 2008*, pp. 438–440, para. 82. The Court cited previous cases including the *Mavrommatis Palestine Concessions* case, the case concerning *Certain German Interests in Polish Upper Silesia*, the *Northern Cameroons* case, the case concerning *Military and Paramilitary Activities in and against Nicaragua*, and the *Application of Genocide Convention* case between Bosnia and

> has ... shown realism and flexibility in certain situations in which the conditions governing the Court's jurisdiction were not fully satisfied when proceedings were initiated but were subsequently satisfied, before the Court ruled on its jurisdiction.
>
> What matters is that, at the latest by the date when the Court decides on its jurisdiction, the applicant must be entitled, if it so wishes, to bring fresh proceedings in which the initially unmet condition would be fulfilled. In such a situation, it is not in the interests of the sound administration of justice to compel the applicant to begin the proceedings anew—or to initiate fresh proceedings—and it is preferable, except in special circumstances, to conclude that the condition has, from that point on, been fulfilled.[44]

This realist and flexible approach to procedural matters has raised some concerns as to the standard of application of the relevant procedural rules. On the issue of the existence of a dispute, if such flexibility is extended a bit too much, it would render the condition almost meaningless.

d *The Subject-matter of a Dispute*

Substantively, the determination of the existence of a dispute also concerns the identification of the subject-matter of the dispute. In practice, the respondent may argue that despite the fact that there were disputes between the parties, none of them relates to the subject-matter as claimed by the applicant. If the Court upholds that argument, the condition for the existence of a dispute is thus not fulfilled. In the *Obligation to Negotiate Access* (*Bolivia* v. *Chile*) case, the Court stated that:

> It is for the Court itself, however, to determine on an objective basis the subject-matter of the dispute between the parties, that is, to "isolate the real issue in the case and to identify the object of the claim" (*Nuclear Tests* (*Australia* v. *France*), *Judgment, I.C.J. Reports 1974*, p. 262, para. 29; *Nuclear Tests* (*New Zealand* v. *France*), *Judgment, I.C.J. Reports 1974*, p. 66, para. 30).

Herzegovina and Yugoslavia. A similar idea is discernible in all these cases: "The Court ... is not bound to attach to matters of form the same degree of importance which they might possess in municipal law." (*Mavrommatis Palestine Concessions, Judgment No. 2, 1924, P.C.I.J., Series A, No. 2*, p. 34.)

44 *Application of the Convention on the Prevention and Punishment of the Crime of Genocide* (*Croatia* v. *Serbia*), *Preliminary Objections, Judgment, I.C.J. Reports 2008*, pp. 438, 441, paras. 81, 85.

> In doing so, the Court examines the positions of both parties, "while giving particular attention to the formulation of the dispute chosen by the [a]pplicant" (*Fisheries Jurisdiction* (*Spain* v. *Canada*), *Jurisdiction of the Court, Judgment, I.C.J. Reports 1998*, p. 448, para. 30; see also *Territorial and Maritime Dispute* (*Nicaragua* v. *Colombia*), *Preliminary Objections, Judgment, I.C.J. Reports 2007* (*II*), p. 848, para. 38).[45]

Therefore, the identification of the subject-matter of the dispute is part of the process of this objective determination by the Court.

In the case concerning *Application of the International Convention on the Elimination of All Forms of Racial Discrimination* (*Georgia* v. *Russia Federation*), Georgia accused Russia of violating its obligations under the International Convention on the Elimination of All Forms of Racial Discrimination (CERD).[46] Georgia relied on Article 22 of CERD, the compromissory clause, as the jurisdictional basis of its application. Obviously, the dispute between the parties must concern the interpretation or application of CERD, otherwise, the Court would have no jurisdiction in the case.

The Court, in determining the subject-matter of the dispute, reaffirmed that when a claim is based on a convention, as a general rule, the subject-matter of the dispute must relate to the interpretation and application of that convention. On that point, it emphasized that,

> in terms of the subject-matter of the dispute, to return to the terms of Article 22 of CERD, the dispute must be "with respect to the interpretation or application of [the] Convention." While it is not necessary that a State must expressly refer to a specific treaty in its exchanges with the other State to enable it later to invoke that instrument before the Court (*Military and Paramilitary Activities in and against Nicaragua* (*Nicaragua* v. *United States of America*), *Jurisdiction and Admissibility, Judgment, I.C.J. Reports 1984*, pp. 428–429, para. 83), the exchanges must refer to the subject-matter of the treaty with sufficient clarity to enable the State against which a claim is made to identify that there is, or may be, a dispute with regard to that subject-matter.[47]

---

45 *Obligation to Negotiate Access to the Pacific Ocean* (*Bolivia* v. *Chile*), *Preliminary Objection, Judgment*, para. 26.

46 *Application of the International Convention on the Elimination of All Forms of Racial Discrimination* (*Georgia* v. *Russian Federation*), *Preliminary Objections, Judgment, I.C.J. Reports 2011*, p. 70.

47 *Ibid.*, p. 85, para. 30.

The Court went on to point out that, for that purpose, an express specification would remove any doubt about one State's understanding of the subject-matter in issue and put the other on notice.[48]

Subsequently the Court found that the exchanges between the representatives of the parties in the Security Council and the allegations of "ethnic cleaning" by Georgia, which was expressly directed at Russia and positively opposed by Russia, constituted a dispute between Georgia and Russia about the latter's compliance with its obligations under CERD as invoked by Georgia in this case.[49]

With regard to the definition of a dispute, Judge Jennings once commented on the general terms "a disagreement on a point of law or fact" or "positive opposition" taken from the *Mavrommatis* judgment. In his view, these phrases may be too simplistic for defining a dispute within the meaning of Articles 36 and 38 of the Statute. They do not mean that every disagreement on a point of law or fact is qualified to meet the criterion, but only refer to those that are suitable for judicial settlement. He explained that,

> the *kind* of legal dispute that the Court can deal with, is much affected by the practices and processes of written and oral pleadings...which [are] designed to reduce the whole case to a series of quite specific issues of fact or law, or both, for the Court to determine. The processing of the case, this reduction, or refinement, is practically a concomitant of an adversarial process. *A "legal dispute" in a technical and realistic sense is accordingly, one which has been thus processed, or reduced, into a form suitable for decision by a court of law; i.e. a series of specific issues for decision.*[50]

He then gave the example of the *Tehran Hostages* case. In that case, Iran did not appear before the Court, because it claimed that the hostage issue could not be studied separately as it only represented a marginal and secondary aspect of an overall problem of the United States' 25 years of interference in Iranian internal affairs, exploitation of its resources and crimes committed against Iranian people in violation of international and humanitarian norms.[51] In Judge Jennings'

48 *Ibid.*

49 *Ibid.*, p. 120, para. 113.

50 Sir Robert Jennings, "Reflections on the Term 'Dispute,'" in Ronald St. John MacDonald (ed.), *Essays in Honour of Wang Tieya*, Martinus Nijhoff Publishers, 1994, p. 403 (emphasis added).

51 *United States Diplomatic and Consular Staff in Tehran* (*United States of America* v. *Iran*), *Judgment, I.C.J. Reports 1980*, p. 19, para.35.

view, the reason why the Court rejected Iran's arguments was not because there was no dispute between the parties: Iran's claim clearly indicated a situation of dispute with the United States and Iran explicitly referred to international law and international humanitarian law. Nor did the Court reject Iran's position because the "overall problem" it referred to covered a span of 25 years of relations between the two governments. Many territorial disputes lasted much longer than that.[52] The reason for the Court's rejection was that Iran's allegations had not been reduced to a series of specific issues such that a court could deal with them. Namely, they had not been reduced to "a disagreement *on a point* of law or fact." Such points of law or fact often exist in an overall complex political and factual situation. That overall situation does not prevent the Court from dealing with the points of law or fact properly presented before the Court.[53]

Judge Jennings actually touches on a deeper aspect of the matter, an aspect that underlines the very nature of the judicial system of international justice and the way in which certain judicial techniques of the Court evolved and developed.

2 Negotiation and Other Preconditions for the Seisin of the Court

States, when they accept the jurisdiction of the Court for the settlement of their disputes, tend to use the recourse to judicial settlement as the ultimate solution in case their own efforts to resolve a dispute fail to bring any fruition. They may lay down certain conditions such as negotiation, arbitration or other means prior to the seisin of the Court. Such conditions may be expressly provided for in the final clause of a bilateral or multilateral treaty, or even laid down in a special agreement, so as to reserve the right of the parties to resort to the Court only after the lapse of a certain time. Oftentimes, however, even without such express provisions, States may still insist on such prior negotiations as a practice of customary law. In order to establish its jurisdiction, the Court has to decide whether such preconditions are required by law, and if so, whether they are met.

a *Prior Negotiation as a Condition*

As is discussed before, States have the freedom to choose any kind of peaceful means as enumerated in Article 33 of the Charter of the United Nations to settle

52 For example, the currently pending case between Bolivia and Chile concerns their boundary treaty and a matter that may trace back to the late 19th century.

53 Sir Robert Jennings, *op. cit. supra* footnote 50, pp. 403–404.

their disputes. From daily issues to most complicated matters, negotiation is, of course, the unfailing method that States most frequently use to resolve international disputes. It is not unusual that, when a State is brought to the Court facing a legal suit for a dispute with another country, it would plead that the matter should be submitted to bilateral negotiations for settlement.

In its jurisprudence, the Court spelled out three aspects about the importance of negotiation as a pre-step for judicial settlement. First, negotiation gives notice to the respondent State that a dispute exists and delimits the scope of the dispute and its subject-matter. Secondly, it encourages the parties to attempt to settle their dispute by mutual agreement, thus avoiding recourse to binding third-party adjudication. Thirdly, negotiation as well as other methods of peaceful dispute settlement help indicate the limit of consent given by States to the judicial settlement. In this aspect, the Court stated in the *Armed Activities* case that:

> [The Court's] jurisdiction is based on the consent of the parties and is confined to the extent accepted by them... When that consent is expressed in a compromissory clause in an international agreement, *any conditions to which such consent is subject must be regarded as constituting the limits thereon.*[54]

The precondition of negotiation or the condition of negotiation attached subsequently to the acceptance of the Court's jurisdiction is always given effect by the Court by virtue of the principle of consent. The Court does not impose any criterion on States as to how and when negotiations should be conducted so long as that is their free choice. As the Court stated in the case concerning *Land and Maritime Boundary between Cameroon and Nigeria*:

> A precondition of this type may be embodied and is often included in compromissory clauses of treaties. It may also be included in a special agreement whose signatories then reserve the right to seise the Court only after a certain lapse of time (*cf. Territorial Dispute* (*Libyan Arab Jamahiriya/Chad*), *Judgment, I.C.J. Reports 1994*, p. 9). Finally, States remain free to insert into their optional declaration accepting the compulsory jurisdiction of the Court a reservation excluding from the latter those

54 *Armed Activities on the Territory of the Congo* (*New Application: 2002*) (*Democratic Republic of the Congo* v. *Rwanda*), *Jurisdiction and Admissibility, Judgment, I.C.J. Reports 2006*, p. 39, para. 88 (emphasis added).

> disputes for which the parties involved have agreed or subsequently agree to resort to an alternative method of peaceful settlement.[55]

Notwithstanding that free choice, once the Court is duly seised by the parties, whether the precondition of negotiation is satisfied will be subject to the determination of the Court.

In practice, in order to object to the jurisdiction of the Court in the case, the respondent may argue that, as negotiations were making headway for the settlement of the dispute, the judicial process should give way to the negotiations. That consideration, of course, is important for the parties before either of them resorts to the Court. However, once the Court is duly seized, that consideration does not constitute a legal reason to object the Court's jurisdiction.

In the *Aegean Sea Continental Shelf* (*Greece* v. *Turkey*) case,[56] Turkey objected to the jurisdiction of the Court and did not appear before it. While the case was pending before the Court, Greece and Turkey resumed their negotiations in accordance with the Security Council resolution and made substantial progress in their negotiation. During the negotiations, Greece proposed to postpone the legal proceedings in the Court, but Turkey insisted that, with a view to creating a favourable political climate for an agreed settlement, the whole proceedings should be discontinued and the case be removed from the list of the Court.[57] In its view, the existence of active negotiations in progress constituted an impediment to the Court's exercise of jurisdiction in the present case.

The Court, nevertheless, did not accept Turkey's claim. It maintained that:

> Negotiation and judicial settlement are enumerated together in Article 33 of the Charter of the United Nations as means for the peaceful settlement of disputes. The jurisprudence of the Court provides various examples of cases in which negotiations and recourse to judicial settlement have been pursued *pari passu*. Several cases, the most recent being that concerning the *Trial of Pakistani Prisoners of War* (*I.C.J. Reports 1973*, p. 347), show that judicial proceedings may be discontinued when such negotiations result in the settlement of the dispute. Consequently, the fact that negotiations are being actively pursued during the present proceedings

55 *Land and Maritime Boundary between Cameroon and Nigeria* (*Cameroon* v. *Nigeria*), *Preliminary Objections, Judgment, I.C.J. Reports 1998*, pp. 303, para. 56.

56 *Aegean Sea Continental Shelf* (*Greece* v. *Turkey*), *Judgment, I.C.J. Reports 1978*, pp. 11–13, paras. 27–31.

57 *Ibid.*, p. 12, para. 28.

> is not, legally, any obstacle to the exercise by the Court of its judicial function.[58]

Although ultimately the Court found that it was without jurisdiction to entertain Greece's application, its decision was based on an entirely different ground. According to the Court, once it is properly seised, negotiations on parallel between the parties should not deprive the jurisdiction of the Court. The Court has no reason to give priority to negotiations under such circumstances.

The Court expressed the same position in subsequent cases.[59] In the case concerning *Military and Paramilitary Activities in and against Nicaragua*, the United States contended that regional dispute resolution processes should first be exhausted. The Court did not accept that there was any requirement of prior exhaustion of regional negotiating processes as a precondition to seising the Court.[60]

The threshold for triggering judicial settlement is usually low, if the jurisdictional ground is based on the Optional Clause. Although States are required under international law to conduct negotiations in good faith for the settlement of international disputes, the Court does not impose such a condition for the resort to judicial settlement, unless otherwise provided for.

b *Precondition Attached to Declarations Accepting Compulsory Jurisdiction of the Court*

A precondition of negotiation can be attached, and often is, to the recourse to judicial settlement. Efforts of negotiations may be made under various circumstances. But at which point of time and the extent of such efforts required for the precondition of negotiation to be deemed satisfied often give rise to contention between States. When one of the parties initiates the legal action in the Court, the other party oftentimes contends that negotiations were not yet exhausted.

In the *Land and Maritime Boundary* (*Cameroon* v. *Nigeria*) case, Nigeria claimed that, for over 24 years prior to the filing of the case, the parties had accepted in their regular dealings a duty to settle all their boundary questions through the existing bilateral machinery. In its view, there was an implicit agreement between them to resort exclusively to such machinery and refrain

58 *Ibid.*, p. 12, para. 29.

59 See, for example, *United States Diplomatic and Consular Staff in Tehran* (*United States of America* v. *Iran*), *Judgment, I.C.J. Reports 1980*, p. 23, para. 43.

60 *Military and Paramilitary Activities in and against Nicaragua* (*Nicaragua* v. *United States of America*), *Jurisdiction and Admissibility, Judgment, I.C.J. Reports 1984*, p. 440, para. 108.

from relying on the ICJ.[61] Cameroon, for its part, contended that there was no such bilateral machinery between the parties and no explicit or implicit agreement had been reached between them with a view to vesting exclusive jurisdiction in such mechanism.[62]

Having examined the evidence submitted by the parties, the Court found that the fact that the two States had attempted to solve the boundary issues through bilateral contacts for a long period of time did not imply that either one had excluded the possibility of bringing the boundary dispute before other fora, particularly the ICJ.[63] Both Cameroon and Nigeria had made declarations under Article 36, paragraph 2, of the Statute, but neither of them had included any reservation, initially or subsequently, to their declaration, which would have precluded boundary matters from the jurisdiction of the Court. Consequently, the Court had jurisdiction in the case.

States may, by agreement, exclude certain disputes from the jurisdiction of the Court, even after they have accepted the compulsory jurisdiction of the Court. That kind of agreement, however, is not a precondition, but a different choice of means of settlement for a particular purpose. States, of course, could set up a precondition of negotiation for the resolution of disputes before resorting to judicial settlement, but they have to do so either by amending their declarations, or by a separate agreement between the relevant States. In the former case, the amendment applies to all those States that have made the same declaration, while in the latter case, the condition only applies to the State with whom such an agreement is concluded.

By the Pact of Bogotá, some American States agreed to accept the compulsory jurisdiction of the Court between the parties to the Pact. Article II of the Pact reads:

> The High Contracting Parties recognize the obligation to settle international controversies by regional pacific procedures before referring them to the Security Council of the United Nations.
>
> Consequently, in the event that a controversy arises between two or more signatory States which, in the opinion of the parties, cannot be settled by direct negotiations through the usual diplomatic channels, the parties bind themselves to use the procedures established in the present Treaty, in the manner and under the conditions provided for in the

61 *Land and Maritime Boundary between Cameroon and Nigeria (Cameroon* v. *Nigeria), Preliminary Objections, Judgment, I.C.J. Reports 1998*, pp. 300–301, para. 48.

62 *Ibid.*, p. 301, para. 49.

63 *Ibid.*, pp. 302–303, para. 56.

> following articles, or, alternatively, such special procedures as, in their opinion, will permit them to arrive at a solution.

This clause includes a term that has been subjected to the Court's interpretation in more than one case: namely, "in the opinion of the parties," the dispute "cannot be settled by direct negotiations through the usual diplomatic channels."

In the *Border and Transborder Armed Actions* case, the parties contested heavily on the linguistic discrepancy between the different texts of the treaty in its four official languages.[64] The French text refers to the opinion of one of the parties ("de l'avis de l'une des parties"), while the other three (English, Portuguese and Spanish) refer to the opinion of both parties. Since Article II contains a precondition of negotiation for the recourse to the Court, the interpretation of this term would have a direct bearing on the legal action instituted by Nicaragua.

The Court first drew a distinction between the preconditions under the Pact and those in the compromissory clauses. In its opinion, under the Pact, what the Court should determine was the opinion of the parties on the possibility of settling their dispute by diplomatic negotiations, but not the objective possibility of such a settlement, which was the term of compromissory clauses. With regard to the linguistic discrepancy, the Court did not consider it necessary to provide a clarification to that term, because, in its view, the Court in any event was not bound by the views of one party or the other. It held that, to discharge its judicial function, it must be free to make its own determination of the issue in question. Based on the examination of the substantive evidence available to it, it would decide whether the parties considered "in good faith" that a dispute could or could not be settled by direct negotiations.[65]

The same issue arose in the *Alleged Violations of Sovereign Rights and Maritime Spaces* (*Nicaragua* v. *Colombia*) case. The Court applied the same standard in determining the opinion of the parties. It examined the positions and conduct of the parties in relation to the claims raised by Nicaragua. In its conclusion, the Court found that:

> No evidence submitted to the Court indicates that, on the date of Nicaragua's filing of the Application, the Parties had contemplated, or were in a position to hold negotiations to settle the dispute concerning the

64 *Border and Transborder Armed Actions* (*Nicaragua* v. *Honduras*), *Jurisdiction and Admissibility, Judgment, I.C.J. Reports 1988*, pp. 92–95, paras. 58–65.

65 *Ibid.*, p. 95, para. 65.

> alleged violations by Colombia of Nicaragua's rights in the maritime zones which, according to Nicaragua, the Court declared in its 2012 Judgment appertain to Nicaragua.[66]

The relevant date for the Court to determine "the opinion of the parties" is the date on which the application is filed, the same date as that for the determination of the existence of a dispute.

c *Precondition in a Compromissory Clause*

There are a large number of treaties which contain a compromissory clause conferring jurisdiction on the Court for the settlement of disputes concerning the interpretation and application of the treaty between the contracting State parties. Many of the clauses include preconditions to the jurisdiction of the Court. These terms vary, but their meaning is more or less the same.

Generally speaking, there are three types of preconditions contained in a compromissory clause: first, negotiation or attempt to settlement by the procedures provided for in the treaty; second, negotiation first, then arbitration with a time limit for settlement; third, attempt to settlement through diplomacy.

The first type can be found in the Convention against Racial Discrimination, CERD. Article 22 of CERD states that any dispute, which is not settled by negotiation or by the procedures expressly provided for in this Convention, shall, at the request of any of the parties to the dispute, be referred to the ICJ for decision, unless the disputants agree to another mode of settlement.[67]

The compromissory clause of the Convention against Torture gives an example of the second type.[68] Article 30 of the Convention provides that if the

---

66 *Alleged Violations of Sovereign Rights and Maritime Spaces in the Caribbean Sea (Nicaragua* v. *Colombia), Preliminary Objections, Judgment*, para. 100.

67 Article 22 of the CERD reads: "Any dispute between two or more States parties with respect to the interpretation or application of this Convention, which is not settled by negotiation or by the procedures expressly provided for in this Convention, shall, at the request of any of the parties to the dispute, be referred to the International Court of Justice for decision, unless the disputants agree to another mode of settlement."

68 Article 30, paragraph 1, of Convention against Torture reads: "Any dispute between two or more States Parties concerning the interpretation or application of this Convention which cannot be settled through negotiation shall, at the request of one of them, be submitted to arbitration. If within six months from the date of the request for arbitration the Parties are unable to agree on the organization of the arbitration, any one of those Parties may refer the dispute to the International Court of Justice by request in conformity with the Statute of the Court."

dispute cannot be settled through negotiation, it shall, at the request of one of the parties to the dispute, be submitted to arbitration. If within six months from the date of the request for arbitration the parties are unable to agree on the organization of the arbitration, the case may be referred to the ICJ.

The last kind of terms is found in the bilateral treaties concluded by the United States with Iran and Nicaragua respectively. For example, Article XXI, paragraph 2, of the Treaty of Amity, Economic Relations, and Consular Rights of 1955 between the United States and Iran states that any dispute not satisfactorily adjusted by diplomacy shall be submitted to the ICJ, unless the parties agree to settlement by some other pacific means.[69]

In practice, counsels for the parties often try to inject special meanings into such different terms as "*is not settled,*" "*cannot be settled,*" and "*not satisfactorily adjusted by diplomacy.*"[70] In evaluating the conduct of the parties, the Court however does not draw much distinction between these terms. Notwithstanding the nuanced emphasis that the Court placed on the importance of preconditions in some cases, these terms generally refer to the situation, where, in the Court's words, "one of the Parties definitely declares himself unable, or refuses, to give way,"[71] "an impasse was reached," or "no reasonable probability

69 Article XXI, paragraph 2, of the Treaty of Amity, Economic Relations, and Consular Rights of 1955 between the United States and Iran reads: "Any dispute between the High Contracting Parties as to the interpretation or application of the present Treaty, not satisfactorily adjusted by diplomacy, shall be submitted to the International Court of Justice, unless the High Contracting Parties agree to settlement by some other pacific means."

70 For the discussions on the term "is not settled," see the following cases: *Mavrommatis Palestine Concessions; South West Africa cases* (*Ethiopia* v. *South Africa; Liberia* v. *South Africa*); *Questions of Interpretation and Application of the 1971 Montreal Convention arising from the Aerial Incident at Lockerbie* (*Libyan Arab Jamahiriya* v. *United States of America*); *Armed Activities on the Territory of the Congo* (*New Application: 2002*) (*Democratic Republic of the Congo* v. *Rwanda*); *Questions relating to the Obligation to Prosecute or Extradite* (*Belgium* v. *Senegal*).

For the discussions on the term "cannot be settled," see the following cases: *Applicability of the Obligation to Arbitrate under Section 21 of the United Nations Headquarters Agreement of 26 June 1947; Armed Activities on the Territory of the Congo* (*New Application: 2002*) (*Democratic Republic of the Congo* v. *Rwanda*).

For the last category, see the following cases: *United States Diplomatic and Consular Staff in Tehran* (*United States of America* v. *Iran*); *Military and Paramilitary Activities in and against Nicaragua* (*Nicaragua* v. *United States of America*); *Oil Platforms* (*Islamic Republic of Iran* v. *United States of America*).

71 *Mavrommatis Palestine Concessions, Judgment No. 2, 1924, P.C.I.J., Series A, No. 2*, p. 13.

exists that further negotiations would have led to a settlement."[72] In the 18 cases so far in which the Court discussed the question of preconditions in a compromissory clause, the Court has always looked at the evidence to see whether, as a matter of fact, the diplomatic efforts were exhausted, either because either party refused to enter into any further discussion, the parties never intended to conduct genuine negotiations, or the negotiations indeed reached a deadlock.

It seems that in its early days the Court attached more importance to the attitude of the parties regarding the possibility of negotiations. In the *Mavrommatis Palestine Concessions* case, it observed that "the Court cannot disregard, amongst other considerations, the views of the States concerned, who are in the best position to judge as to political reasons which may prevent the settlement of a given dispute by diplomatic negotiation."[73] In the more recent cases, the Court gave more consideration to the actual relations between the parties and the possibility to continue the negotiation process.[74]

In determining whether the precondition of negotiation is satisfied, the Court normally takes several elements into consideration.

First, for the fulfilment of the precondition, a genuine attempt to solve the dispute is necessary. As the Court stated in the *Georgia* v. *Russian Federation* case, "[m]anifestly, in the absence of evidence of a genuine attempt to negotiate, the precondition of negotiation is not met."[75] The parties carry the burden of proof to show to the Court whether such efforts have been exercised in good faith.

Secondly, the subject-matter of the negotiation must relate to the subject-matter of the dispute. This link between the negotiation and the dispute has long been highlighted in the Court's jurisprudence. In the *Mavrommatis Palestine Concessions* case, the Court pointed out that "before a dispute can be made the subject of an action at law, its subject-matter should have been

72 *South West Africa cases (Ethiopia* v. *South Africa; Liberia* v. *South Africa), Preliminary Objections, Judgment of 21 December 1962, I.C.J. Report: 1962*, p. 345.

73 *Mavrommatis Palestine Concessions, Judgment No. 2, 1924, P.C.I.J., Series A, No. 2*, p. 15.

74 See, for example, *Applicability of the Obligation to Arbitrate under Section 21 of the United Nations Headquarters Agreement of 26 June 1947, Advisory Opinion, I.C.J. Reports 1988*, p. 33, paras. 53–55; *Application of the International Convention on the Elimination of All Forms of Racial Discrimination (Georgia* v. *Russian Federation), Preliminary Objections, Judgment, I.C.J. Reports 2011*, pp. 134–140, paras. 163–184.

75 *Application of the International Convention on the Elimination of All Forms of Racial Discrimination (Georgia* v. *Russian Federation), Preliminary Objections, Judgment, I.C.J. Reports 2011*, p. 133, para. 159.

clearly defined by means of diplomatic negotiations."[76] In more recent Court's practice, however, this requirement is often subject to treaty interpretation.

In invoking a compromissory clause of a treaty as the jurisdictional basis of the Court, the absence of express reference to that treaty in the dispute between the parties does not constitute a bar for the applicant to institute proceedings.[77] However, there must be a link between the subject-matter of the dispute and the subject-matter of the treaty. Negotiations often provide a means to examine that connection. In the above-mentioned case between Georgia and Russia, the Court elaborated on this point:

> to meet the precondition of negotiation in the compromissory clause of a treaty, these negotiations must relate to the subject-matter of the treaty containing the compromissory clause. In other words, the subject-matter of the negotiations must relate to the subject-matter of the dispute which, in turn, must concern the substantive obligations contained in the treaty in question.[78]

Thirdly, negotiations must have clearly failed or reached a deadlock. The Court noted that genuinely attempted negotiations need not be successful. Referring to its earlier jurisprudence, the Court stated that,

> Clearly, evidence of such an attempt to negotiate—or of the conduct of negotiations—does not require the reaching of an actual agreement between the disputing parties. In this regard, in its *Advisory Opinion on Railway Traffic between Lithuania and Poland*, the Permanent Court of International Justice characterized the obligation to negotiate as an obligation "not only to enter into negotiations, but also to pursue them as far as

76 *Mavrommatis Palestine Concessions, Judgment No. 2, 1924, P.C.I.J., Series A, No. 2*, p. 15.

77 *Application of the International Convention on the Elimination of All Forms of Racial Discrimination (Georgia* v. *Russian Federation), Preliminary Objections, Judgment, I.C.J. Reports 2011*, p. 133, para. 161. See also *Military and Paramilitary Activities in and against Nicaragua (Nicaragua* v. *United States of America), Jurisdiction and Admissibility, Judgment, I.C.J. Reports 1984*, p. 428, para. 83, where the Court stated that "it does not necessarily follow that, because a State has not expressly referred in negotiations with another State to a particular treaty as having been violated by conduct of that other State, it is debarred from invoking a compromissory clause in that treaty."

78 *Application of the International Convention on the Elimination of All Forms of Racial Discrimination (Georgia* v. *Russian Federation), Preliminary Objections, Judgment, I.C.J. Reports 2011*, p. 133, para. 161.

> possible, with a view to concluding agreements [even if] an obligation to negotiate does not imply an obligation to reach agreement..."[79]

Regarding the argument that to meet the requirement of negotiation, the parties to a dispute must formally hold talks and conduct negotiations for some time with a view to resolving the dispute, the Court's jurisprudence does not support such a formalistic approach. As a practical matter, the Court examines whether there existed a relative prospect of settling the dispute, but not necessarily a final solution.[80]

Negotiations could be carried out through various means, including by exchange of diplomatic Notes, multilateral conferences, parliamentary diplomacy, official correspondences, etc. Failure in the negotiation has to be objectively determined on the basis of evidence. In the cases where the parties were highly hostile to each other, the attitude of the parties and the nature of the dispute can lead the Court to the conclusion that negotiations would be futile.[81]

The preconditions is a very important point of departure for the consideration of the question of jurisdiction. Strictly speaking, these preconditions are more substantive matters than procedural requirements; they indicate the extent to which States have given their consent to the jurisdiction of the Court.

---

79 *Application of the International Convention on the Elimination of All Forms of Racial Discrimination* (*Georgia* v. *Russian Federation*), *Preliminary Objections, Judgment, I.C.J. Reports 2011*, pp. 132–133, para. 158.

80 *Mavrommatis Palestine Concessions, Judgment No. 2, 1924, P.C.I.J., Series A, No. 2*, p. 13.

81 For instance, the *Tehran Hostages* case, the *Lockerbie* cases, and the *Military and Paramilitary Activities* case.

CHAPTER VI

Competent Parties—Jurisdiction *ratione personae*

The most frequently asked question from the general public about the ICJ is who can bring a case to the Court. Indeed, every year the Registry of the Court receives a huge number of letters from individuals for grievances against their governments. They appeal to the Court with the anticipation that the ICJ, as the "supreme court of the world," would exercise its judicial power over their governments. This innocent mistake largely derives from the name we usually give to the ICJ, "the World Court." Under the Charter and the Statute, these individual complaints will not, of course, enter the General List of cases of the Court, for the simple reason that individuals do not have legal standing before the Court. As is mentioned previously, only States are qualified to file contentious cases in the Court.

The Court has the competence to exercise jurisdiction in two kinds of cases: contentious cases and requests for advisory opinions. In both types of cases, there are strict rules on the competence of the parties to a dispute to file a case in the Court and the organs that may request the Court to render an advisory opinion.

1 States—Access to the Court and Jurisdiction *ratione personae*

In contentious cases, the first matter that the Court shall deal with is to examine the competence of the party which institutes the legal action and the party against whom the application is filed. According to Article 34 of the Statute, only States may be parties in cases before the Court. They can bring cases only against other States. International organizations, private entities and individuals can neither institute contentious cases in the Court, nor can they be sued therein, even if the subject-matter of their disputes concerns matters of international law. This is very different from international criminal courts and tribunals, which prosecute and punish individual criminal offences.

Competence to start a legal action in the Court is often characterized as "access," although Article 34 does not specifically use that term. Under Article 35, the parties that have access to the Court usually fall into three categories: member States of the United Nations, parties to the Statute of the Court, and

 | DOI 10.1163/9789004342767_007

States which are specifically permitted to have access to the Court under Article 35, paragraph 2, of the Statute.[1]

The Statute of the Court, following the example of its predecessor, the PCIJ, grants States exclusive access to the Court for contentious proceedings, which largely reflects the attributes of the State-system based on sovereignty. Article 34, paragraph 1, in absolute terms, explicitly excludes entities other than States from the jurisdiction of the Court for dispute settlement. Given the contemporary development of international law, it is not surprising that this clause has received many criticisms for its exclusiveness. Some scholars comment that Article 34, paragraph 1, is more about what it precludes than what it actually states.[2]

Statehood is the essential prerequisite for an entity to have access to the Court. In other words, only States are qualified to appear before the Court, either as the principal parties, applicant or respondent, in a contentious case, or to intervene as a third party, or for any other purpose. That condition precedes the question of consent for the consideration of jurisdiction. Access concerns the qualifications of an entity to seise the Court; it is therefore based on an objective criterion of statehood, whereas consent stems from a subjective expression of a party, the determination of which depends on the interpretation of the acts of the party.

The term "access to the Court" is developed from the jurisprudence of the Court on Article 35, paragraph 1, of the Statute, which reads as follows: "[t]he Court shall be open to the States parties to the present Statute." This clause is a historical heritage of the Permanent Court, as well as a guarantee of the continuity of the PCIJ and ICJ. The question whether access to the Court should be expanded does not fall within the purview of this special course.

a *Members of the United Nations*

The first category of eligible parties before the Court in a contentious case is the member States of the United Nations.

---

1 Article 35 of the Statute reads:

1 The Court shall be open to the states parties to the present Statute.

2 The conditions under which the Court shall be open to other states shall, subject to the special provisions contained in treaties in force, be laid down by the Security Council, but in no case shall such conditions place the parties in a position of inequality before the Court.

3 When a state which is not a Member of the United Nations is a party to a case, the Court shall fix the amount which that party is to contribute towards the expenses of the Court. This provision shall not apply if such state is bearing a share of the expenses of the Court.

2 Pierre-Marie Dupuy, "Article 34," in Andreas Zimmermann, Karin Oellers-Frahm, Christian Tomuschat, and Christian J. Tams (eds.), *The Statute of the International Court of Justice: A Commentary*, Oxford University Press, 2006, p. 586.

Access to the Permanent Court was not linked with the membership of the League of Nations. Its Statute was not part of the Covenant. A State that signed the Protocol of 16 December 1920, thus becoming a party to the Statute of the PCIJ did not necessarily have to be a State party to the League Covenant and a member of the League of Nations. In order to have access to the Permanent Court, a member State of the League also had to become a party to the Statute of the Court. Its membership of the League was not related to its status to the Statute of the PCIJ.

In the case of the ICJ, its Statute constitutes an integral part of the UN Charter. The Court is the principal judicial organ and one of the six major organs of the United Nations. This is the major distinction between the ICJ and the PCIJ. According to Article 93, paragraph 1, of the Charter, "[a]ll members of the United Nations are *ipso facto* parties to the Statute of the International Court of Justice." When a State ratifies or accedes to the Charter, it automatically becomes a party to the Statute of the Court. This closer institutional link between the United Nations and the Court is designed to strengthen the role of the Court in the peaceful settlement of international disputes. Formally speaking, member States, when they are committed to the Purposes and Principles of the United Nations, undertake to settle disputes through peaceful means. To pursue that lofty goal, access to the Court should automatically be made available to all the members.

According to the Charter, UN member States are distinguished as original members under Article 3 of the Charter or new members under Article 4. The original members refer to those that participated in the San Francisco Conference or signed the 1942 Declaration by United Nations. Due to historical reasons, some of the original members did not have full sovereign status under international law when they obtained full membership of the United Nations, e.g. the Philippines (the Commonwealth of the Philippines at that time) and India before their independence,[3] as well as the Byelorussian Soviet Socialist Republic (BSSR) and the Ukrainian Soviet Socialist Republic (UkSSR).[4] Their statehood during the critical period may be questionable under international law, but for the purposes of the Charter and the Statute, they were treated without any distinction from other member States. In other words, if any of such States instituted proceedings in the Court, the respondent State as well as the Court could not reject its access to the Court on the ground of its non-sovereign

3 The Philippines obtained its independence in 1946, while India did so in 1947.

4 In order to maintain a numerical balance in the United Nations, the Soviet Union insisted on these federal entities being admitted as members of the Organization, although internally they were subject to the supreme organs of the USSR. See Robert Kolb, *The International Court of Justice*, Hart Publishing, 2013, pp. 281–282.

status. Otherwise, any judgment on their status deviated from their membership in the United Nations could imply a legal challenge to the provisions of the Charter or the decisions of the General Assembly and the Security Council. The Charter and the Statute were not designed to provide for such judicial review by the Court of the decisions of the political organs of the Organization.

In the practice of the United Nations,[5] the original members that did not possess full sovereign status such as the BSSR and the UkSSR, never instituted proceedings in the Court. For those non-independent States that were also members of the United Nations, such as the Philippines and India, there were no cases, either. For matters relating to colonies, it was always the metropolitan State which appeared before the Court, representing the interests of the trust territory or protected State. For instance, in the *Case concerning rights of nationals of the United States of America in Morocco*, in December 1948, the Shereefian Government of Morocco adopted measures to licence imports of certain products for the purpose of protection of its economy. The Government of the United States complained that such measures affected its rights under the treaties it had with Morocco. It contended that no Moroccan law or regulation could be applied to American nationals in Morocco without its previous consent. France filed an application in the Court against the United States. It made it clear that it was proceeding the case both on its own account and as the Protecting Power of Morocco and the judgment of the Court would be binding upon France and Morocco.[6]

In case where the exercise of the rights and privileges of membership of a State is suspended in accordance with Article 5 of the Charter, should its access to the Court be automatically blocked as well? As is observed, that would in fact put that State in an even less favourable position than a non-member State, thus going against the basic policy of wider access to the Court. Moreover, such State, even when suspended of its rights and privileges, is not discharged from its international obligations, which implies that suspension does not automatically have the effect of relieving its previous acceptance of the jurisdiction of the Court. Supposedly, if another State files a case against this State, it seems arguable that it may object to the jurisdiction of the Court on

5 In the years of the Permanent Court, the question of access to the Court involved some entities that did not enjoy full sovereignty under international law at that time, for instance, the Dominions of the British Empire. They could be parties to the Peace Treaties of 1919, members of the League of Nations, or signatories to the Statute. In practice, no case was ever brought by or against such a State.

6 *Case concerning rights of nationals of the United States of America in Morocco* (*France* v. *United States of America*), *Judgment of August 27th, 1952: I.C.J. Reports 1952*, p. 178.

the ground of the suspension. In a reverse position, however, whether such State can institute proceedings in the Court against another State remains an uncertain issue. Under the principle of reciprocity, access to the Court should not be affected by such suspension in any way.[7] So far this is a purely theoretical question, as the political organs of the United Nations—the General Assembly and the Security Council—have never exercised their power to suspend the membership of a State.

When a State becomes a member of the United Nations, by virtue of Article 93, paragraph 1, of the Charter, it is automatically a party to the Statute. This means that that State possesses the *capacity*, or *competence* to be a party in a contentious case before the Court. Such capacity, however, does not mean that it would, in and by itself, provide the ground for jurisdiction. For the purpose of jurisdiction, it requires the second condition, namely, the consent of the State to specifically confer jurisdiction on the Court, either for all cases or for certain groups or types of cases by accepting the compulsory jurisdiction of the Court under Article 36, paragraph 2, of the Statute, or just for one particular case or type of cases by virtue of a special agreement or a compromissory clause. These two conditions form the basis for personal jurisdiction. In reality, many member States of the United Nations, although party to the Statute, have not yet accepted the jurisdiction of the Court.

A member State, in becoming a party to the Statute, shall undertake other obligations under the Charter in relation to the jurisdiction of the Court. According to Article 94, it shall comply with the decision of the Court in any case to which it is a party. If any party to a case fails to implement the judgment of the Court, the other party may bring the matter to the Security Council for measures of enforcement.

The term "State" in Article 34 is invariably interpreted as referring to an independent sovereign State. What constitutes such a State is governed by general international law. As is pointed out by Rosenne, "[i]t is in this aspect of the law relating to litigation in the International Court that the classic concepts of public international law have exerted their greatest influence."[8]

b *Non-members of the United Nations*

Apart from member States of the United Nations, the Court is also open to other States. Such States can be further divided into two categories. One is non-member States of the United Nations that are party to the Statute. The other

7 The issue is more complicated than it seems. See Robert Kolb, *op. cit. supra* footnote 4, pp. 282–283.

8 Shabtai Rosenne, *The Law and Practice of the International Court, 1920–2005, Vol. II, Jurisdiction,* 4th edition, Martinus Nijhoff Publishers, 2006, p. 591.

is States which are neither UN members nor parties to the Statute, but wish to have access to the Court. Under Article 35, paragraph 2, of the Statute, such States may be given access to the Court under certain conditions. These two categories will be discussed in turn.

1 A Party to the Statute

With regard to non-member States of the United Nations, Article 93, paragraph 2, of the Charter provides that:

> A State which is not a Member of the United Nations may become a party to the Statute of the International Court of Justice on conditions to be determined in each case by the General Assembly upon the recommendation of the Security Council.

The intention of the clause is to offer judicial means of settlement to a broader international community of States. Policy-wise, this is to facilitate the widest possible recourse to pacific settlement of international disputes by judicial means.

In the history of the United Nations, there have been five States that were granted such status by the General Assembly upon the recommendation of the Security Council on a case-by-case basis: Switzerland, Liechtenstein, Japan, San Marino and Nauru. Switzerland was the first State that went through the process.

The matter of non-member States' access to the Court was raised at the outset of the United Nations. The Security Council referred it to the Committee of Experts for studies. The Committee recognized its analogy with the problem which had confronted the Council of the League of Nations in 1922. On 17 May 1922 the League Council adopted a resolution under Article 35, paragraph 2, of the Statute of the PCIJ, which laid down the conditions for the non-member and non-party States to accept the jurisdiction of the Permanent Court by a declaration.[9] Largely on the basis of that precedent, the Committee of Experts submitted its report. The Security Council adopted the recommendations of the Committee in resolution 11 of 15 October 1946. It provided the conditions for Switzerland to become a party to the Statute as a non-member State of the United Nations. These conditions were further adopted by the General Assembly in its resolution 91 (I) of 11 December 1946 for Switzerland.

The first condition for a non-member State to become a party to the Statute of the Court is that the State in question must deposit with the Secretary-General

9 PCIJ, Statute and Rules of Court, Series D, No.1, fourth edition—April 1940, p. 44.

of the United Nations the instrument of adherence, accepting all the provisions of the Statute. This comprises all the rights and obligations of a party to the Statute, including the provisions on jurisdiction.

Secondly, a non-member State must accept the conditions as laid down in Article 94 of the Charter. That is to say, it shall comply with the judgment of the Court in any case to which it is a party. The decision of the Court is final and binding on it. In case it fails to perform the obligations incumbent upon it under a judgment rendered by the Court, the other party may have recourse to the Security Council. If it deems necessary, the Security Council may make recommendations or decide upon measures to be taken to give effect to the judgment. Conversely, the non-member State equally has the right to have such recourse against the other party in similar situations. In that regard, Article 25 and Article 103 of the Charter would also be applicable. Should the Security Council decide to take measures for the implementation of the judgment, the non-member State would be obliged to carry out the Security Council's decision in accordance with the Charter. Such obligations prevail over other treaty obligations which that State may have previously undertaken.

Thirdly, the State concerned shall undertake to contribute to the expenses of the Court in equitable amounts as assessed by the General Assembly in consultation with that State. The assessment is based on the percentage which that State would have to contribute to the expenses of the United Nations if it were a member State. In the 1950s when these non-member States' status to the Statute was considered, the contribution required from them was rather modest.[10]

The General Assembly adopted resolutions for each of these five non-member States to become a party to the Statute. Conditions for each of them were identical.[11] Notwithstanding their power to do so, the Security Council and the General Assembly would be unlikely to amend such conditions, unless there were compelling reasons. Out of these five non-member States, three of them had cases in the Court in that status; Nauru had a case against Australia after it became a member of the United Nations, but the case concerned activities that took place before its independence when it was under the administration of the Trusteeship Agreement. Liechtenstein instituted proceedings against Guatemala, and Switzerland filed an application against

10 Under General Assembly resolution 1308 (XIII), for all of them, the percentage was below 1%. See Robert Kolb, *op. cit. supra* footnote 4, pp. 94–95.

11 Switzerland became a party to the Statute in 1948; Liechtenstein in 1950; San Marino in 1954; Japan in 1954; and Nauru in 1988. International Court of Justice, *Yearbook 2012–2013*, No. 67, p. 18.

the United States.[12] Now these five States are all members of the United Nations. The conditions for them thus become obsolete.

A non-member State is entitled to the same right as that of a member State to nominate candidates for the election of the members of the Court and participate in the elections of the members of the Court in the General Assembly. They can also take part in the process of amending the Statute just as any member State of the United Nations.[13] Equally, if they get into arrears of payment, equal to or greater than their contributions for the two preceding years, their right to participate in the election of the members of the Court may be suspended by the General Assembly, subject to the same conditions as those for the member States.[14]

2 A Non-party to the Statute

With regard to the second type of States which are neither UN members nor parties to the Statute, Article 35, paragraph 2, of the Statute applies. This kind of situation mainly arose during the early period of the United Nations. As almost all the States are now members of the United Nations and parties to the Statute, this provision is rarely applied.

Article 35, paragraph 2, reads:

> The condition under which the Court shall be open to other States shall, subject to the special provisions contained in treaties in force, be laid down by the Security Council, but in no case shall such conditions place the parties in a position of inequality before the Court.

During the time of the League of Nations, the Permanent Court on two occasions dealt with the access question with regard to a State which was neither a member of the League of Nations nor a party to the Statute.[15] The Statute of

---

12 *Nottebohm case* (*Liechtenstein* v. *Guatemala*); *Interhandel* (*Switzerland* v. *United States of America*); *Certain Phosphate Lands in Nauru* (*Nauru* v. *Australia*).

13 See General Assembly resolution 264 (III) of 8 October 1948 and General Assembly resolution 2520 (XXIV) of 4 December 1969.

14 Article 19 of the Charter provides that: "A Member of the United Nations which is in arrears in the payment of its financial contributions to the Organization shall have no vote in the General Assembly if the amount of its arrears equals or exceeds the amount of the contributions due from it for the preceding two full years. The General Assembly may, nevertheless, permit such a Member to vote if it is satisfied that the failure to pay is due to conditions beyond the control of the Member."

15 Case of the *S.S. "Wimbledon," Judgments, 1923, P.C.I.J., Series A, No. 1*, p. 15; Case concerning *Certain German Interests in Polish Upper Silesia, Jurisdiction, Judgment No. 6, 1925, P.C.I.J.*,

the PCIJ left the possibility for the settlement of international disputes arising from the interpretation or application of the Peace Treaties of 1919 and 1920, regardless of whether the parties, applicant or respondent, were members of the League or parties to the Statute. Article 37 of the Statute of the PCIJ stipulates that, "[w]hen a Treaty or Convention in force provides for the reference of a matter to a tribunal to be instituted by the League of Nations, the Court will be such tribunal."

In the *S.S. "Wimbledon"* case, Great Britain, France, Italy and Japan instituted proceedings against Germany for the interdiction imposed by Germany on the transit through the Kiel Canal. Germany claimed that S.S. "Wimbledon" headed for Poland and Russia carrying military goods, thus breaking the rules of neutrality. The parties disputed about the interpretation and application of Articles 380 to 386 of the Peace Treaty of Versailles of 28 June 1919. Article 386 (1) of that Treaty provides that, "[i]n the event of violation of any of the conditions of Articles 380 to 386, or of disputes as to the interpretation of these articles, any interested Power can appeal to the jurisdiction instituted for the purpose by the League of Nations." When the proceedings were instituted in that case against Germany, Germany was not a member of the League of Nations; nor was it mentioned in the Annex to the Covenant. As the case concerned the interpretation and application of the Peace Treaties, in accordance with Article 35, paragraph 2, of the Statute, the Court founded its jurisdiction.[16]

In the case concerning *Certain German Interests in Polish Upper Silesia*, the proceedings were instituted by Germany, before its admission to the League of Nations, against Poland on the basis of Article 23 of the Convention relating to Upper Silesia of 15 May 1922.[17] The Permanent Court noted that Poland "[did] not dispute the fact that the suit has been duly submitted to the Court in accordance with Articles 35 and 40 of the Statute." The Permanent Court exercised jurisdiction without requiring Germany's special declaration accepting the jurisdiction of the Court as provided for in the Council Resolution.[18]

Article 35, paragraph 2, of the ICJ Statute was adopted on the model of Article 35, paragraph 2, of the PCIJ Statute. The conditions for a non-party State

Series A, No. 6, p. 3. See Andreas Zimmermann, "Article 35," in Andreas Zimmermann, Karin Oellers-Frahm, Christian Tomuschat, and Christian J. Tams (eds.), *op. cit. supra* footnote 2, p. 611, paras. 13–14.

16 Case of the *S.S. "Wimbledon," Judgments, 1923, P.C.I.J., Series A, No. 1*, p. 15.

17 Case concerning *Certain German Interests in Polish Upper Silesia, Jurisdiction, Judgment No. 6, 1925, P.C.I.J., Series A, No. 6*, p. 3.

18 *Annual Report of the Permanent Court of International Justice (1 January 1922–15 June 1925), P.C.I.J., Series E, No. 1*, p. 261.

to have access to the ICJ are laid down in the Security Council resolution 9 of 15 October 1946. The State in question shall deposit with the Registrar of the Court a declaration accepting the jurisdiction of the Court. The certified copies of the declaration shall be transmitted to all the State parties to the Statute, to all the States which have made similar declarations and to the Secretary-General of the United Nations.

Such a declaration may be general with respect to all disputes or to certain classes of disputes that may arise in the future. It may also be particular to one specific dispute which has already arisen. The State may by the declaration recognize as compulsory, *ipso facto* and without special agreement, the jurisdiction of the Court. Such declaration must be accepted by the States which had already accepted the compulsory jurisdiction of the Court under Article 36, paragraph 2, of the Statute. This is because there could otherwise be a situation, where the State in question made the declaration just for instituting a particular case against another State which had already accepted the jurisdiction of the Court. In that case, the latter State would thus be placed in a disadvantageous position, as it could not have done the same to the State non-party to the Statute. In other words, the principle of reciprocity equally applies to the State non-party to the Statute.

The Security Council reserved the right to rescind or amend the resolution by a new resolution to be communicated to the Court. Upon receiving the new resolution, the existing declarations shall cease to be effective, except in regard to disputes which are already before the Court. All the questions as to the validity or the effect of a declaration made under the terms of the Security Council resolution shall be decided by the Court. The State in question, of course, shall undertake to comply with the decision of the Court. It is clear that the conditions for the States party to the Statute and the conditions for the States not party to the Statute are in principle the same.

In the formative years of the ICJ, jurisdictional issues with the non-member States of the United Nations were handled with certain flexibility. In the *Corfu Channel* case, Albania was not a party to the Statute of the ICJ. The Security Council adopted resolution 22 on 9 April 1947, recommending that the parties to the dispute, namely, the United Kingdom and Albania, "should immediately refer the dispute" to the Court. Albania formally communicated to the Court, stating that it fully accepted the jurisdiction of the Court for that case. Under such circumstances, Albania's communication was taken as a declaration accepting the jurisdiction of the Court. Although Albania's acceptance occurred after the adoption of the Security Council's resolution 9 of 15 October 1946, it did not express its acceptance of the conditions as set out in the aforesaid resolution. The Court initially based its jurisdiction on *forum prorogatum*;

Albania's communication was regarded also as an act accepting the jurisdiction of the Court. The issue of jurisdiction was eventually resolved with the conclusion of a special agreement between the United Kingdom and Albania.[19]

In 1978, the Rules of Court were revised. Article 41 specifies the terms of a non-party State's acceptance of the Court's jurisdiction as follows:

> the institution of proceedings by a State which is not a party to the Statute but which, under Article 35, paragraph 2, thereof, has accepted the jurisdiction of the Court by a declaration made in accordance with any resolution adopted by the Security Council under that Article, shall be accompanied by a deposit of the declaration in question, unless the latter has previously been deposited with the Registrar. If any question of the validity or effect of such declaration arises, the Court shall decide.

Today, the practical value of this provision is diminishing in the settlement of international disputes, as there are hardly any States that fall into that category. However, the term "treaties in force" in Article 35, paragraph 2 proves to be still relevant under special circumstances.[20]

Once qualified as a party in a case before the Court, a State, either non-member State of the United Nations, or non-party to the Statue, enjoys all the rights and privileges on an equal footing with the other party in the case. Its qualification as a State shall not be put into question before the Court. The Statute and the Rules of Court shall apply to it in strict equality.

The questions of access to the Court and jurisdiction *ratione personae* are not identical but interconnected. A State must first satisfy the conditions for the access to the Court before the question of personal jurisdiction in a particular case can be considered. That is to say, it has to be party to the Statute of the Court, or if otherwise, to have accepted the conditions and made the declaration accepting the jurisdiction of the Court. If a State does not have access to the Court, as was the situation of Serbia in the *Legality of Use of Force* cases, the Court is certainly without jurisdiction in the case. In other words, access to the Court is a condition of qualification, a condition that has a general application to all States that may institute proceedings in the Court.

---

19 As indicated in the previous chapter, Albania objected to the jurisdiction of the Court with regard to the third phase on the reparation of damages. In its view, the Special Agreement did not include that matter.

20 As mentioned below, this term was discussed in the cases relating to the Federal Republic of Yugoslavia during the period from 1992 to 2000.

Personal jurisdiction, on the other hand, as one of the aspects of jurisdiction, can only arise in a particular case. It has to be examined with the specific parties. Under a normal situation, the question of access seldom arises, because the parties are UN member States; they are *ipso facto* party to the Statute of the Court. The parties do not even have to mention that fact, nor does the Court have to examine it *proprio motu*. Therefore, access to the Court normally does not present itself as an issue. In the history of the ICJ, the question of access arose only in the cases concerning Serbia after the dissolution of the former Socialist Federal Republic of Yugoslavia, which will be discussed separately.

c *Access to the Court in Case of State Succession*

In the 1990s, the question of access arose in the cases involving the newly independent Republics of the former Yugoslavia. In these cases, the status of these States, particularly the Federal Republic of Yugoslavia (the FRY, later Serbia and Montenegro, Serbia) gave rise to complicated issues of State succession with regard to treaties and the States access to the Court.

In the early 1990s, ethnic conflicts among the republics of the former Socialist Federal Republic of Yugoslavia (the SFRY) led to the eventual dissolution of the State. During the course of the process, serious international crimes were committed in these republics. After their independence, a number of cases were instituted in the Court, either by one of the new States against the FRY, or filed by the FRY against one of the other States.

The FRY, upon its proclamation on 27 April 1992, declared that, as the continuator of the SFRY, it "shall strictly abide by all the commitments that the Socialist Federal Republic of Yugoslavia assumed internationally."[21] On the same day it sent through its Permanent Mission in the United Nations to the Secretary-General a Note stating, *inter alia*:

> Strictly respecting the continuity of the international personality of Yugoslavia, the Federal Republic of Yugoslavia shall continue to fulfil all the rights conferred to, and obligations assumed by, the Socialist Federal Republic of Yugoslavia in international relations, including its membership in all international organizations and participation in international treaties ratified or acceded to by Yugoslavia.[22]

21 Annex II to the "Letter dated 6 May 1992 from the Chargé d'affaires a.i. of the Permanent Mission of Yugoslavia to the United Nations addressed to the Secretary-General," UN doc. A/46/915, 7 May 1992.

22 Annex I to the "Letter dated 6 May 1992 from the Chargé d'affaires a.i. of the Permanent Mission of Yugoslavia to the United Nations addressed to the Secretary-General," UN doc. A/46/915, 7 May 1992.

The FRY's claim to continue the former Yugoslavia was neither accepted by the other newly independent republics, nor recognized by the United Nations. Its request to continue the former Yugoslavia's membership of the United Nations went aground. It was required to apply for membership under the Security Council resolution 777 (1992) and the General Assembly resolution 47/1. As the FRY insisted on its claim, the situation became a dilemma. That dilemma persisted until 27 October 2000, 8 years after the adoption of the relevant resolutions, when the FRY ultimately changed its position and applied for the membership of the United Nations.[23]

On 1 November 2000, the FRY was admitted to the United Nations. Subsequently on 6 March 2001, it deposited the instrument of accession to the Genocide Convention with the UN Secretary-General, with a reservation to the effect that the FRY did not consider itself bound by Article IX of the Convention, precluding the jurisdiction of the Court. On 15 March 2001, the Secretary-General issued a depositary notification, indicating that the accession of the FRY to the Genocide Convention took effect on 12 March 2001. Soon after that, Croatia, Bosnia and Herzegovina, and Sweden made objections to the FRY's deposit of the instrument of accession, claiming that the FRY, as a successor State, was bound by the Convention from the date of its independence.

From the FRY's establishment in 1992 till it was admitted to the United Nations in 2000, there were several cases filed in the Court that involved the FRY.[24] Whether it was qualified to have access to the Court and its treaty status to the Genocide Convention had a direct bearing on the personal jurisdiction of the Court in these cases.

In 1993, Bosnia and Herzegovina filed an application in the Court against the FRY for alleged violations of the Genocide Convention. In due course, the FRY raised several preliminary objections to the jurisdiction of the Court and the admissibility of the application. In its third preliminary objection, the FRY contended that as Bosnia and Herzegovina had not established its independent statehood and had not become a State party to the Genocide Convention in accordance with the provisions of the Convention before the alleged acts occurred, it was not a State party to the Convention at the relevant time, and

23 "Letter dated 27 October 2000 from the President of the Federal Republic of Yugoslavia to the Secretary-General," Annex to "Application of the Federal Republic of Yugoslavia for admission to membership in the United Nations," UN doc. A/55/528-S2000/1043, 30 October 2000.

24 *Application of the Convention on the Prevention and Punishment of the Crime of Genocide* (*Bosnia and Herzegovina* v. *Serbia and Montenegro*); *Application of the Convention on the Prevention and Punishment of the Crime of Genocide* (*Croatia* v. *Serbia*); *Legality of Use of Force* cases (Serbia and Montenegro against 10 NATO member States).

consequently the Court had no personal jurisdiction, *ratione personae*, in this case.[25]

Reviewing the sequence of events, the Court noted that the FRY (Serbia and Montenegro), at the time of its proclamation of independence, declared that it shall strictly abide by all the commitments that the former Yugoslavia assumed internationally. This intention thus expressed by the FRY to remain bound by the international treaties to which the former Yugoslavia was party was confirmed by its official Note of 27 April 1992 sent to the UN Secretary-General. The Court observed that the parties did not contest that the FRY was party to the Genocide Convention.[26]

The Court further noted that Bosnia and Herzegovina, for its part, on 29 December 1992, sent an official Note of Succession to the UN Secretary-General, stating that it "wishes to succeed to the same [Genocide Convention] and undertakes faithfully to perform and carry out all the stipulations therein contained with effect from March 6, 1992, the date on which the Republic of Bosnia and Herzegovina became independent."[27] Therefore, from the time of its independence and admission to the UN, Bosnia and Herzegovina, under the terms of Article XI of the Genocide Convention, became a party to the Convention through the mechanism of State succession. The Court concluded that, regardless of the nature of the Convention concerned, at all events, Bosnia and Herzegovina was a party to the Genocide Convention on the date of the filing of its application.

By founding its jurisdiction in the case, the Court determined that the FRY was party to the Convention and had access to the Court. The Court delivered its judgment on preliminary objections on 11 July 1996.

In December 2000, the FRY was admitted into the United Nations as a new member.[28] Based on this "new fact," it filed an application for revision of the

---

25 *Application of the Convention on the Prevention and Punishment of the Crime of Genocide, Preliminary Objections, Judgment, I.C.J. Reports 1996*, pp. 606–607, para. 15.

26 *Ibid.*, p. 610, para. 17.

27 *Ibid.*, p. 610, para. 18.

28 By the Security Council resolution 777 (1992) and the General Assembly resolution 47/1, the FRY's membership of the United Nations as a continuator of the former Yugoslavia was not recognized by the United Nations. It was requested to apply for new membership. It could not participate in the activities of the United Nations, although the nameplate and the last flag of Yugoslavia were maintained. It still had to contribute its fees to the Organization. Regarding its status under international treaties, it was excluded from the major human rights treaty meetings, but some States insisted on its continued undertaking of its international obligations under those treaties. Serbia and Montenegro itself

1996 judgment. It claimed that "this new fact is of such a nature as to be a decisive factor regarding the question of jurisdiction *ratione personae* over the FRY."[29]

The Court took note of the new development and characterized the position of the FRY during the period from 1992 to 2000 as "*sui generis.*" It went to great lengths reviewing the legal status of the FRY in the United Nations and its treaty status during this *sui generis* period. The Court concluded that by its own conduct the FRY considered itself bound by the Genocide Convention during this *sui generis* period.[30] Its admission to the United Nations in 2000 did not constitute a new fact within the meaning of Article 61 of the Statute, capable of founding a request for the revision of the 1996 judgment. The Court in particular pointed out that,

> [r]esolution 47/1 did not *inter alia* affect the FRY's right to appear before the Court or to be a party to a dispute before the Court under the conditions laid down by the Statute. Nor did it affect the position of the FRY in relation to the Genocide Convention. To "terminate the situation created by resolution 47/1," the FRY had to submit a request for admission to the United Nations as had been done by the other Republics composing the SFRY. All these elements were known to the Court and to the FRY at the time when the Judgment was given.[31]

In light of the foregoing reasons, the Court rejected the FRY's request for revision of the 1996 judgment in its judgment of 3 February 2003.

In the *Legality of Use of Force* cases, however, the Court took a different turn. On 29 April 1999, the FRY instituted separate proceedings in the Court against ten member States of NATO for the military bombing of the territory of

---

insisted its automatic continued international personality and commitment to its treaty obligations. The FRY deposited a declaration accepting the compulsory jurisdiction of the ICJ with the Secretary-General on 25 April 1999.

29 *Application for Revision of the Judgment of 11 July 1996 in the Case concerning* Application of the Convention on the Prevention and Punishment of the Crime of Genocide (Bosnia and Herzegovina *v.* Yugoslavia), Preliminary Objections (*Yugoslavia* v. *Bosnia and Herzegovina*), *Judgment, I.C.J. Reports 2003*, p. 12, para. 18.

30 The Court referred to the Note of the FRY upon its proclamation on 27 April 1992 and its legal actions taken during the *Bosnian Genocide* case. It participated in the proceedings for provisional measures, and submitted a Counter-Memorial containing counter-claims. See *ibid.*, pp. 26–30, paras. 54–64.

31 *Ibid.*, p. 31, para. 70.

Yugoslavia and other alleged illegal acts in violation of international law.[32] The United Kingdom and other respondent States raised preliminary objections to the jurisdiction of the Court.[33]

In considering the issue of jurisdiction, the Court noted that "the question whether Serbia and Montenegro was or was not a party to the Statute of the Court at the time of the institution of the present proceedings is a fundamental one."[34] In its view, the fact that the FRY was admitted to the United Nations in 2000 raised the question of access in the case.

During the proceedings, several respondents argued that Serbia and Montenegro "cannot rely on its acquiescence as respondent in one case in order to found jurisdiction as Applicant in this case." Belgium concluded that it "relie[d] on both the letter and the spirit of Article 35 of the Statute" and "[did] not acquiesce to the bringing of a claim against it by an applicant for whom the Court was not open at the relevant time."[35] Moreover, Italy observed that "the question is still whether the Court could … regard itself as having jurisdiction *ratione personarum* pursuant to Article 35, paragraph 2, because Serbia and Montenegro was allegedly a party to a 'treaty in force' laying down the jurisdiction of the Court." It further emphasized that,

> [i]n particular, Italy maintained that the mere presence of a clause conferring jurisdiction in a treaty in force between two States, one of which, the Applicant, is not at the same time a party to the Statute, could not give that State the right to appear before the Court, unless it met the conditions laid down by the Security Council in its resolution No. 9 of 15 October 1946. This Serbia and Montenegro has not done and does not claim ever to have done.[36]

The Court first discussed the situation with the FRY's legal status in the United Nations during the period from 1992–2000. It noted that the Court's

---

32 See, for example, *Legality of Use of Force* (*Serbia and Montenegro* v. *United Kingdom*), *Preliminary Objections, Judgment, I.C.J. Reports 2004*, p. 1307.

33 The FRY filed the case against the United States and Spain on *forum prorogatum*, but the two States did not accept it. As a result, eight States participated in the proceedings as respondents. In each case, the FRY invoked as the title of jurisdiction of the Court Article IX of the Genocide Convention; in five cases, it also invoked its own acceptance of the jurisdiction of the Court under the Optional Clause of Article 36, paragraph 2, of the Statute.

34 *Legality of Use of Force* (*Serbia and Montenegro* v. *Belgium*), *Preliminary Objections, Judgment, I.C.J. Reports 2004*, p. 293, para. 30.

35 *Ibid.*, p. 317, para. 97.

36 *Ibid.*

characterization of the FRY's position as "*sui generis*" during that period in the 2003 judgment on Request for Revision was largely due to the "amorphous state of affairs" surrounding the legal status of the FRY in the United Nations prior to its membership in the United Nations. The term "*sui generis*" was descriptive, but not prescriptive, without any defined legal consequence intended by the Court. In its view, the 2003 judgment only ruled that one of the conditions for the application of Article 61 of the Statute was not satisfied. It did not pronounce on the legal status of the FRY vis-à-vis the United Nations, nor in relation to the Statute of the Court.[37]

In regard to the observation concerning the term "subject to the special provisions contained in treaties in force" in Article 35, paragraph 2, the Court examined in great detail the drafting history of the Article from the time of the PCIJ to the ICJ and concluded that Article 35, paragraph 2, of the ICJ Statute was intended to refer to treaties in force at the date the ICJ Statute entered into force, not to any treaties concluded since that date.[38] Therefore, whether or not the FRY was considered a party to the Genocide Convention at the time when the case was filed in 1999, the matter was irrelevant for the consideration of the question of access, as the Convention only entered into force on 12 January 1951. Based on this analysis, the Court decided that:

> Serbia and Montenegro did not, at the time of the institution of the present proceedings, have access to the Court under either paragraph 1 or paragraph 2 of Article 35 of the Statute, makes it unnecessary for the Court to consider the other preliminary objections filed by the Respondents to the jurisdiction of the Court.[39]

37 *Ibid.*, pp. 308–309, paras. 73–74.

38 *Ibid.*, p. 324, para. 113. In the history of the ICJ, unlike the case of its predecessor, there has never been a case where the jurisdiction of the Court was based on a special provision of a treaty in force under Article 35, paragraph 2, of the Statute.

39 *Ibid.*, pp. 327–328, para. 127. Right after filing the Applications, the FRY requested the Court to indicate provisional measures to order the NATO members to stop bombing the territory of the FRY. For example, in the case against the United Kingdom, the Court, however, found that it had no jurisdiction *prima face* and dismissed the request. In the reasoning, it avoided dealing with the claim of the United Kingdom that the FRY was not a member of the United Nations, thus not a party to the Statute, and therefore it had no capacity to participate in the proceedings. The FRY contended that the General Assembly resolution 47/1 neither terminated nor suspended its membership. The FRY partly based the jurisdiction of the Court on Article 36, paragraph 2, as both parties had made the declaration accepting the compulsory jurisdiction of the Court. However, the United Kingdom's declaration precluded any dispute in respect of which

Based on the same ground, the Court found that it had no jurisdiction in eight cases filed by the FRY (Serbia and Montenegro).

In 1999, Croatia instituted proceedings against the FRY (Serbia) for alleged violations of the Genocide Convention. It invoked Article IX of the Convention as the basis of the jurisdiction of the Court. The FRY raised preliminary objections to the jurisdiction of the Court.[40] It asked the Court to adjudicate and declare that it lacked jurisdiction over the claims brought against the FRY by the Republic of Croatia and the claims based on acts or omissions which took place before the FRY came into being (i.e., before 27 April 1992) were inadmissible.

During the proceedings, Serbia, on the basis of the 2004 judgments in the cases concerning *Legality of Use of Force,* claimed that as Croatia filed its application at the time when the FRY was not admitted to the United Nations, it was not a party to the Statute and the conditions under Article 35, paragraph 2, of the Statute were not met. Moreover, it argued that the Court could not have jurisdiction on the basis of Article IX of the Genocide Convention, because the FRY did not become bound by the Convention in any way before 10 June 2001. Furthermore, with its reservation to Article IX of the Convention, the FRY did not accept the jurisdiction of the Court for the purpose of the Convention.

On Serbia's capacity to participate in the proceedings, the Court first recalled the declaration of the FRY upon its proclamation of independence on 27 April 1992 with the commitment to honour international obligations assumed by the SFRY and the subsequent events relating to the status of the FRY. It noted that some of the facts and legal issues that had been dealt with in the previous cases also arose in the present case. However, the Court considered that as none of those decisions were given between the same parties of the present case, by virtue of Article 59 of the Statute, the previous judgments had no effect of *res judicata* for the present case.[41]

With regard to the meaning of Article 35, paragraph 2, the Court gave the following interpretation:

---

any other party to the dispute has accepted the Court's compulsory jurisdiction solely for the purpose of instituting a particular case. Moreover, the FRY made the declaration only three days before the filing, less than 12 months as required in the United Kingdom's declaration. Hence that ground was not accepted by the Court. See *Legality of Use of Force (Yugoslavia* v. *United Kingdom), Provisional Measures, Order of 2 June 1999, I.C.J. Reports 1999*, pp. 833–836, paras. 21–28.

40 *Application of the Convention on the Prevention and Punishment of the Crime of Genocide (Croatia* v. *Serbia), Preliminary Objections, Judgment, I.C.J. Reports 2008,* p. 412.

41 The Court also stressed that "while those decisions are in no way binding on the Court, it will not depart from its settled jurisprudence unless it finds very particular reasons to do so." *Ibid.*, p. 428, para. 53.

> That paragraph on the one hand empowers the Security Council to lay down the conditions under which the Court shall be open to such States and on the other contains a reservation for "special provisions contained in treaties in force." Pursuant to the authority thus conferred upon it, the Security Council adopted resolution 9 (1946) of 15 October 1946, providing in substance that the Court shall be open to any State not a party to the Statute which has previously deposited a declaration, either in respect of one or more particular matters or with a more general ambit, whereby the State undertakes to accept the jurisdiction of the Court in accordance with the Charter and to comply in good faith with the decisions of the Court.[42]

That interpretation of Article 35, paragraph 2, apparently did not maintain the emphasis on the legal status of Serbia in relation to the Statute at the time of the filing of the application, as the Court did in the *Legality of Use of Force* cases.

Given the fact that Croatia was a member of the United Nations and the FRY was admitted to the Organization on 1 November 2000, the Court maintained that both parties at present were States within the meaning of Article 35, paragraph 1. It stated that, had Croatia's application been filed on 2 November 2000, instead of 2 July 1999, no objection to jurisdiction could have been based on lack of access to the Court under Article 35 of the Statute. While acknowledging the established rule of the Court on the critical date for the assessment of jurisdiction,[43] the Court nevertheless considered that there were certain situations where realism and flexibility were called for. Unlike the practice in municipal law, international adjudication did not impose strict requirement on matters of form.[44] In the Court's view, as Croatia could have instituted a new proceeding to overcome the issue of access, the question of access should not

42 *Ibid.*, p. 430, para. 58.

43 It is a well-established principle of the Court that the jurisdiction of the Court must normally be assessed on the date of the filing of the application instituting proceedings. For the analysis of the Court on this point, see *ibid.*, pp. 437–438, paras. 79–80.

44 See *Mavrommatis Palestine Concessions, Judgment No. 2, 1924, P.C.I.J., Series A, No. 2*, p. 34; *Certain German Interests in Polish Upper Silesia, Jurisdiction, Judgment No. 6, 1925, P.C.I.J., Series A, No. 6*, p. 14; *Case concerning the Northern Cameroons* (*Cameroon* v. *United Kingdom*), *Preliminary Objections, Judgment of 2 December 1963: I.C.J. Reports 1963*, p. 28; *Military and Paramilitary Activities in and against Nicaragua* (*Nicaragua* v. *United States of America*), *Jurisdiction and Admissibility, Judgment, I.C.J. Reports 1984*, pp. 428–429, para. 83.

be an obstacle to the jurisdiction of the Court.[45] It therefore concluded that on 1 November 2000 the Court was open to the FRY. Therefore, as the Court found that Serbia was bound by Article IX of the Convention on 2 July 1999, the date on which proceedings in the present case were instituted, and remained bound by that Article until at least 1 November 2000, the Court was in a position to uphold its jurisdiction and the question whether the conditions laid down in Article 35, paragraph 2, had been fulfilled had no pertinence in the present case.

The Court's jurisprudence on the question of access in these cases with regard to Serbia's status cannot be deemed consistent and coherent. This is the first time that the Court applied Article 35, paragraph 2, of the Statute. Individual opinions appended to the judgments in each case, particularly in the *Legality of Use of Force* cases[46] and the *Genocide Convention* case (*Croatia* v. *Serbia*)[47] reveal how divided the Court was on each issue relating to the status

45 The Court drew a distinction between the *Legality of Use of Force* cases and the present case; Serbia was the applicant in the former case, while in the latter case, it was the respondent. Moreover, the Court relied on two facts for its conclusion. First, Croatia had exercised care in instituting the proceedings. At the time when Croatia filed this case, the FRY had filed the cases against NATO countries. Apparently Serbia considered that it had the capacity to participate in the Court's proceedings. Secondly, Croatia submitted its Memorial after 2000. Therefore, the Court concluded that the conditions under Article 35, paragraph 1 were satisfied. Thus, the Court turned the question of access to the Court into an issue of premature action. *Application of the Convention on the Prevention and Punishment of the Crime of Genocide* (*Croatia* v. *Serbia*), *Preliminary Objections, Judgment, I.C.J. Reports 2008*, pp. 437–444, paras. 79–90.

46 In the *Legality of Use of Force* cases, seven judges in their Joint Declaration took the view that if the Court found that, on two or more grounds, its jurisdiction was not well founded, it might choose the most appropriate ground on which to base its decision of lack of competence. They did not think that the personal jurisdiction prevailed over other grounds. They believed that there were three criteria that must guide the Court in making a selection among the possible options, namely, consistency, the principle of certitude and possible implications for the other pending cases. In their opinion, to find that the Court lacked jurisdiction on the basis of Article 35, paragraph 2, was inconsistent with the jurisprudence as established by the previous judgments. See *Legality of Use of Force* (*Serbia and Montenegro* v. *United Kingdom*), *Preliminary Objections, Judgment, I.C.J. Reports 2004*, Joint Declaration of Vice-President Ranjeva, Judges Guillaume, Higgins, Kooijmans, Al-Khasawneh, Buergenthal and Elaraby, p. 1353.

47 Four judges appended a joint declaration, critically stating that the judgment "not only lacks legal validity and consistency but is even *contra legem* and untenable." In their opinion, "[t]his Court is not entitled to exercise jurisdiction based on a *contra legem* interpretation of a convention, such as the United Nations Charter or the Statute of the Court. Any such Judgment cannot but be extra-legal. It is regrettable that this Court, as a court

of the FRY (Serbia). On the meaning of Article 35, paragraph 2, the Court virtually gave conflicting interpretations to the term "treaties in force." Although the Court repeatedly asserted that, as these cases concerned different parties and different subject-matters, by virtue of Article 59, no question of *res judicata* arose, it is questionable that for the same party the Court may draw different conclusions on its legal status at the same particular point in time. The *sui generis* position of the FRY from 1992 to 2000 indeed posed difficult legal questions of international law in case of State succession.

On the relations between jurisdiction *ratione personae* with other jurisdictional grounds, *ratione materiae* and *ratione temporis*, the Court in the *Legality of Use of Force* cases considered that jurisdiction *ratione personae* should be dealt with before other jurisdictional issues.[48] In its view, unless there is jurisdiction *ratione personae*, there is no point to consider jurisdiction *ratione materiae* and *ratione temporis*. This position, however, was not shared by some judges. They maintained that the Court should base its judgment on a safer and more solid ground to dismiss a case if there were other jurisdictional options.[49]

d *The Role of States in Advisory Proceedings*

Under the Charter and the Statute, States cannot request an advisory opinion from the Court, nor can they do so through the organs of the United Nations, which is different from the practice of the PCIJ. As is discussed below, this is to avoid that States use the advisory procedure to circumvent the principle of consent.

That said, under Article 66 of the Statute, States may still participate in the advisory proceedings. When a request for advisory opinion is properly submitted to the Court by one of the organs or specialized agencies of the United Nations, States which have access to the Court may raise objections to the competence of the Court in the case and give their observations on the legal question concerned.[50] They may either submit written statements only, or take part in both written and oral proceedings.

of law, should have taken such a position." See *Application of the Convention on the Prevention and Punishment of the Crime of Genocide (Croatia* v. *Serbia), Preliminary Objections, Judgment, I.C.J. Reports 2008*, Joint Declaration of Judges Ranjeva, Shi, Koroma and Parra-Aranguren, p. 472, para. 1.

48 *Legality of Use of Force (Serbia and Montenegro* v. *United Kingdom), Preliminary Objections, Judgment, I.C.J. Reports 2004*, pp. 1324–1325, para. 44.

49 See above, footnote 46.

50 In accordance with Article 66, paragraph 2, of the Statute, the States considered likely to be able to furnish information on the question in the advisory proceedings will receive a special communication from the Registrar, inviting them to submit their views to the

2 International Organizations

International organizations, as States, are competent to take part in both contentious cases and advisory proceedings, but their competence in the two kinds of jurisdiction and the conditions attached to their participation are quite different from those for States.

a *The Role in Contentious Cases*

Under the Charter and the Statute, international organizations refer to public, inter-governmental organizations. As a matter of principle, an international organization does not have access to the Court in contentious cases. In other words, it cannot institute legal proceedings as a party in the Court. Their participation in the contentious cases, as will be explained below, is a limited one.

First of all, by legal implication of Article 34, paragraph 1, of the Statute, international organizations are not competent to appear before the Court as a party in a contentious case, either as the applicant or the respondent, or to intervene as a third party. Under the Statute of the PCIJ, Article 34 only had the content of what is now the first paragraph about the exclusive competence of States to have access to the Court. Paragraphs 2 and 3 concerning international organizations were added to the Statute of the ICJ at the San Francisco Conference. This development shows the growing role of international organizations in world affairs after WWII. Such role, however, as practice proves, was not fully envisaged and recognized by the draftsmen of the Statute at the San Francisco Conference. The Article was criticized for lack of vision in this respect.[51]

During the time of the League of Nations, there were only a few international organizations composed of States. Their mandate usually was limited to one particular area, e.g. post, labour. In the PCIJ's practice, the International Labour Organization (ILO) might furnish information to the Permanent Court in cases involving labour matters. For that purpose, the Director of the ILO should receive copies of all written proceedings of the relevant cases.[52] In 1944, the ILO suggested that the jurisdiction of the PCIJ be expanded to cover disputes between organizations, implying that international organizations would have

---

Court. Paragraph 3 further provides that a State which has not received a special communication may express a desire to submit a written statement or to be heard, and the Court will decide. In practice, the Court has been very liberal in this respect and very deferential to States' wishes under paragraph 3. See Robert Kolb, *op. cit. supra* footnote 4, pp. 1106–1107.

51 See Pierre-Marie Dupuy, "Article 34," in Andreas Zimmermann, Karin Oellers-Frahm, Christian Tomuschat, and Christian J. Tams (eds.), *op. cit. supra* footnote 2, pp. 596–598.

52 Article 26 of the Statute of the PCIJ.

legal standing in the Court.[53] Its proposal did not receive sufficient support from States.

At the San Francisco Conference, the idea to give international organizations access to the Court for contentious cases was brought up again. Unfortunately, it failed to fly one more time. The Committee of Jurists responsible for the drafting of the Statute, at the initiative of the United States, proposed to add one new paragraph, as a compromise, to Article 34, which reads,

> [t]he Court may, subject to and in conformity with its own Rules, request of public international organizations information relevant to cases before it, and it shall receive such information voluntarily presented by such organizations.[54]

In presenting this draft, the Committee clarified that, "[i]n doing so, the Committee has not wished to go so far as to admit, as certain delegations appear disposed to do so, that public international organizations may become parties to a case before the Court."[55] Later the third paragraph was added to Article 34 on the proposal of the British delegation.[56] Compared with Article 26 of the PCIJ Statute on the provision of information by the ILO on labour matters, these additional paragraphs substantially enlarged the coverage of international organizations for the purpose of furnishing information.

Starting with the International Civil Aviation Organization (ICAO), the Court has requested and received information from different international organizations. In the case concerning *Appeal Relating to the Jurisdiction of the ICAO Council (India v. Pakistan)*,[57] India instituted proceedings in the Court to appeal from the decisions rendered by the Council of the ICAO on the preliminary objections raised by India in a case brought by Pakistan in the Council. In order to found the jurisdiction of the Court, the application relied on

53 Pierre-Marie Dupuy, "Article 34," in Andreas Zimmermann, Karin Oellers-Frahm, Christian Tomuschat, and Christian J. Tams (eds.), *op. cit. supra* footnote 2, p. 590.

54 *Documents of the United Nations Conference on International Organization*, UNCIO XIV, pp. 323, 325–337.

55 *Ibid.*, pp. 139, 839.

56 See Shabtai Rosenne, *op. cit. supra* footnote 8, *Vol. II, Jurisdiction* p. 622. That paragraph reads as follows: "[w]henever the construction of the constituent instrument of a public international organization or of an international convention adopted there-under is in question in a case before the Court, the Registrar shall so notify the public international organization concerned and shall communicate to it copied of all the written proceedings."

57 *Appeal Relating to the Jurisdiction of the ICAO Council (India v. Pakistan), Judgment, I.C.J. Reports 1972*, p. 46.

Article 84 of the Convention on International Civil Aviation signed at Chicago on 7 December 1944 (the Chicago Convention), and Article II of the International Air Services Transit Agreement opened for signature at Chicago on 7 December 1944. As the Chicago Convention is a constitutive instrument of the ICAO, the ICAO was notified of the application and furnished with copies of the written pleadings in accordance with Article 34, paragraph 3, of the Statute. The Registrar also informed the Secretary General of the ICAO that in accordance with Article 57 of the Rules of Court, the ICAO could submit its observations in writing on the case. Within the fixed time-limit, the Secretary General of the ICAO informed the Court that his Organization did not intend to submit observations.

After this case, the Court amended its Rules on the procedure of furnishing information by international organizations. Under Article 69 of the Rules of Court, the Court may either by its own decision, *proprio motu*, or at the request of one of the parties, request an international organization to furnish information relevant to the case which is pending before the Court. In consultation with the chief administrator of the organization, the Court shall fix the time limits for the presentation of the information.

Under Article 69, an international organization may take the initiative to furnish information relating to a pending case to the Court. Such information shall be presented in the form of a Memorial to be filed with the Registrar before the closure of written proceedings. It shall be transmitted to the parties for their comments. The Court may request supplementary information from that organization during the proceedings, and authorize the parties to comment on the information.

If a case concerns the interpretation of the Charter or any constituent instrument of an organization or a multilateral convention which was concluded under the auspices of an international organization, the Registrar shall notify the organization concerned and communicate to it copies of all the written pleadings of the case. The Court shall, in consultation with the chief administrator of the organization, fix the time limit within which the latter may submit to the Court its observations in writing. Such observations shall be passed on to the parties. The parties and the representative of the organization may comment on these observations during the oral hearings.

In 2005, the Court amended Article 43 of the Rules of Court. It provides the procedure for public international organizations and third States to furnish information to the Court for the construction of a treaty. According to Article 63 of the Statute, if the Court needs to construe a treaty in dealing with a case, the Registrar shall notify the State parties to the treaty. Should any State party wish to present its view on the construction of the treaty, it may intervene for that purpose. Article 43 of the Rules of Court is a corresponding clause for the international organizations for the same purpose.

The organization so notified shall confine its observations on the particular provisions of the treaty that the Court is to construe. In submitting such observations, the organization shall follow the procedure provided in Article 69, paragraph 2, of the Rules of Court.

Up to date, the practice of the Court with regard to international organizations is still limited. First, the Rules of Court only apply to public, intergovernmental organizations. Non-governmental organizations (NGOs) and other entities do not have the right to submit information to the Court.

Secondly, the role of international organizations in the contentious proceedings is restricted to furnishing information and providing observations. Although the Statute and the Rules of Court only provide that information should relate to the case in the Court and do not specifically require that it should fall within the mandate and function of the organization, the functional link between the organization and the information thus provided is self-evident.

Thirdly, an organization may either furnish information upon the request by the Court, or do so on its own initiative. On both accounts, furnishing information is not mandatory for the organization. Even if requested by the Court, the organization may choose not to provide information or make observations. The Rules of Court leave the discretion to international organizations to measure their action in the specific circumstances of each case.

Since the Rules of Court were thus amended, there have been a number of cases involving requests from the Court to international organizations to provide observations on the construction of certain multilateral international treaties.[58] In very few cases, however, have international organizations really

58 In the case concerning *Border and Transborder Armed Actions* (*Nicaragua* v. *Honduras*), the Court notified the Secretary General of the Organization of American States (OAS) as the Pact of Bogotá was invoked by the parties as the basis of jurisdiction. In the case concerning *Aerial Incident of 3 July 1988* (*Islamic Republic of Iran* v. *United States of America*), the Court notified the Secretary General of the ICAO, which in due time submitted its observation, consisting of a factual description of earlier proceedings in the ICAO Council. In the case concerning *Application of the Convention on the Prevention and Punishment of the Crime of Genocide* (*Bosnia and Herzegovina* v. *Serbia and Montenegro*), the Court notified the Secretary-General of the United Nations, as the construction of the Genocide Convention would be in question. This was the first time that the Court applied Article 34, paragraph 3, to the United Nations. In the recent cases between Nicaragua and Costa Rica over the San Juan River, the Court notified the Ramsar Convention Secretariat for its observations, as the parties both referred to the interpretation and application of the Ramsar Convention on Wetlands of International Importance.

showed interest in furnishing information in contentious cases.[59] It reveals, in an indirect way, the dominant role that States play in treaty interpretation and application.

For many years there has been strong advocacy for widening access to the Court, including allowing international organizations to appear in contentious cases.[60] It is regarded as a way to strengthen the role of the Court as well as that of international organizations in the field of international law. So far, however, there has been little progress.

b *Requests for Advisory Opinions*

According to Article 96 of the Charter, the General Assembly and the Security Council may request the Court to give an advisory opinion on any legal question. Other organs of the United Nations and specialized agencies, with the authorization of the General Assembly, may also request advisory opinions of the Court on legal questions arising from their activities.

Although the Statutes of the PCIJ and ICJ both provide advisory jurisdiction, their practice is quite distinct. Article 96 of the Charter in a way is an innovative clause, a deviation from the practice of the PCIJ.

1 PCIJ Practice

Advisory jurisdiction of the Permanent Court stemmed from Article 14 of the League Covenant. The Statute of the PCIJ, however, did not contain any articles to that effect.[61] Under Article 14 of the Covenant, "[t]he Court may also give an advisory opinion upon any dispute or question referred to it by the Council or by the Assembly." Accordingly, only the Council and the Assembly were competent to request advisory opinions from the Court, although, in fact,

---

59 For instance, in the *East Timor* case (*Portugal* v. *Australia*), the *Gabčíkovo-Nagymaros Project* case (*Hungary/Slovakia*), the *Fisheries Jurisdiction* case (*Spain* v. *Canada*), the case concerning the *Vienna Convention on Consular Relations* (*Paraguay* v. *United States of America*), the *LaGrand* case (*Germany* v. *United States of America*), the *Legality of Use of Force* cases, none of the relevant organizations gave their observations. See Pierre-Marie Dupuy, "Article 34," in Andreas Zimmermann, Karin Oellers-Frahm, Christian Tomuschat, and Christian J. Tams (eds.), *op. cit. supra* footnote 2, pp. 595–596.

60 The *Institut de droit international* in 1954 already proposed that "[i]t is a matter of urgency to widen the terms of Article 34 of the Statute so as to grant access to the Court to international organizations of States of which at least a majority are members of the United Nations or parties to the Statute of the Court." *Annuaire De l'Institut de Droit International*, Vol. 45, 1954, Part II, p. 296, Part I, p.43.

61 This gap was only filled in 1936 by the revised Rules of Court.

all the opinions that were put forward to the Permanent Court were requested by the Council. As the requests might relate to "any dispute or question," the matters put forward were either disputes between two or more States submitted to the Court through the Council, or questions that an individual State or an international organization requested the Council to transmit to the Court on its behalf.[62] The Council normally adopted the decision to request an advisory opinion by unanimity.

The idea of advisory competence at the time of the League of Nations was rather flexible.[63] By its vague terms, it actually allowed States, whether they were party or not to the Statute of the PCIJ, or otherwise had access to the Court, to request an advisory opinion of the Court through the two organs on a dispute pending between them. As advisory opinions rendered by the Court had no binding force on them, such opinion could at least help them avoid head-on binding decisions and give them a better chance to assess their position so as to facilitate the final settlement. This practice equally led to some apprehensions that such advisory procedure could indirectly lead to a compulsory adjudication of international disputes without the consent of both parties to the dispute.[64]

In practice, the Permanent Court did exercise caution not to cross the bounds of its jurisdiction in an advisory case. In the *Eastern Carelia* case, the Court declined to exercise its advisory jurisdiction to give an opinion, as it concluded that the question submitted to it for an opinion formed the subject of a dispute, and that to give a reply would be tantamount to giving a judicial decision on that dispute.[65]

---

62 In 29 advisory opinion cases, the Court rendered 27 advisory opinions. Six cases were requested by the ILO, and the rest concerned disputes between two or more States, application of the Covenant, and legal advice to other international organs for the implementation of the peace settlement of 1919.

63 It is also considered that, largely due to the fact that there were no specific rules on advisory opinion, the Court was left with general discretion in all aspects of its advisory competence. See Shabtai Rosenne, *op. cit. supra* footnote 8, *Vol. II, Jurisdiction*, p. 950.

64 Shabtai Rosenne, *op. cit. supra* footnote 8, *Vol. I, The Court and the United Nations,* p. 274.

65 See *Status of Eastern Carelia, Advisory Opinion of July 23rd, 1923, Series B, No. 5*. The question concerned a legal dispute between Finland and Russia over the interpretation of the terms of the Peace Treaty of 1920 concluded between the two countries. After the question was submitted to the Court, Finland requested a hearing, but Russia refused. The Court considered that without the consent of Russia, the Court would be in a disadvantageous position to ascertain the necessary facts. It was against the principle of consent to render an opinion that was tantamount to a judicial settlement.

2 ICJ Practice

As far as advisory jurisdiction is concerned, the ICJ has substantially changed the practice of the PCIJ. First of all, as the principal judicial organ of the United Nations, the Court has defined its advisory function as part of its participation in the activities of the United Nations. By virtue of Article 96 of the Charter and Article 65 of the Statute, all the organs, alongside the General Assembly and the Security Council, may request advisory opinions from the Court, provided that such request is duly authorized by the General Assembly and falls within the scope of the requesting organ's activities. Procedurally, all the requests should be communicated to the Secretary-General, who shall pass them on to the Court. The General Assembly in adopting the resolution for the request of advisory opinion only needs a majority voting rather than unanimity.[66] This will allow certain requests to pass through political controversy in the Assembly.

The resolution of the General Assembly by itself does not mean that the Court automatically has the power to exercise its advisory function. Member States may still, by communication to the Court, raise objections to the competence of the Court in a particular advisory case. The Court has to examine, either *proprio motu* or by addressing the contentions of States, its competence, as is the case with its contentious jurisdiction. The Court must be satisfied that the requesting organ, if other than the two major organs of the United Nations, is duly authorized by the General Assembly. The legal question put forward to the Court must clearly lie within the scope of the requesting organ's mandate. For that matter, the Court may have to examine the constituent instrument of the organization concerned.

Oftentimes the legal question submitted to the Court in essence relates to a legal dispute between two or more States or between a State and an international organization. This does not by itself deprive the Court of its competence to give an advisory opinion. As is time and again reaffirmed in the Court's jurisprudence, an advisory opinion is given not to the States, but to the organ requesting it. In this sense, the Court is acting as an "organ of the United Nations." To give an advisory opinion represents its participation in the activities

66 Most of the resolutions requesting for an advisory opinion were adopted by a majority in excess of two thirds of the members present and voting. The one relating to the *Reparation* case in 1948 was adopted by unanimity. The resolution requesting opinion on the use or threat of use of nuclear weapons was adopted by a vote of 78 to 43, with 38 abstentions, out of a total of 185 members. See Shabtai Rosenne, *op. cit. supra* footnote 8, *Vol. I, The Court and the United Nations*, pp. 296–297.

of the Organization. Therefore, in principle, requests duly authorized by the General Assembly should not be refused.[67]

On the concept of "legal question" that falls within the meaning of Article 96 of the Charter, the Court's interpretation tends to be rather broad. According to the Court, the political nature of a request does not by itself deprive the Court of its competence to address the request. In the *Interpretation of Peace Treaties* case, for example, the power of the Court to exercise its advisory function was contested by Bulgaria, Hungary, Romania, and some other States. They argued that the request for an opinion was an action *ultra vires* on the part of the General Assembly because, in dealing with the question of the observance of human rights and fundamental freedoms in the three mentioned States, the Court was "interfering" or "intervening" in matters essentially within the domestic jurisdiction of States. The Court considered that that argument was based on a misunderstanding. It observed that the object of the request was much more limited. The Court was not called upon to deal with the charges brought before the General Assembly against the three countries, but requested to give certain clarifications to the applicability of the procedure for the settlement of disputes by the treaty commissions. The Court stated that:

> The interpretation of the terms of a treaty for this purpose could not be considered as a question essentially within the domestic jurisdiction of a State… It is a question of international law which, by its very nature, lies within the competence of the Court.[68]

With regard to the concern over the risk that an advisory procedure may turn into a factual compulsory judicial process without the consent of the parties in question, the Court emphasized that:

---

67 *Interpretation of Peace Treaties, Advisory Opinion: I.C.J. Reports 1950*, p. 71. This has been confirmed in a series of subsequent cases. See *Reservations to the Convention on the Prevention and Punishment of the Crime of Genocide, Advisory Opinion: I.C.J. Reports 1951*, p. 19; *Judgments of the Administrative Tribunal of the ILO upon Complaints Made Against Unesco, Advisory Opinion of October 23rd, 1956: I.C.J. Reports 1956*, p. 86; *Certain expenses of the United Nations (Article 17, paragraph 2, of the Charter), Advisory Opinion of 20 July 1962: I.C.J. Reports 1962*, p. 155; *Applicability of Article VI, Section 22, of the Convention on the Privileges and Immunities of the United Nations, Advisory Opinion, I.C.J. Reports 1989*, p. 189, para. 31; *Legality of the Threat or Use of Nuclear Weapons, Advisory Opinion, I.C.J. Reports 1996*, p. 235, para. 14; *Legal Consequences of the Construction of a Wall in the Occupied Palestinian Territory, Advisory Opinion, I.C.J. Reports 2004*, p. 157, para. 47.

68 *Interpretation of Peace Treaties, Advisory Opinion: I.C.J. Reports 1950*, pp. 70–71.

> The consent of States, parties to a dispute, is the basis of the Court's jurisdiction in contentious cases. The situation is different in regard to advisory proceedings even where the Request for an Opinion relates to a legal question actually pending between States. The Court's reply is only of an advisory character: as such, it has no binding force.[69]

The distinction between the contentious jurisdiction and the advisory jurisdiction focuses on the nature of the decisions of the Court. An advisory opinion, although non-binding in nature, can nevertheless have great impact on the dispute settlement, as such opinion comes from the principal judicial organ of the United Nations. Compared with the PCIJ, the ICJ plays a much more active role in providing advisory opinions on issues of contemporary international law. Through its advisory opinions, the Court has made a series of far-reaching pronouncements on international law issues. Apart from its early opinions such as those on international personality of international organizations,[70] the effect of treaty reservation,[71] and legal questions relating to South West Africa,[72] one of its recent advisory opinions, among others, is of particular importance.

In the *Legality of the Threat or Use of Nuclear Weapons* case, the Court was requested by resolution 49/75 K adopted by the General Assembly on 15 December 1994 to render an advisory opinion on the following question: "Is the threat or use of nuclear weapons in any circumstance permitted under international law?"[73]

Before that case, in 1993, the World Health Organization (WHO) by the decision of its Assembly submitted a similar request to the Court for an advisory opinion.[74] Its question was stated as follows: "In view of the health and environmental effects, would the use of nuclear weapons by a State in war or other

69 *Ibid.*, p. 71.

70 *Reparation for Injuries Suffered in the Service of the United Nations, Advisory Opinion: I.C.J. Reports 1949*, p. 174.

71 *Reservations to the Convention on the Prevention and Punishment of the Crime of Genocide, Advisory Opinion: I.C.J. Reports 1951*, p. 15.

72 *International status of South West Africa, Advisory Opinion: I.C.J. Reports 1950*, p. 128; *Legal Consequences for States of the Continued Presence of South Africa in Namibia (South West Africa) notwithstanding Security Council Resolution 276 (1970), Advisory Opinion, I.C.J. Reports 1971*, p. 16.

73 *Legality of the Threat or Use of Nuclear Weapons, Advisory Opinion, I.C.J. Reports 1996*, p. 228, para 1.

74 *Legality of the Use by a State of Nuclear Weapons in Armed Conflict, Advisory Opinion, I.C.J. Reports 1996*, p. 66.

armed conflict be a breach of its obligations under international law including the WHO Constitution?"

The Court first examined the three conditions for a specialized agency to request an advisory opinion from the Court: the agency must be duly authorized by the General Assembly of the United Nations; the opinion must be on a legal question; the question must be one arising from the activities of the requesting agency.

On the first condition, the Count noted Article 76 of the WHO Constitution. It reads as follows:

> Upon authorization by the General Assembly of the United Nations or upon authorization in accordance with any agreement between the Organization and the United Nations, the Organization may request the International Court of Justice for an advisory opinion on any legal question arising within the competence of the Organization.

This provision, among others, provides due authorization to the WHO to make such request.

On the legal nature of the question raised in the request, the Court held that the political aspects of a dispute did not suffice to deprive the Court of a competence expressly conferred on it by its Statute.[75] The Court referred to its earlier ruling in the Opinion it gave in the case concerning the *Interpretation of the Agreement of 25 March 1951 between the WHO and Egypt*, where it stated that,

> [i]ndeed, in situations in which political considerations are prominent it may be particularly necessary for an international organization to obtain an advisory opinion from the Court as to the legal principles applicable with respect to the matter under debate, especially when these may include the interpretation of its constitution.[76]

The Court ascertained that political motive or implication of a request was of no relevance in establishing the jurisdiction of the Court.

Lastly, the Court examined the question whether the WHO's request fell within the scope of its activities. It interpreted the terms of the WHO Constitution in accordance with the rules of treaty law. The Court observed that although, under the mandate of Article 2 of its Constitution, the WHO was

75 *Ibid.*, p. 73, para. 16.

76 *Interpretation of the Agreement of 25 March 1951 between the WHO and Egypt, Advisory Opinion, I.C.J. Reports 1980*, p. 87, para. 33.

responsible to deal with the effects on health of the use of nuclear weapons, or of any other hazardous activity, the question raised by the WHO related *not to the effects* of the use of nuclear weapons on health, but to the legality of the use of such weapons *in view of their health and environmental effects*. Whatever effects nuclear weapons may have, the competence of the WHO to deal with them was not dependent on the legality of the acts that caused them. Accordingly, the Court did not consider that Article 2 of the WHO Constitution could be understood as conferring upon the Organization a competence to address the legality of the use of nuclear weapons, and thus in turn a competence to ask the Court about that.[77]

The Court further analysed the specific mandates of the Organization in the prevention of the effects of nuclear weapons on the health and environment and any possible "implied" power rested with the WHO to address the legality of the use of such weapons. The Court observed that "[i]f, according to the rules on which the United Nations system is based, the WHO has, by virtue of Article 57 of the Charter, 'wide international responsibilities', those responsibilities are necessarily restricted to the sphere of public 'health' and cannot encroach on the responsibilities of other parts of the United Nations system. And there is no doubt that questions concerning the use of force, the regulation of armaments and disarmament are within the competence of the United Nations and lie outside that of the specialized agencies."[78] Besides, the practice of the WHO further bore out that the request did not fall within its activities.

Two years after the WHO made the request for advisory opinion of the Court on the legality of the use of nuclear weapons in armed conflict, the General Assembly decided to raise the question itself to the Court.[79] In both cases, a large number of States submitted written statements. The oral hearings for the two cases were joined. The WHO and 20 States appeared before the Court in the first case and 22 States in the second case.[80]

77 *Legality of the Use by a State of Nuclear Weapons in Armed Conflict, Advisory Opinion, I.C.J. Reports 1996*, p. 76, para. 21.

78 *Ibid.*, p. 80, para. 26.

79 It is interesting to note that the Court delivered its Advisory Opinion on the two cases relating to the legality of the use of nuclear weapons on the same date, i.e. 8 July 1996.

80 In the first case, 35 States made written statements, the WHO and 20 States appeared before the Court in the oral hearings. In the latter case, 28 States submitted written statements, 22 States made oral statements. As the hearings of the two cases were joined, States were invited to state their positions on both requests, if they had submitted written statements in both cases; otherwise, they were only to address the case in which they had chosen to participate. Among the five permanent members of the Security Council, only China did not participate in either case.

Some States raised objections to the competence of the Court in the case, contending that the question was totally unrelated to the activities of the General Assembly.[81] The Court, in addressing that issue, stated that,

> the General Assembly has competence in any event to seise the Court. This is because, Article 10 of the Charter has conferred upon the General Assembly a competence relating to "any questions or any matters" within the scope of the Charter. Article 11 of the Charter has specifically provided the General Assembly with a competence to "consider the general principles... in the maintenance of international peace and security, including the principles governing disarmament and the regulation of armaments."[82]

Moreover, the Court considered that the General Assembly had a longstanding interest in the disarmament process. It has adopted resolutions on nuclear weapons, held three special sessions on disarmament (1978, 1982 and 1988), and commissioned studies on the effects of the use of nuclear weapons.

On the legal nature of the question, the Court reiterated its established jurisprudence that,

> the political nature of the motives which may be said to have inspired the request and the political implications that the opinion given might have are of no relevance in the establishment of its jurisdiction to give such an opinion.[83]

The Court considered that it was competent to give advisory opinion on *any* legal question, abstract or otherwise.[84] It was not up to the Court to decide

81 The States which raised objections to the competence of the Court in the case argued that the question presented was vague and abstract. Such complex issues were the subject of consideration among interested States and within the other bodies of the United Nations which have an express mandate to deal with such matters. An opinion by the Court in regard to this question would provide no practical assistance to the General Assembly in carrying out its functions under the Charter. Such an opinion had the potential of undermining the progress already achieved or being achieved, therefore, to do so was contrary to the interests of the United Nations Organization. *Legality of the Threat or Use of Nuclear Weapons, Advisory Opinion, I.C.J. Reports 1996*, p. 236, para. 15.

82 *Ibid.*, p. 233, para. 11.

83 *Ibid.*, p. 234, para. 13.

84 *Ibid.*, p.236, para. 14. See also *Conditions of Admission of a State to Membership in the United Nations (Article 4 of the Charter), Advisory Opinion: I.C.J. Reports 1948*, p. 61; *Effect*

whether and to what extent an opinion may be of use for the General Assembly. The Court maintained that, unless there were compelling reasons, the Court should not refuse to exercise its advisory competence; as the principal juridical organ, such function represented its participation in the activities of the Organization.[85]

On the nature of its opinion, the Court clarified that it just stated the existing law, but did not legislate. In stating and applying the law, the Court necessarily had to specify its scope and sometimes note its general trend.[86] Thus, the Court upheld its competence to deliver an opinion on the question presented by the General Assembly.

As in contentious cases, in advisory proceedings, the Court will determine its competence first. It has the power to clarify or reformulate the question presented to it. Unless there are compelling reasons, it should not refuse to discharge its judicial task by addressing the question submitted to it by the competent organs or specialized agencies of the United Nations, as that exercise represents its participation in the work of the United Nations.

There are certain situations, however, in which the Court is mindful of judicial propriety by declining to exercise its competence. The most relevant principle is *audiatur et altera pars*; that is to say, if a request relates to a pending dispute between two States or between a State and an international organization, the Court, without the consent of the States concerned, would not exercise its advisory power to give an opinion. This is to avoid the possibility

---

of Awards of Compensation Made by the United Nations Administrative Tribunal, Advisory Opinion, I.C.J. Reports 1954, p. 51; *Legal Consequences for States of the Continued Presence of South Africa in Namibia (South West Africa) notwithstanding Security Council resolution 276 (1970), Advisory Opinion, I.C.J. Reports 1971*, p. 27, para. 40.

85 In the Opinion, the Court cited the following precedents: *Interpretation of Peace Treaties with Bulgaria, Hungary and Romania, First Phase, Advisory Opinion, I.C.J. Reports 1950*, p. 71; *Reservations to the Convention on the Prevention and Punishment of the Crime of Genocide, Advisory Opinion, I.C.J. Reports 1951*, p. 19; *Judgments of the Administrative Tribunal of the ILO upon Complaints Made against Unesco, Advisory Opinion, I.C.J. Reports 1956*, p. 86; *Certain Expenses of the United Nations (Article 17, paragraph 2, of the Charter), Advisory Opinion, I.C.J. Reports 1962*, p. 155; *Applicability of Article VI, Section 22, of the Convention on the Privileges and Immunities of the United Nations, Advisory Opinion, I.C.J. Reports 1989*, p. 189, para. 31.

86 *Legality of the Threat or Use of Nuclear Weapons, Advisory Opinion, I.C.J. Reports 1996*, p. 236, para. 18.

that advisory proceedings be misused or abused for contentious cases. The basic principle of consent also applies to the advisory jurisdiction.[87]

It should be noted that the effects of advisory opinions are *erga omnes*. The Court's pronouncement on the state of the rules of international law and its trend of development has broad implications for international law. The competence of the Court in advisory proceedings should therefore be taken seriously.

Apart from instituting advisory proceedings, an international organization may also, upon the invitation of the Court, furnish information to the Court in advisory proceedings instituted by other international organizations.[88]

3 Jurisdictional Issues in Incidental Proceedings

This sub-section will briefly discuss some incidental proceedings, where the question of jurisdiction may also arise. Jurisdiction is provided for in the Statute and the Rules of Court for some incidental actions, but not all. The Court has developed a set of case law for such proceedings.

a *Interim Protection*

Under Article 41 of the Statute and Article 75 of the Rules of Court,[89] the Court has the power to indicate provisional measures during the legal proceedings.

87 The first case in which the principle was applied was *Eastern Carelia case* by the Permanent Court. The case concerned a dispute between a State and the requesting international organization. However, in some cases, where a dispute involving the relevant question was pending, the Court did not decline to exercise its competence on the ground of judicial propriety. See *Applicability of Article VI, Section 22, of the Convention on the Privileges and Immunities of the United Nations, Advisory Opinion, I.C.J. Reports 1989*, pp. 190–191, paras. 37–39; *Legal Consequences of the Construction of a Wall in the Occupied Palestinian Territory, Advisory Opinion, I.C.J. Reports 2004*, p. 159, para. 50.

88 See Article 66, paragraph 2, of the Statute. For example, in the case concerning *Legal Consequences of the Construction of a Wall in the Occupied Palestinian Territory*, the Court permitted the League of Arab States and the Organization of the Islamic Conference to submit both written and oral statements. See *Legal Consequences of the Construction of a Wall in the Occupied Palestinian Territory, Advisory Opinion, I.C.J. Reports 2004*, p. 142, para. 6.

89 Article 41, paragraph 1, of the Statute reads: "The Court shall have the power to indicate, if it considers that circumstances so require, any provisional measures which ought to be taken to preserve the respective rights of either party."
Article 75, paragraphs 1 and 2, of the Rules of Court provide:

It may, at the request of one of the parties, or by itself, *proprio motu*, after examining the circumstance of the case, indicate such measures. The Court will determine whether and what provisional measures should be granted in light of the particular circumstances of the case. It may wholly or partly satisfy the request of the applicant. Moreover, even if the provisional measures are requested by the applicant, the Court may nevertheless order both of the parties to comply with the measures it has indicated. In short, the power of the Court in providing interim protection is quite substantial.[90]

It is clear that a request for the indication of provisional measures can be raised only after an application is instituted. Subject to the special circumstances of the case, the applicant may submit a request for the indication of provisional measures immediately after the filing of the application, when the Court has not yet decided whether it has jurisdiction on the merits of the case. This kind of situation often occurs in cases concerning armed conflicts, serious human rights violations, and environmental damage.[91]

Once a request for the indication of provisional measures is duly submitted to the Court, the Court should immediately consider it. According to Article 74, paragraph 1, of the Rules of Court, a request for the indication of provisional measures shall have priority over all other cases. In other words, the Court should put aside all the other cases at hand and deal with the request without any delay.

After the Court indicates provisional measures, a party may, upon a change of circumstances, request the Court to modify the order. The Court

---

1 The Court may at any time decide to examine *proprio motu* whether the circumstances of the case require the indication of provisional measures which ought to be taken or complied with by any or all of the parties.

2 When a request for provisional measures has been made, the Court may indicate measures that are in whole or in part other than those requested, or that ought to be taken or complied with by the party which has itself made the request....

90 On the binding effect of an order indicating provisional measures, see *LaGrand* (*Germany* v. *United States of America*), *Provisional Measures, Order of 3 March 1999, I.C.J. Reports 1999*, p. 16, para. 28.

91 For instance, *LaGrand* (*Germany* v. *United States of America*), *Provisional Measures, Order of 3 March 1999, I.C.J. Reports 1999*, p. 9; *Military and Paramilitary Activities in and against Nicaragua* (*Nicaragua* v. *United States of America*), *Provisional Measures, Order of 10 May 1984, I.C.J. Reports 1984*, p. 169; *Certain Activities Carried Out by Nicaragua in the Border Area* (*Costa Rica* v. *Nicaragua*), *Provisional Measures, Order of 8 March 2011, I.C.J. Reports 2011*, p. 6; *Pulp Mills on the River Uruguay* (*Argentina* v. *Uruguay*), *Provisional Measures, Order of 13 July 2006, I.C.J. Reports 2006*, p. 113.

will examine the facts and decide whether to change or maintain the measures.[92]

As required by Article 38, paragraph 2, of the Rules of Court, the applicant should "specify as far as possible the legal grounds upon which the jurisdiction of the Court is said to be based." In the case of a request for provisional measures, the question of jurisdiction is also the preliminary issue that the Court has to dispose first. Together with the jurisdictional grounds, the Court should also determine whether the necessary preconditions are satisfied, e.g. the existence of a legal dispute at the time of the filing of the application, prior negotiations or other conditions that should be fulfilled. However, at this stage, the Court need not finally satisfy itself that it has jurisdiction on the merits of the case, but only decide whether it has *prima facie* jurisdiction for the purpose of considering the request.

In the *Pulp Mills* (*Argentina* v. *Uruguay*) case, Argentina made a request for the indication of provisional measures on the same date it filed the application.[93] It based the jurisdiction of the Court on Article 36, paragraph 1, of the Statute of the Court and on the first paragraph of Article 60 of the 1975 Statute of the River Uruguay, a treaty it had concluded with Uruguay. Article 60 of the said treaty provided: "Any dispute concerning the interpretation or application of the [1961] Treaty and the [1975] Statute which cannot be settled by direct negotiations may be submitted by either party to the International Court of Justice." Argentina claimed that negotiations had failed.

The Court stated in its Order of 13 July 2006 that,

> in dealing with a request for provisional measures, the Court need not finally satisfy itself that it has jurisdiction on the merits of the case, but will not indicate such measures unless the provisions invoked by the applicant appear, prima facie, to afford a basis on which the jurisdiction of the Court might be established (see *Armed Activities on the Territory of the Congo* (*New Application: 2002*) (*Democratic Republic of the Congo* v. *Rwanda*), *Provisional Measures, Order of 10 July 2002, I.C.J. Reports 2002*, p. 241, para. 58).[94]

---

92 See *Certain Activities Carried Out by Nicaragua in the Border Area* (*Costa Rica* v. *Nicaragua*); *Construction of a Road in Costa Rica along the San Juan River* (*Nicaragua* v. *Costa Rica*), *Order of 16 July 2013, Provisional Measures, I.C.J. Reports 2013*, p. 230.

93 *Pulp Mills on the River Uruguay* (*Argentina* v. *Uruguay*), *Provisional Measures, Order of 13 July 2006, I.C.J. Reports 2006*, p. 113.

94 *Ibid.*, pp. 128–129, para. 57.

The term used by the Court in this order, "appear, prima facie, to afford a basis on which the jurisdiction of the Court might be established," suggests a very low threshold on the question of jurisdiction.

The Court noted that Uruguay did not deny that the Court had jurisdiction under Article 60 of the 1975 Statute, but contended such jurisdiction did not cover the rights claimed by Argentina. The Court further noted, however, that the parties were in agreement that the Court had jurisdiction with regard to the rights to which Article 60 of the 1975 Statute applied. The Court considered that it needed not at this stage of the proceedings further address the issue raised by Uruguay, and therefore, it found that it had *prima facie* jurisdiction under Article 60 of the 1975 Statute to deal with the merits and could address Argentina's request for provisional measures.[95]

As the Court does not give a final ruling on the question of jurisdiction during the proceedings for provisional measures, the respondent may none the less subsequently raise preliminary objections to the jurisdiction of the Court. Only at that stage will the Court finally decide on the jurisdictional issue. There can be situations where the Court finds at the provisional measures stage that it has *prima facie* jurisdiction, but decides later that the jurisdictional ground as claimed by the applicant is unfounded.

For example, in the case concerning *Application of the International Convention on the Elimination of all Forms of Racial Discrimination*, after filing its application, Georgia asked the Court to indicate provisional measures.[96] It relied on the sole jurisdictional ground of Article 22, the compromissory clause of the International Convention on the Elimination of All Forms of Racial Discrimination (CERD). Georgia claimed that both States were party to CERD and neither of them appended any reservation to Article 22. Regarding subject-matter jurisdiction, it argued that ethnic discrimination was and had been a key aspect in the conflicts in South Ossetia and Abkhazia and the present case was particularly about the ethnic cleansing.

Upon examination of the facts presented by the parties, the Court first drew the conclusion that there existed a dispute between the parties capable of falling within the provisions of CERD at the time of the filing of the application, which was a necessary condition for the Court to have *prima facie* jurisdiction under Article 22 of CERD. Next, the Court ascertained whether the preconditions provided for in Article 22 were satisfied. On the negotiation requirement,

95 *Ibid.*, p. 129, para. 59.

96 *Application of the International Convention on the Elimination of all Forms of Racial Discrimination (Georgia* v. *Russian Federation), Provisional Measures, Order of 15 October 2008, I.C.J. Reports 2008*, p. 353.

it is interesting to note the following paragraph from the Order of 15 October 2008:

> Whereas it is apparent from the case file that such issues (racial discrimination) have been raised in bilateral contacts between the Parties, and, that these issues have manifestly not been resolved by negotiation prior to the filing of the Application; whereas, in several representations to the United Nations Security Council in the days before the filing of the Application, those same issues were raised by Georgia and commented upon by the Russian Federation; whereas therefore the Russian Federation was made aware of Georgia's position in that regard; and whereas the fact that CERD has not been specifically mentioned in a bilateral or multilateral context is not an obstacle to the seisin of the Court on the basis of Article 22 of the Convention.[97]

This paragraph apparently suggested that the precondition of negotiation was met. The Court, in light of the above considerations, concluded that, *prima facie*, it had jurisdiction under Article 22 of CERD to deal with the case to the extent that the subject-matter of the dispute related to the "interpretation or application" of the Convention.[98]

Subsequently Russia raised preliminary objections to the jurisdiction of the Court, and the case entered the preliminary stage to address the question of jurisdiction first.[99] After examining the evidence submitted to the Court, the Court found that there existed a dispute between the parties relating to Russia's compliance with its obligations under CERD. On the meaning of Article 22, the Court specifically addressed what constituted negotiations; their adequate form and substance; and the extent of negotiations that was required for the fulfilment of the precondition under Article 22. In light of those considerations, the Court concluded that the facts in the record showed that during the relevant period, namely, between 9 August and 12 August 2008, when there existed between the parties a legal dispute capable of falling under CERD, Georgia did not attempt to negotiate CERD-related matters with Russia. Consequently, Georgia and Russia did not engage in negotiations or resort to other means indicated in Article 22 with respect to the latter's compliance with its

97 *Ibid.*, p. 388, para. 115.

98 *Ibid.*, p. 388, para. 117.

99 *Application of the International Convention on the Elimination of All Forms of Racial Discrimination (Georgia* v. *Russian Federation), Preliminary Objections, Judgment, I.C.J. Reports 2011*, p. 70.

substantive obligations under CERD. Based on that finding, the Court decided that, as the preconditions in Article 22 were not met, the Court's jurisdiction in the present case was not founded. By virtue of this final decision, the Order of 15 October 2008 on provisional measures ceased to be effective.

b *Intervention*

In municipal legal systems, when a third party's right or interest is involved, the court may order the third party to appear so as to defend its own right or interest. In international law, however, no State is under an obligation to appear before the Court, as the Court affirmed in the *Continental Shelf* (*Libyan Arab Jamahiriya/Malta*) case: in the Court's procedure, there is no compulsory intervention system whereby a third State could be cited by the Court to come in as a party.[100] Whether to submit a request for intervention is a voluntary act on the part of a third State. The principal parties in the case may raise objections to such intervention, but it is for the Court to decide whether the request should be permitted.[101]

1 Intervention under Article 62

Under Article 62 of the Statute, a third State may request a permission to intervene in a contentious case.[102] By the case law of the Court, a third State may request to intervene as a party or a non-party. In the former case, the consent of the parties must be obtained so as to found the necessary jurisdictional link between the intervening State and the principal parties. In other words, the intervening procedure should also satisfy the consensual basis of jurisdiction. In the case concerning *Land, Island and Maritime Frontier Dispute*, the Court stated that, "the competence given to the Court in Article 62 of the Statute is not extendable to making an intervener a party to the case unless the parties

100 *Continental Shelf* (*Libyan Arab Jamahiriya/Malta*), *Application to Intervene, Judgment, I.C.J. Reports 1984*, p. 25, para. 40.

101 Even when all the conditions are satisfied under Article 62 or 63 of the Statute, the Court retains certain discretion to reject an application. This is because for the good administration of justice, the Court may consider that to permit the intervention may not be conducive to the conduct of its judicial function. Notwithstanding, the Court has to make sure that the legal interest of the third party will not be adversely affected by its decision in the case.

102 Article 62 provides that: "Should a State consider that it has an interest of a legal nature which may be affected by the decision in the case, it may submit a request to the Court to be permitted to intervene."

to the case have consented to the change."[103] If the intervening State becomes a party to the case, the decision of the Court in the case will have the same binding effect on the intervening party as on the principal parties. All the procedural rights and obligations equally apply to the third party.

In the latter case, if a third State only wishes to intervene as a non-party to provide information in order to protect its rights and interests, Article 62 of the Statute will sufficiently serve as the jurisdictional basis between the intervening party and the principal parties. No additional jurisdictional basis is needed. On its rationale, the Court, again, in the case concerning *Land, Island and Maritime Frontier Dispute*, gave the following explanation:

> [P]rocedures for a "third" State to intervene in a case are provided in Articles 62 and 63 of the Court's Statute. The competence of the Court in this matter of intervention is not, like its competence to hear and determine the dispute referred to it, derived from the consent of the parties to the case, but from the consent given by them, in becoming parties to the Court's Statute, to the Court's exercise of its powers conferred by the Statute... the Court has the competence to permit an intervention even though it be opposed by one or both of the parties to the case; as the Court stated in 1984, "the opposition [to an intervention] of the parties to a case is, though very important, no more than one element to be taken into account by the Court" (*I.C.J. Reports 1984*, p. 28, para. 46.)[104]

When two States are in a dispute, for example, about land or maritime boundary, it often happens that their claims may overlap with the claim of a third State or third States. Such situation certainly arises not only in the event of territorial disputes, but also in other disputes as well. Naturally the third State can institute separate proceedings on the same subject to obtain its own judgment. That would nevertheless likely give rise to complicated situations. Economically speaking, it would not be wise to have multiple litigations for the same subject-matter. Besides, in practice, the judgments obtained may not always be consistent. So far as the Court is concerned, it must refrain from making any pronouncement in a judgment that may prejudice the right of a third State.

103 *Land, Island and Maritime Frontier Dispute (El Salvador/Honduras), Application for Permission to Intervene, Judgment, I.C.J. Reports 1990*, p. 135, para. 99.

104 *Ibid.*, p. 133, para. 96.

In practice, under certain circumstances, the Court may not be aware of the existence of the interests of a third party or the Court's decision would in any event have an irreversible effect on the interest of a third State. As is observed, intervention procedure serves

> the need for the avoidance of repetitive litigation as well as the need for harmony of principle, for a multiplicity of cases involving the same subject-matter could result in contradictory determinations which obscure rather than clarify the applicable law.[105]

The third party intervention, as an incidental procedure, depends on the principal case. If the Court decides that it has no jurisdiction in the case, or the claim of the application is inadmissible, the third party intervention automatically lapses. In the *Nuclear Tests* cases, for example, on 16 May 1973 Fiji filed in the Registry of the Court a request under Article 62 of the Statute to be permitted to intervene in the main proceedings. As the Court had to first deal with France's objections to the jurisdiction of the Court, it decided to defer its consideration of Fiji's request until the Court had pronounced upon the question of jurisdiction.[106] The Court ultimately found that the claim of Australia no longer had any object and that the Court was therefore not called upon to give a decision thereon. As a result, Fiji's request to intervene became moot.

Articles 81 to 86 of the Rules of Court lay down the specific rules for the application for intervention. Among others, the requesting party must submit its request as soon as possible, but not later than the closure of the written proceedings. Only under exceptional circumstances may a late submission be admitted.

Third party intervention was rarely practiced during the time of the PCIJ. Starting with the *Nuclear Tests* cases, there have been nine cases in which requests for permission to intervene under Article 62 were formally submitted to the Court, among which three requests were granted.[107] The first case is the

105 *Sovereignty over Pulau Ligitan and Pulau Sipadan (Indonesia/Malaysia), Application for Permission to Intervene, Judgment, I.C.J. Reports 2001*, Separate Opinion of Judge *ad hoc* Weeramantry, p. 636, para. 17.

106 *Nuclear Tests (Australia* v. *France), Judgment, I.C.J. Reports 1974*, p. 255, para. 7; *Nuclear Tests (New Zealand* v. *France), Judgment, I.C.J. Reports 1974*, p. 459, para. 7.

107 Nicaragua was granted permission to intervene in the *Land, Island and Maritime Frontier Dispute (El Salvador/Honduras)*; Equatorial Guinea intervened in the *Land and Maritime Boundary between Cameroon and Nigeria (Cameroon* v. *Nigeria)*; Greece did so in *Jurisdictional Immunities of the State (Germany* v. *Italy)*.

Land, Island and Maritime Frontier Dispute (*El Salvador/Honduras*).[108] At the request of the parties by a special agreement, a Chamber was formed with five judges to adjudicate the dispute between the parties over land boundary, title over islands and maritime spaces. In due course, Nicaragua filed an application in the Registry for permission to intervene. It first raised the issue whether its request should be heard by the full Court or by the Chamber. The Court found that it was for the Chamber to decide whether Nicaragua's request should be granted. Of the two parties, Honduras raised no objection to Nicaragua's request, while El Salvador asked the Court to deny Nicaragua's request.

Pursuant to Article 84, paragraph 2, of the Rules of Court, in case there is any objection from the parties or one of the parties to a request for intervention, oral hearings should be held. During the hearings, Nicaragua asked the Court to limit the scope of its jurisdiction to land boundary between the parties and refrain from exercising its power to determine the maritime area within the Gulf of Fonseca and in the Pacific Ocean. It claimed that, otherwise, such delimitation would affect Nicaragua's interests.

In the judgment, the Chamber affirmed the principle that if a State could satisfy the Court that it had an interest of a legal nature which may be affected by the decision in the case, it may be permitted to intervene. Such permission, however, should be limited to that State's interests only. The intervening party is not permitted to make excursions into other aspects of the case.

If a State intervenes as a party, it will be bound, as the parties to the case, by the judgment of the Court with regard to the decision relating to its interests. If it intervenes as a non-party, simply to furnish information to the Court as to where its interests lie, it is not bound by the judgment. So far, all the intervening States that were permitted to intervene under Article 62 entered the respective cases as a non-party.

2 Intervention under Article 63

In addition to Article 62, there is another kind of intervention provided under Article 63. A State intervening under that provision may not have a legal interest in the case, but has an interest in the interpretation of a treaty which would be construed by the Court in the case.[109]

108 *Land, Island and Maritime Frontier Dispute* (*El Salvador/Honduras*), *Application for Permission to intervene, Judgment, I.C.J. Reports 1990*, p. 92.

109 Article 63 states that
"1. Whenever the construction of a convention to which States other than those concerned in the case are parties is in question, the Registrar shall notify all such States forthwith.

Intervention under Article 63 can be regarded as a special intervention. The interest of the intervening party only relates to the construction of a convention for the adjudication of the dispute. All the State parties to the convention have the right to intervene in such capacity. For that purpose, the Registrar of the Court is under a legal obligation to notify the State parties to the convention in question of the case.

In the *Nuclear Tests* (*New Zealand* v. *France*) case (Request for an Examination of the Situation), New Zealand in 1995 filed an application against France in the Court, with a request to examine the situation of France's nuclear tests in the region.[110] Five States requested to intervene, under Article 62 and Article 63.[111] The Court did not permit any of these requests.

In the *Whaling in the Antarctic* (*Australia* v. *Japan*) case, Australia filed an application in the Court against Japan's scientific whaling programmes for the alleged violations of the 1946 International Convention for the Regulation of Whaling. New Zealand filed with the Registry of the Court a Declaration of Intervention in the case under Article 63, paragraph 2, of the Statute. In its Declaration, New Zealand stated that it "avail[ed] itself of the right ... to intervene as a non-party in the proceedings brought by Australia against Japan in this case."[112] As neither of the parties raised any objection to New Zealand's Declaration, no oral hearings were held, but the parties made written observations on the Declaration. With the Court's permission to intervene, New Zealand further submitted written observations on the construction of the Convention, on which Japan made observations. Australia reserved its right to make observations on some points in New Zealand's written observations during the oral proceedings. New Zealand took part in the oral proceedings to present its views on the construction of the Whaling Convention.

According to Article 63, paragraph 2, once into the case, New Zealand as an intervening State was bound by the construction of the Convention as given by the Court in the final judgment.

---

2. Every State so notified has the right to intervene in the proceedings; but if it uses this right, the construction given by the judgment will be equally binding upon it."

110 *Request for an Examination of the Situation in Accordance with Paragraph 63 of the Court's Judgment of 20 December 1974 in the* Nuclear Tests (New Zealand *v.* France) *Case (New Zealand* v. *France), I.C.J. Reports 1995*, p. 288.

111 Australia requested to intervene under Article 62, while Samoa, the Solomon Islands, the Marshall Islands and Micronesia requested to intervene under Article 62 and Article 63.

112 *Whaling in the Antarctic (Australia* v. *Japan: New Zealand intervening), Judgment, I.C.J. Reports 2014*, p. 235, para. 8.

In the case concerning *Fisheries Jurisdiction* (*Spain* v. *Canada*), the 1978 Convention on Future Multilateral Cooperation in the Northwest Atlantic Fisheries might have been in question in the case.[113] Due to its exclusive competence in matters relating to fisheries for the member States, the European Community was a party to the Convention. At the jurisdictional stage, no notification was sent to the European Community. Whether it could intervene under Article 63 is an interesting question, because there is no provision on that issue in the Statute and the Rules of Court. Ultimately, the Court found that it had no jurisdiction in the case, so the matter did not come up in practice.

That event led to the subsequent amendment to Article 43 of the Rules of Court in 2005. Two new paragraphs that were added to the Article read as follows:

> 2. Whenever the construction of a convention to which a public international organization is a party may be in question in a case before the Court, the Court shall consider whether the Registrar shall so notify the public organization concerned. Every public international organization notified by the Registrar may submit its observations on the particular provisions of the convention the construction of which is in question in the case.
>
> 3. If a public organization sees fit to furnish its observations under paragraph 2 of this Article, the procedure to be followed shall be that provided for in Article 69, paragraph 12, of these Rules.

This amendment extends the scope of intervention under Article 63 of the Statute to all public international organizations. It should be noted, however, that the Court still has to take a decision on the matter in each case.

c *Counter-Claims*

In the case of counter-claims, Article 80 of the Rules of Court provides that "the Court may entertain a counter-claim only if it comes within the jurisdiction of the Court and is directly connected with the subject-matter of the claim of the other party." A counter-claim should be contained in the Counter-Memorial of the respondent. The applicant therefore preserves its right to give its views on the counter-claim. The applicant may raise objections to the jurisdiction

113 *Fisheries Jurisdiction (Spain* v. *Canada), Jurisdiction of the Court, Judgment, I.C.J. Reports 1998*, p. 432.

of the Court over the subject-matter of the counter-claims and the admissibility of the counter-claims, if it deems that the counter-claims are not directly connected with the subject-matter of the claims in the principal proceedings. In that case, the Court will take a decision on the admissibility of the counter-claims after hearing the parties.

In the case concerning *Certain Activities Carried Out by Nicaragua in the Border Area* (*Costa Rica* v. *Nicaragua*), Nicaragua, the respondent, in its Counter-Memorial raised four counter-claims against the applicant. Costa Rica raised objections to the admissibility of three of the counter-claims, while reserving its right to comment on the fourth.[114]

In its Order on counter-claims, the Court first recalled the two requirements under Article 80 of the Rules of Court and its judicial practice in that regard. It noted that counter-claims were autonomous legal acts the object of which was to submit new claims to the Court. Therefore, the Court had to first of all decide whether it had jurisdiction to adjudicate these new claims. Moreover, as new claims, the subject-matter of the counter-claims must be directly connected with the subject-matter of the principal claims of the case. These two requirements have been followed in the jurisprudence of the Court.[115] The Court underscored that, in the earlier cases, the matter was mostly considered as of admissibility, but in this context the issue concerned both jurisdiction and admissibility.[116]

On the question of jurisdiction, the Court found that the first counter-claim was the same as the issue raised by Nicaragua in the case concerning *Construction of a Road in Costa Rica along the San Juan River* (*Nicaragua* v.

114 *Certain Activities Carried Out by Nicaragua in the Border Area* (*Costa Rica* v. *Nicaragua*); *Construction of a Road in Costa Rica along the San Juan River* (*Nicaragua* v. *Costa Rica*), *Counter-Claims, Order of 18 April 2013, I.C.J. Reports 2013*, p. 202, para. 10.

115 See, for example, *Application of the Convention on the Prevention and Punishment of the Crime of Genocide* (*Bosnia and Herzegovina* v. *Yugoslavia*), *Counter-Claims, Order of 17 December 1997, I.C.J. Reports 1997*, pp. 257–258, para. 31.

116 *Certain Activities Carried Out by Nicaragua in the Border Area* (*Costa Rica* v. *Nicaragua*); *Construction of a Road in Costa Rica along the San Juan River* (*Nicaragua* v. *Costa Rica*), *Counter-Claims, Order of 18 April 2013, I.C.J. Reports 2013*, p. 208, para. 20. The Court noted that in the earlier cases, the Court usually treated the issue as a matter of admissibility, see *Oil Platforms* (*Islamic Republic of Iran* v. *United States of America*), *Counter-Claim, Order of 10 March 1998, I.C.J. Reports 1998*, p. 203, para. 33; *Armed Activities on the Territory of the Congo* (*Democratic Republic of the Congo* v. *Uganda*), *Counter-Claims, Order of 29 November 2001, I.C.J. Reports 2001*, p. 678, para. 35.

Costa Rica). Since that case was joined with the present case by the Court,[117] the Court considered it appropriate to address that question in the joint cases. On the other two counter-claims, the Court mainly examined whether they were directly connected with the subject-matter of the claims in the principal proceedings.[118]

117 *Construction of a Road in Costa Rica along the San Juan River* (*Nicaragua* v. *Costa Rica*), *Joinder of Proceedings, Order of 17 April 2013, I.C.J. Reports 2013*, p. 184.

118 *Certain Activities Carried Out by Nicaragua in the Border Area* (*Costa Rica* v. *Nicaragua*); *Construction of a Road in Costa Rica along the San Juan River* (*Nicaragua* v. *Costa Rica*), *Counter-Claims, Order of 18 April 2013, I.C.J. Reports 2013*, pp. 208–215, paras. 22–38.

CHAPTER VII

Subject-matter Jurisdiction and Temporal Jurisdiction

In this part, two classifications of jurisdictional bases, subject-matter jurisdiction, *ratione materiae,* and temporal jurisdiction, *ratione temporis,* will be discussed. Temporal jurisdiction normally arises when the obligation in question has temporal limitations; therefore, it is often examined together with the question of the subject-matter jurisdiction and the admissibility of the claims.

1 Jurisdiction *ratione materiae*

a *The Concept of Subject-matter Jurisdiction*

The subject-matter jurisdiction refers to the substance of a case over which the Court has the competence to adjudicate. When a State seises the Court, instituting proceedings, it has to make sure that the subject-matter it wishes the Court to adjudicate falls within the scope of the jurisdiction of the Court. In the jurisprudence of the Court, the concept of the subject-matter jurisdiction is often linked with the following concepts: "the subject of an application," "the subject(-matter) of a dispute" and "the subject(-matter) of a case." These concepts are not identical, but inherently interconnected. So it is not surprising that they are often used interchangeably in legal writings. The term "the subject of an application" refers to the legal matter upon which the applicant wishes the Court to adjudicate. It underscores the substance of the whole case, for example, the boundary delimitation, or maritime disputes, etc. In contrast with the term "the subject of the case," which should be determined by the Court, the subject of an application is defined by the applicant. The two may, or may not, refer to the same matter. For instance, in the case concerning *Obligation to Prosecute or Extradite*, Belgium claimed that the subject of the dispute between Senegal and itself concerned Senegal's violations of its obligations under the Convention against Torture and customary international law.[1] On the basis of the evidence, however, the Court found that the subject of the dispute was about Senegal's alleged violations of the Convention

1 *Questions relating to the Obligation to Prosecute or Extradite* (*Belgium* v. *Senegal*), *Judgment, I.C.J. Reports 2012*, p. 422.

 | DOI 10.1163/9789004342767_008

against Torture, but not related to international obligations with regard to other international crimes under customary international law.

The term "the subject of a dispute" is a general reference to the matter on which the parties have conflicting legal claims. Because the essence of judicial adjudication is about settlement of a dispute, the subject of a dispute is also referred to as the subject of a case. In that sense there is no difference between the two terms. When the Court refers to "the subject-matter" of a dispute, its emphasis is on the specific substance with which that dispute is concerned, for instance, use of force, territorial disputes, overlapping maritime claims, State succession, diplomatic protection, sovereign immunity, etc. When a case involves complicated matters with various issues in dispute, the Court has to identify whether any, some, or all, of the claims fall within its jurisdiction. In the *Georgia* v. *Russian Federation* case, the situation between the parties involved use of force, repatriation of refugees, peace-keeping operations, and internal ethnic conflicts. Because Georgia based the jurisdiction of the Court on the compromissory clause of the International Convention on the Elimination of All Forms of Racial Discrimination (CERD), the Court had to find whether any dispute between the parties related to racial discrimination, the subject-matter of CERD. If so, that subject-matter would be covered by CERD, thus falling within the jurisdiction of the Court. If the dispute was about armed conflict and peace-keeping operations, it would not concern the interpretation or application of CERD, thus falling outside the Court's jurisdiction.

The terms "the subject of a case," "the subject of a dispute," or "the subject-matter of a case" in a specific case, once determined by the Court, often refer to the same substance. It is in the examination of a specific dispute that the Court will be able to consider and determine whether the parties have, by any of the means as provided for in the Statute and the Rules of Court, conferred jurisdiction *ratione materiae* on the Court.

Article 36, paragraph 1, of the Statute defines the scope of the subject-matter jurisdiction of the Court in a broadest possible term. It covers "*all cases* which the parties refer to it and *all matters* specially provided for in the Charter of the United Nations or in treaties and conventions in force." These terms "all cases" and "all matters" literally mean that the Court can deal with all categories of cases that are governed by international law. This scope is more specifically spelt out in the following paragraph of Article 36; such jurisdiction concerns:

a. the interpretation of a treaty;
b. any question of international law;
c. the existence of any fact which, if established, would constitute a breach of an international obligation;

d. the nature or extent of the reparation to be made for the breach of an international obligation.

In accepting the compulsory jurisdiction of the Court, a State, subject to the reservations and conditions it may attach to its declaration, confers jurisdiction on the Court for any subject-matter that is governed by international law.

This mandate of the Court is apparently very different from that of municipal courts, the jurisdiction of which is divided by the subject-matters, e.g. criminal, civil, administrative, family, labour, intellectual property, juvenile crimes, etc. It is also different from other international judicial organs, for example, the International Tribunal for the Law of the Sea (ITLOS), the International Criminal Tribunal for the former Yugoslavia (ICTY), the International Criminal Court (ICC), the European Court of Justice and regional courts of human rights. ITLOS specially deals with maritime matters relating to the interpretation and application of the United Nations Convention on the Law of the Sea. In a way, it is a special court on the law of the sea. The ICTY is an *ad hoc* tribunal for the prosecution and punishment of crimes committed in the former Yugoslavia during its dissolution process. The ICC is a permanent international criminal court. Both of these criminal courts are concerned with individual criminal responsibility. The subject-matter jurisdiction of these courts is limited to criminal offences of individuals.[2] With regard to regional courts, their subject-matter jurisdiction is restricted to their regional affairs or human rights matters in the region.

The ICJ, as the principal judicial organ of the United Nations, is empowered by the Statute to adjudicate upon any cases that States may wish to bring to the Court for settlement in accordance with international law. That explains why States, after ITLOS was founded, may still choose to institute proceedings in the ICJ to settle their maritime disputes. The Court has also dealt with human rights cases, but the subject-matter of such cases directly relates to the responsibility of States for the violation of their international obligations.[3]

2 Although the ICJ has also dealt with cases on genocide, the subject-matter of these cases mainly concerns the interpretation and application of the Genocide Convention and the State responsibility for any breach of the obligations thereunder.

3 For example, *LaGrand (Germany* v. *United States of America), Judgment, I.C.J. Reports 2001*, p. 466; *Avena and Other Mexican Nationals (Mexico* v. *United States of America), Judgment, I.C.J. Reports 2004*, p. 12; *Ahmadou Sadio Diallo (Republic of Guinea* v. *Democratic Republic of the Congo), Preliminary Objections, Judgment, I.C.J. Reports 2007*, p. 582.

Since its inception, the Court has dealt with a wide range of cases, covering almost every field of international law. This is particularly evident in the cases that were instituted in the Court in the post-Cold War period.

b *The Title of Jurisdiction*

Another concept connected to the subject-matter jurisdiction is the title of jurisdiction. In the Court's judgments, the term "the title of jurisdiction" occasionally appears. It refers to the source of power by which the Court has the right to adjudicate. In its broad sense, the term covers various legal instruments, including the Charter, the Statute, the Rules of Court, and the particular instrument(s), on the basis of which the applicant party submits its case to the Court. In the narrow sense, it specifically refers to "the legal grounds upon which the jurisdiction of the Court is said to be based."[4] In interpreting these legal instruments, the Court would examine the subject-matter of the case and decide whether it is governed by the relevant instrument. Therefore, the title of jurisdiction concerns the jurisdictional grounds in each case.[5]

Generally speaking, jurisdictional grounds based on the Optional Clause declarations by the parties mainly concern the reciprocal scope of the consent of the parties. However, if the reservations attached thereto intend to exclude certain subject-matters from the scope of the jurisdiction of the Court, or set a time limit for the application of the declaration, the Court may have to decide whether the subject-matter of the dispute between the parties is excluded by such reservations from the jurisdiction *ratione materiae* or *ratione temporis* of the Court. In the case concerning *Obligations concerning Negotiations relating to Cessation of the Nuclear Arms Race and to Nuclear Disarmament* (*Marshall Islands* v. *India*), India invoked its reservations attached to its Optional Clause declaration, arguing that the application filed by the Marshall Islands fell outside the jurisdiction of the Court, because the subject-matter of the dispute is excluded by India's reservations. In its pleadings, India referred to, *inter alia*, the following reservations:

> India ... accept[s] ... the jurisdiction of the International Court of Justice over all disputes other than:
>
> (3) disputes in regard to matters which are essentially within the domestic jurisdiction of the Republic of India;
>
> (4) disputes relating to or connected with facts or situations of hostilities, armed conflicts, individual or collective actions taken in

4 Article 38, paragraph 2, of the Rules of Court.

5 See Shabtai Rosenne, *The Law and Practice of the International Court, 1920–2005*, *Vol. II, Jurisdiction*, 4th edition, Martinus Nijhoff Publishers, 2006, pp. 903–906.

> self-defence, resistance to aggression, fulfilment of obligations imposed by international bodies, and other similar or related acts, measures or situations in which India is, has been or may in future be involved.[6]

So far as jurisdiction *ratione materiae* is concerned, the question depends on the determination of the subject-matter of the dispute.

On the subject-matter jurisdiction, the Pact of Bogotá, although providing for compulsory jurisdiction of the Court for the State parties, excludes certain matters from the subject-matter jurisdiction of the Court. Notwithstanding its similar terms with Article 36, paragraph 2, its scope of subject-matter jurisdiction is narrower both in time and in substance. According to Article VI of the Pact,[7] matters that were "already settled by arrangement between the parties" or "governed by agreements or treaties in force" on the date of the conclusion of the Pact, namely, 30 April 1948, should not be subject to the procedures laid down therein, including recourse to the ICJ. In the *Obligation to Negotiate Access* (*Bolivia* v. *Chile*) case, Bolivia relied on the Pact of Bogotá as the basis of the Court's jurisdiction.[8] Chile raised objections to the subject-matter jurisdiction of the Court. It claimed that the matters between Bolivia and itself had already been settled by the 1904 Peace Treaty between the two countries. According to Article VI of the Pact, therefore, the Court lacked jurisdiction *ratione materiae* to decide on the merits of the case.

After examining the positions of the parties, the Court was of the view that, given the subject-matter of the dispute it had identified, the 1904 Peace Treaty did not address the question raised by Bolivia. Therefore, the matters in dispute were neither "settled by arrangement between the parties, or by arbitral award or by decision of an international court" nor "governed by agreements or treaties in force on the date of the conclusion of the [Pact of Bogotá]" within the meaning of Article VI of the Pact. This necessarily led to the Court's conclusion that the dispute fell within the subject-matter jurisdiction of the Court.

Normally, the issue of subject-matter jurisdiction should not arise if a case is submitted to the Court by a special agreement concluded between the parties,

6 *Obligations concerning Negotiations relating to Cessation of the Nuclear Arms Race and to Nuclear Disarmament* (*Marshall Islands* v. *India*), Counter-Memorial of India, p. 25, para. 51.

7 Article VI of the Pact of Bogotá reads: "The ... procedures [laid down in the Pact of Bogotá] ... may not be applied to matters already settled by arrangement between the parties, or by arbitral award or by decision of an international court, or which are governed by agreements or treaties in force on the date of the conclusion of the present Treaty."

8 *Obligation to Negotiate Access to the Pacific Ocean* (*Bolivia* v. *Chile*), *Preliminary Objections, Judgment.*

as the subject-matter of their dispute should be specified in the agreement. In practice, what should be submitted to the Court for settlement could by itself have been the very subject-matter of bilateral negotiations between the parties. In the *Pedra Branca* (*Malaysia/Singapore*) case, the parties spent several years negotiating to find an agreement as to how many disputed territorial features they should include in the special agreement for the settlement by the ICJ. When they reached the agreement clarifying the scope of the dispute, the subject-matter jurisdiction of the Court was thereby ascertained. The Court, in determining its jurisdiction in the case, gave effect to the terms of the agreement.

In practice, however, there are also cases, where the parties hold different views as to the scope of the jurisdiction they had conferred on the Court.[9] Before proceeding to the merits, the Court has to ascertain its jurisdiction *ratione materiae*. In the case concerning the *Land, Island and Maritime Frontier Dispute*, the parties agreed to submit their territorial dispute over islands to the Chamber for settlement.[10] During the proceedings, however, Honduras took the view that, by the terms of the General Treaty of Peace and the same terms of Article 2, paragraph 2, of the special agreement, the jurisdiction of the Chamber should be limited to the islands which were in dispute at the time that the General Treaty of Peace was concluded, namely, islands of Meanguera and Meanguerita, but not El Tigre, El Salvador's claim over which was made only after the General Treaty was concluded.

The Chamber considered that, under both instruments, the task for the settlement explicitly extended to "all the islands." The question whether a given island was in dispute was relevant, not to the question of the existence of such jurisdiction, but to that of its exercise. The Chamber considered the date for the determination of the matter should be the date at which the parties concluded the special agreement, rather than the date at which the General Treaty was concluded.

Obviously, Honduras' claim essentially challenged the scope of the Court's jurisdiction, but not the jurisdiction *per se*, in other words whether the Court should extend its jurisdiction to determine the sovereignty over the El Tigre Island.[11]

9 For example, in the *Corfu Channel* case, Albania contended that the special agreement between the parties did not include the question of compensation, therefore, the Court did not have jurisdiction in the third phase of the case. Consequently Albania refused to appear before the Court. See *Corfu Channel case* (*United Kingdom* v. *Albania*), *Judgment of December 15th, 1949: I.C.J. Reports 1949*, p. 244.

10 *Land, Island and Maritime Frontier Dispute* (*El Salvador/Honduras: Nicaragua intervening*), *Judgment, I.C.J. Reports 1992*, p. 351.

11 *Ibid.*, pp. 553–557, paras. 323–330.

In the case of *forum prorogatum*, after the respondent reacts positively to the application, the case enters the General List of the Court. Theoretically, when the respondent accepts the invitation of the applicant to submit their dispute to the jurisdiction of the Court, it means that the parties have reached a kind of agreement by two "intersecting unilateral declarations." The scope of the subject-matter should be defined by the terms of the application. However, in reality if the respondent does not have the same understanding as the applicant of the description of the dispute in the application, the parties would likely end up in a dispute over the scope of the subject-matter that they wish the Court to settle. In the case concerning *Certain Questions of Mutual Assistance*, the parties held different positions on the scope of the Court's jurisdiction *ratione materiae*.[12] France gave a narrow interpretation to the subject of the dispute, confining it solely to France's refusal to execute the letter rogatory issued by Djibouti on 3 November 2004, and excluding all other allegations. It maintained that Djibouti's Memorial went beyond the claims formulated in the application, expanding the subject of the dispute. It insisted that the Court's jurisdiction "must be determined exclusively on the basis of the submissions," not on the claims.[13]

Djibouti, for its part, acknowledged that the extent of the Court's jurisdiction was "strictly delimited" *ratione materiae* by the terms of the application. It, however, rejected France's claim that its expansion of claims in the Memorial had changed the subject of the application.[14]

The Court noted that "[t]he consent allowing for the Court to assume jurisdiction must be certain. That is so, no more and no less, for jurisdiction based on *forum prorogatum*."[15] Although the applicant is required to state "the precise nature of the claim" and "the facts and grounds on which the claim is based" in the application, the Court emphasized that in determining the subject of the dispute, one should discern it from reading the whole application, and not confining oneself to the section heading of the application.

This is the first case where the Court's jurisdiction was established on the basis of *forum prorogatum* under Article 38, paragraph 5, of the Rules of Court. The Court took a quite liberal stand on the scope of the subject-matter of the dispute by including all the relevant legal actions conducted by the French authorities against the high-ranking officials of Djibouti. Thus it had a relatively broad scope of jurisdiction *ratione materiae* on the merits of the case.

---

12 *Certain Questions of Mutual Assistance in Criminal Matters (Djibouti* v. *France), Judgment, I.C.J. Reports 2008*, p. 177.

13 *Ibid.*, pp. 201–202, paras. 51–55.

14 *Ibid.*, pp. 202–203, paras. 56–59.

15 *Ibid.*, p. 204, para. 62.

When the title of jurisdiction is a compromissory clause of a treaty, the subject-matter of the dispute often concerns interpretation or application of the treaty. To determine whether the Court has jurisdiction *ratione materiae* in the case, the Court has to determine whether the dispute between the parties, if extant, concerns the interpretation or application of the treaty. The compromissory clause of the treaty in question gives the title of jurisdiction to the Court.

In the *Oil Platforms* case, Iran filed claims against the United States in respect of a dispute "aris[ing] out of the attack [on] and destruction of three offshore oil production complexes, owned and operated for commercial purposes by the National Iranian Oil Company, by several warships of the United States Navy on 19 October 1987 and 18 April 1988, respectively."[16] These acts, in its view, constituted a "fundamental breach" of various provisions of the Treaty of Amity, Economic Relations and Consular Rights between the United States of America and Iran concluded in 1955 (the 1955 Treaty). Iran invoked the compromissory clause, Article XXI, paragraph 2, of the Treaty as the basis of the Court's jurisdiction. Within the time-limit fixed for the filing of the Counter-Memorial, the United States raised a preliminary objection to the jurisdiction of the Court. It maintained that the application bore no relation to the 1955 Treaty. The dispute between the parties did not fall within the provisions of Article XXI, paragraph 2, of the Treaty, and consequently the Court lacked jurisdiction to deal with it.[17]

On the substance of the matter, the United States' objection was two-fold. One concerned the applicability of the 1955 Treaty in the event of use of force. The other related to the scope of the articles invoked by Iran. Both of them dictated the scope of the Court's jurisdiction *ratione materiae*.

On the first aspect, the United States argued that, regardless of the characterization of the incidents of armed conflict, the dispute between the parties related to the lawfulness of actions by naval forces of the United States that "involved combat operations," while the Treaty of Amity and Commerce was intended to regulate and assure fair and non-discriminatory treatment of the nationals of one of the parties in the territory of the other. It maintained that there was no relationship between these two different matters. Therefore, the 1955 Treaty was not applicable.[18]

16 *Oil Platforms* (*Islamic Republic of Iran* v. *United States of America*), *Preliminary Objection, Judgment, I.C.J. Reports 1996*, p. 805, para. 1.

17 *Ibid.*, p. 809, para. 14.

18 *Ibid.*, pp. 810–811, para. 18.

Iran contended that the dispute related to the interpretation and application of the 1955 Treaty, and that, therefore, the objection raised by the United States should be rejected.[19]

The Court first noted that the 1955 Treaty had a broad scope of provisions governing the relations between the two countries. It did not preclude any matters from the scope of the Treaty. By its nature, the Court considered that:

> The Treaty of 1955 imposes on each of the Parties various obligations on a variety of matters. Any action by one of the Parties that is incompatible with those obligations is unlawful, regardless of the means by which it is brought about. A violation of the rights of one party under the Treaty by means of the use of force is as unlawful as would be a violation by administrative decision or by any other means. Matters relating to the use of force are therefore not *per se* excluded from the reach of the Treaty of 1955.[20]

The second aspect of the United States' position was conditional on the answer to the first one. If the Court decided that the 1955 Treaty was applicable to the dispute, the next issue would be whether the provisions invoked by Iran were applicable to the case, a question which required the interpretation of the Treaty.

Iran claimed that the actions which it alleged against the United States were such as to constitute a breach of the provisions of the Treaty and the Court consequently had jurisdiction *ratione materiae* to entertain the application.[21]

Based on the rules of customary international law on treaty interpretation as expressed in Article 31 of the 1969 Vienna Convention on the Law of Treaties, the Court examined, one by one, the three provisions referred to by Iran,

---

19 *Ibid.*, p. 811, para. 19.

20 *Ibid.*, pp. 811–812, para. 21.

21 In its application, Iran invoked Article I, Article IV, paragraph 1, and Article X, paragraph 1, of the Treaty.

Article I reads: "There shall be firm and enduring peace and sincere friendship between the United States ... and Iran."

Article IV, paragraph 1, provides that: "Each High Contracting Party shall at all times accord fair and equitable treatment to nationals and companies of the other High Contracting Party, and to their property and enterprises; shall refrain from applying unreasonable or discriminatory measures that would impair their legally acquired rights and interests; and shall assure that their lawful contractual rights are afforded effective means of enforcement, in conformity with the applicable laws."

Article X, paragraph 1, stipulates that: "Between the territories of the two High Contracting Parties there shall be freedom of commerce and navigation."

in light of the object and purpose of the Treaty. On the first provision, Article I, the Court found that the objective of peace and friendship proclaimed in Article I of the 1955 Treaty was to throw light on the interpretation of the other Treaty provisions, and by itself it could not, taken in isolation, be a basis for the jurisdiction of the Court.[22] With regard to the second article, Article IV, paragraph 1, the Court considered that the article mainly dealt with the treatment of natural and legal persons in the exercise of their private or professional activities. It did not cover the alleged actions in the case, so it could not form the basis of the Court's jurisdiction.[23]

The third provision, Article X, paragraph 1, concerned the freedom of commerce and navigation. The whole debate between the parties focused on the term "commerce." Iran argued that the term "commerce" was a general reference, not limited to maritime commerce. The United States, on the other hand, contended that the word must be understood as being confined to maritime commerce between the two countries, referring solely to the actual sale or exchange of goods.[24]

Upon the examination of the other articles in the 1955 Treaty, the Court considered that although the provision primarily concerned maritime commerce, the 1955 Treaty as a whole related to trade and commerce in general, and was not one restricted purely to maritime commerce. The provision should therefore be interpreted in that light.[25] The Court then gave an elaborate interpretation to the word "commerce," observing that whether the word "commerce" was taken in its ordinary sense or in its legal meaning, at the domestic or international level, it had a broader meaning than the mere reference to purchase and sale.[26] Moreover, the Treaty itself covered a wide variety of matters ancillary to

22 *Oil Platforms (Islamic Republic of Iran* v. *United States of America), Preliminary Objection, Judgment, I.C.J. Reports 1996*, pp. 813–815, paras. 27–31.

23 *Ibid.*, p. 816, paras. 35–36.

24 *Ibid.*, p. 817, paras. 39–40.

25 *Ibid.*, p. 817, paras. 41–43.

26 In its judgment, the Court cited a series of authoritative dictionaries with regard to the term "commerce." It stated that "The word 'commerce' is not restricted in ordinary usage to the mere act of purchase and sale; it has connotations that extend beyond mere purchase and sale to include 'the whole of the transactions, arrangements, etc., therein involved' (Oxford English Dictionary, 1989, Vol. 3, p. 552)." It further referred to the law dictionary to define it in legal terms: according to *Black Dictionary*, "this term is not restricted to mere purchase and sale because it can refer to 'not only the purchase, sale, and exchange of commodities, but also the instrumentalities and agencies by which it is promoted and the means and appliances by which it is carried on, and transportation of persons as well as of goods, both by land and sea' (*Black's Law Dictionary*, 1990,

trade and commerce. Additionally, Article X, paragraph 1, was intended to protect "the freedom of commerce"; any act which would impede that "freedom" was thereby prohibited. The Court noted that Iran's oil production, a vital part of the country's economy, constituted an important component of its foreign trade. The acts of destruction of the oil platform by the United States was capable of causing adverse effect on Iran's freedom as guaranteed by Article X, paragraph 1, of the 1955 Treaty. The lawfulness of the acts could be evaluated in relation to that paragraph.[27] The Court thereby concluded that there existed a dispute relating to the interpretation and application of Article X, paragraph 1, of the 1955 Treaty. The dispute fell within the scope of the compromissory clause of the Treaty, and consequently the Court had the jurisdiction *ratione materiae* to entertain the case.

This case illustrates that when the title of jurisdiction is a compromissory clause of a treaty, the question of jurisdiction *ratione materiae* often requires treaty interpretation on the basis of law and fact.

c *Multiple Titles of Jurisdiction*

It is not uncommon that an application may indicate more than one jurisdictional ground for its case. For example, a State may invoke the declarations made under the Optional Clause and a bilateral agreement as the jurisdictional bases of the Court in the case. If the respondent raises objections to the jurisdiction of the Court, it has to address both titles. Failing to do so with one of the grounds, it would likely be regarded by the Court as an acceptance of that ground as a jurisdictional basis.

When multiple titles of jurisdiction are ascertained by the Court, the subject-matter jurisdiction under each title will be determined by the scope of the relevant instrument. In the *Military and Paramilitary Activities* case, Nicaragua invoked the Optional Clause declarations of the parties as the jurisdictional ground in its application and added as a complementary jurisdictional ground in its Memorial Article XXIV of the 1956 Treaty of Friendship,

---

p. 269)." Furthermore, it looked at the French interpretation: "Similarly, the expression 'international commerce' designates, in its true sense, 'all transactions of import and export, relationships of exchange, purchase, sale, transport, and financial operations between nations' and sometimes even 'all economic, political, intellectual relations between States and between their nationals' (Jules Basdevant (ed.), *Dictionnaire de la terminologie du droit international*, Sirey, 1960, p. 126 [translation by the Registry])." See *ibid.*, p. 818, para. 45.

27 *Ibid.*, p. 820, para. 51.

Commerce and Navigation between the United States of America.[28] After the Court found that it had jurisdiction in the case under the Optional Clause declarations and the reservation attached by the United States to its Optional Clause declaration did not affect the jurisdiction of the Court under the 1956 Treaty, it went on to examine Nicaragua's second jurisdictional ground.[29]

In rejecting the applicability of Article XXIV of the Treaty to the case,[30] the United States contended that, if the basis of jurisdiction of the Court was limited to the Treaty, since Nicaragua's application presented no claims of any violations of it, there were no claims properly before the Court for adjudication. In order to establish the Court's jurisdiction over the present dispute under the Treaty, Nicaragua must establish a reasonable connection between the Treaty and the claims submitted to the Court. However, in its view, Nicaragua could not establish such a connection.[31]

Nicaragua argued that the Treaty in question provided a subsidiary, but independent, basis for the Court's jurisdiction to adjudicate the claims presented in the application. It argued that the United States indeed breached its obligations under Articles I, XIV, XVII, XIX and XX of the Treaty by conducting military and paramilitary activities in and against Nicaragua.[32]

The Court first of all stated that although the Statute provided that the applicant should in its application indicate "as far as possible" the legal grounds it wished to rely on for the Court's adjudication of the case, it may nevertheless bring to the attention of the Court an additional ground of jurisdiction later, provided that it met two conditions: it intended to proceed on that basis; the result of the addition was not to transform the dispute brought before the Court into another dispute, which was different in character.[33]

---

28 The Treaty was signed at Managua on 21 January 1956. See *Military and Paramilitary Activities in and against Nicaragua (Nicaragua* v. *United States of America), Jurisdiction and Admissibility, Judgment, I.C.J. Reports 1984*, p. 392.

29 *Ibid.*, p. 426, para. 77.

30 Article XXIV, paragraph 2, of the 1956 Treaty reads as follows: "Any dispute between the Parties as to the interpretation or application of the present Treaty, not satisfactorily adjusted by diplomacy, shall be submitted to the International Court of Justice, unless the Parties agree to settlement by some other pacific means."

31 *Military and Paramilitary Activities in and against Nicaragua (Nicaragua* v. *United States of America), Jurisdiction and Admissibility, Judgment, I.C.J. Reports 1984*, p. 427, para. 81.

32 *Ibid.*, p. 428, para. 82. These articles relate to freedom of commerce and navigation, non-discriminative treatment of imports and exports, freedom of transit, and equitable treatment of interests and property of natural and legal persons.

33 *Ibid.*, p. 427, para. 80, citing *Société Commerciale de Belgique, P.C.I.J., Series A/B, No. 78*, p. 173.

Regarding the subject-matter jurisdiction, the Court noted that the subject-matter of the Treaty related to the freedom of commerce and navigation and the Preamble of the Treaty referred to peace and friendship. Given the circumstances of the case and the facts stated in the application, it was of the view that there was clearly a dispute between the parties relating to the interpretation or application of the Treaty. Moreover, the fact that Nicaragua had not expressly referred in the negotiation with the United States to the 1956 Treaty for the violations by the United States did not bar Nicaragua from invoking the compromissory clause of the Treaty. By its conduct, the United States should have been aware of Nicaragua's allegation before the case was instituted. That procedural defect did not constitute an obstacle to the jurisdiction of the Court.[34] Consequently the Court concluded that it had jurisdiction under that Treaty to entertain the claims in the application.

The factual background of this case shows that the reason why Nicaragua added one more jurisdictional basis is that it feared that, should its declaration made under the Optional Clause be found defective,[35] the Court could dismiss the case for lack of jurisdiction. The 1956 Treaty would be a more reliable jurisdictional basis to secure that the case would be heard by the Court. The military and paramilitary activities conducted in and against Nicaragua apparently related to the question of peace and security, and normal conduct of commerce and trade between the two countries.

There are also situations where an application indicates two titles of jurisdiction, but the Court finds that the subject-matter of the dispute submitted by the applicant only falls within the scope of one ground. For instance, in the case concerning *Obligation to Prosecute or Extradite*, to establish the Court's jurisdiction, Belgium relied on the compromissory clause of the Convention against Torture and the parties' declarations under Article 36, paragraph 2, of the Statute.[36] Neither party had attached any reservation that excluded the subject-matter of torture from the scope of the Court's jurisdiction. Senegal's

34 On that point, the Permanent Court held that "the Court cannot allow itself to be hampered by a mere defect of form, the removal of which depends solely on the party concerned." *Certain German Interests in Polish Upper Silesia, Jurisdiction, Judgment No. 6, 1925, P.C.I.J., Series A, No. 6*, p. 14.

35 It was believed that the instrument of ratification of the Court's jurisdiction by Nicaragua by mistake was never sent. In this case, however, Nicaragua argues otherwise, expressly reiterating its acceptance of the Court's jurisdiction. *Military and Paramilitary Activities in and against Nicaragua (Nicaragua* v. *United States of America), Jurisdiction and Admissibility, Judgment, I.C.J. Reports 1984*, pp. 413–415, paras. 48–51.

36 *Questions relating to the Obligation to Prosecute or Extradite (Belgium* v. *Senegal), Judgment, I.C.J. Reports 2012*, p. 422.

objections to the jurisdiction of the Court mainly concerned the existence of a dispute and the preconditions as set forth in the compromissory clause of the Convention against Torture.

The Court found that, at the time when Belgium instituted proceedings, the dispute between the parties did not relate to breaches of obligations under customary international law, but only to Senegal's obligation to prosecute or extradite Mr. Habré under the Torture Convention. Therefore, the subject-matter of the dispute, in the Court's view, concerned only crimes of torture, but not other international crimes under customary international law.[37] The subject-matter jurisdiction of the Court in the case was thus limited to the interpretation and application of the Convention against Torture.

In order to rely on multiple bases of jurisdiction, a party should expressly indicate in the application or even at a later stage that it intends to proceed on those grounds for the adjudication of the case. In the case of *Certain Norwegian Loans* (*France* v. *Norway*), France filed an application against Norway in the Court for certain loans.[38] It referred to the parties' declarations under Article 36, paragraph 2, of the Statute as the basis of the Court's jurisdiction. Norway in due course raised preliminary objections, claiming that France's application was inadmissible. In its observations and submissions on Norway's preliminary objections and during the oral proceedings, France also relied on the Franco-Norwegian Arbitration Convention of 1904 and the General Act of Geneva of September 26th, 1928, to which both France and Norway were parties, as additional grounds of jurisdiction. France argued that the two Governments had agreed to submit their disputes to arbitration or judicial settlement in certain circumstances.[39] The Court, however, did not accept France's position. Referring to the two conventions mentioned by France, the Court stated that:

> Neither of these references, however, can be regarded as sufficient to justify the view that the Application of the French Government was, so far as the question of jurisdiction is concerned, based upon the Convention or the General Act. If the French Government had intended to proceed upon that basis it would expressly have so stated.[40]

37 *Ibid.*, p. 445, para. 55.

38 *Case of Certain Norwegian Loans, Judgment of July 6th, 1957: I.C.J. Reports 1957*, p. 9.

39 *Ibid.*, pp. 24–25.

40 *Ibid.*, p. 25.

It is apparent that in this case the Court did not consider France's reference to the two conventions as an indication of additional jurisdictional grounds. The question is not only about its belated reference to the two conventions. More importantly, France failed to show any intention that it would proceed upon those jurisdictional grounds, in addition to the parties' declarations.

d *Identification of the Subject-matter*

So far as the subject-matter jurisdiction is concerned, the Court has to determine the subject-matter of the dispute based on the facts presented before it and identify the link between the subject-matter of the dispute as stated in the application and the subject-matter of the applicable law as invoked. A typical case is the *Georgia* v. *Russian Federation* case. With regard to the applicability of the compromissory clause, the parties did not dispute that they were party to CERD and that at the time when the alleged acts occurred, CERD was applicable to both of them. What was really at issue was whether the dispute between the parties concerned racial discrimination. Therefore, what had to be decided for the jurisdiction of the Court was whether the Court had the subject-matter jurisdiction on the basis of the compromissory clause of CERD.

The question of jurisdiction *ratione materiae* also arose in the *Pulp Mills* (*Argentina* v. *Uruguay*) case.[41] In that case, Argentina relied on Article 60 of the 1975 Statute of the River Uruguay as the jurisdictional ground. The 1975 Statute was concluded between the parties after they drew the boundary in 1961 as a measure of protection of their boundary river—River Uruguay.[42] Article 60 of the 1975 Statute reads:

> Any dispute concerning the interpretation or application of the Treaty 1 and the Statute which cannot be settled by direct negotiations may be submitted by either party to the International Court of Justice.

In the proceedings, the parties differed as to whether all the claims advanced by Argentina fell within the ambit of the compromissory clause.

Uruguay accepted that the Court's jurisdiction under the compromissory clause extended to claims concerning any pollution or type of harm caused to River Uruguay, or to organisms living there, in violation of the 1975 Statute. It also acknowledged that the lawfulness of its operation of the pulp mills could be evaluated in accordance with the 1975 Statute. However, it disagreed

41 *Pulp Mills on the River Uruguay* (*Argentina* v. *Uruguay*), *Judgment, I.C.J. Reports 2010*, p. 14.

42 The Montevideo Treaty of 7 April 1961, concerning the boundary constituted by the River Uruguay (635 *UNTS* 98).

that Argentina could rely on the compromissory clause to submit claims regarding every type of environmental damage, such as air pollution, noise, visual and general nuisance, as well as the specific impact on the tourism sector, because they did not concern the interpretation or the application of the 1975 Statute. Therefore, in its opinion, the Court did not have jurisdiction over these matters.[43]

Argentina maintained that Uruguay's position on the scope of the Court's jurisdiction was too narrow. According to Argentina, the 1975 Statute was intended to protect not only the quality of the waters, but more generally its "régime" and the areas affected by it.[44]

To address the differences between the parties on the scope of the subject-matter jurisdiction, the Court considered that the essential criterion for the determination was whether such issues concerned the interpretation or application of the 1975 Statute. In that regard, it stated that:

> In order to determine whether Uruguay has breached its obligations under the 1975 Statute, as alleged by Argentina, the Court will have to interpret its provisions and to determine their scope *ratione materiae*.[45]

That means that the scope of the subject-matter jurisdiction of the Court must coincide with the scope *ratione materiae* of the applicable treaty provisions.

e *Jurisdiction* ratione materiae *and Obligations* erga omnes

With the development of human rights law, in several recent cases,[46] the applicants put forward the claim that given the serious character of the international crimes concerned and universal condemnation, the obligations to prevent and punish such crimes are now obligations *erga omnes*. They further claimed that when dealing with obligations of such character or peremptory

43 *Pulp Mills on the River Uruguay (Argentina* v. *Uruguay), Judgment, I.C.J. Reports 2010*, pp. 40–41, para. 49.

44 *Ibid.*, p. 41, para. 50.

45 *Ibid.*, p. 41, para. 52.

46 See *East Timor (Portugal* v. *Australia), Judgment, I.C.J. Reports 1995*, p. 102, para. 29; *Application of the Convention on the Prevention and Punishment of the Crime of Genocide (Bosnia and Herzegovina* v. *Yugoslavia), Preliminary Objections, Judgment, I.C.J. Reports 1996 (II)*, p. 616, para. 31; *Armed Activities on the Territory of the Congo (New Application: 2002) (Democratic Republic of the Congo* v. *Rwanda), Provisional Measures, Order of 10 July 2002, I.C.J. Reports 2002*, p. 245, para. 71, and *Jurisdiction and Admissibility, Judgment, I.C.J. Reports 2006*, pp. 31–32, para. 64.

norms of international law (*jus cogens*), the Court should exercise its jurisdiction, regardless of the principle of consent.

In 2002, the Democratic Republic of the Congo (the DRC) filed an application in the Court against Rwanda in respect of a dispute concerning "massive, serious and flagrant violations of human rights and of international humanitarian law" which resulted from alleged acts of armed aggression perpetrated by Rwanda on the territory of the DRC. Apart from a number of jurisdictional bases invoked in the application, the DRC claimed that, "Article 66 of the Vienna Convention on the Law of Treaties of 23 May 1969 established the jurisdiction of the Court to settle disputes arising from the violation of peremptory norms (*jus cogens*) in the area of human rights, as those norms were reflected in a number of international instruments."[47] Moreover, it argued that Rwanda's reservation to the compromissory clause of the Genocide Convention was without legal effect.

The Court first of all reaffirmed the principle pronounced in its case law recognizing that certain obligations in international law possessed the character of *erga omnes*.[48] The Court, however, pointed out that "the *erga omnes* character of a norm and the rule of consent to jurisdiction are two different things."[49] The mere fact that rights and obligations *erga omnes* may be at issue in a dispute would not give the Court jurisdiction to entertain that dispute. The same was true with peremptory norms (*jus cogens*). The fact that a dispute related to compliance with a norm having such a character, which was assuredly the case with regard to the prohibition of genocide, could not of itself provide a basis for the jurisdiction of the Court. Under the Court's Statute, jurisdiction was always based on the consent of the parties.[50] The Court further stated that:

47 *Armed Activities on the Territory of the Congo* (*New Application: 2002*) (*Democratic Republic of the Congo* v. *Rwanda*), *Jurisdiction and Admissibility, Judgment, I.C.J. Reports 2006*, p. 12, para. 1.

48 *Reservations to the Convention on the Prevention and Punishment of the Crime of Genocide, Advisory Opinion, I.C.J. Reports 1951*, p. 23.

49 *Armed Activities on the Territory of the Congo* (*New Application: 2002*) (*Democratic Republic of the Congo* v. *Rwanda*), *Jurisdiction and Admissibility, Judgment, I.C.J. Reports 2006*, p. 32, para. 64, referring to *East Timor* (*Portugal* v. *Australia*), *Judgment, I.C.J. Reports 1995*, p. 102, para. 29.

50 *Armed Activities on the Territory of the Congo* (*New Application: 2002*) (*Democratic Republic of the Congo* v. *Rwanda*), *Jurisdiction and Admissibility, Judgment, I.C.J. Reports 2006*, p. 32, para. 64.

> When a compromissory clause in a treaty provides for the Court's jurisdiction, that jurisdiction exists only in respect of the parties to the treaty who are bound by that clause and within the limits set out therein.[51]

On the basis of the above-mentioned principle, the Court decided that Rwanda's reservation to the Genocide Convention could not be regarded as lacking legal effect. Ultimately, the Court found that none of the jurisdictional grounds on which the DRC relied could be established.[52]

2 Jurisdiction *ratione temporis*

As is mentioned above, the title of jurisdiction, be it a declaration, a compromissory clause or any other title, must be valid between the parties at the time when the case is instituted in the Court. The Court's jurisdiction is restricted by the terms of limitation *ratione temporis* attached therein. However, withdrawal or expiration of a declaration under the Optional Clause after the Court is properly seised will not by itself deprive the Court of its jurisdiction.

In the *Nottebohm* case, Guatemala accepted the compulsory jurisdiction of the Court for a period of five years from 27 January 1947 to 26 January 1952.[53] On 17 December 1951, before that period expired, Liechtenstein instituted proceedings against it in the Court. On the question of jurisdiction *ratione temporis*, Guatemala claimed that as its declaration expired on 26 January 1952, from that moment the ICJ had no jurisdiction to treat, elucidate or decide cases which would affect Guatemala, except if Guatemala prolonged the duration of its declaration, or deposited a new declaration with the UN Secretary-General, or signed a special protocol of submission with any other interested State.[54] In other words, it suggested that the case instituted by Liechtenstein be discontinued, since the Court no longer had jurisdiction in the case.

The Court observed that, at the time when the case was filed, the declarations of the parties were both in force. They did not dispute the regularity of the legal action. It was in light of this regularity that the subsequent lapse of the declaration of Guatemala, by reason of the expiry of the period for which it

51 *Ibid.*, p. 32, para. 65.

52 *Ibid.*, p. 52, para. 126.

53 *Nottebohm case (Liechtenstein* v. *Guatemala) (Preliminary Objection), Judgment of November 18th, 1953: I.C.J. Reports 1953*, p. 111.

54 *Ibid.*, p. 115.

was subscribed, in the Court's view, could not invalidate the application.[55] As a consequence, the lapse of Guatemala's declaration could not deprive the Court of the jurisdiction. The Court stated that:

> An extrinsic fact such as the subsequent lapse of the Declaration, by reason of the expiry of the period or by denunciation, cannot deprive the Court of the jurisdiction already established.[56]

The question of temporal jurisdiction may also arise when the jurisdictional basis has a limitation *ratione temporis*. This often happens in the case where a treaty or a declaration specifically states that it does not apply to acts that took place before a certain date. Although generally speaking, treaties, unless otherwise provided, do not apply retroactively,[57] this kind of clause has a particular effect to bar legal actions against certain acts that were supposedly done away with in the past. If the applicant nevertheless files a case for such acts on the basis of a compromissory clause of that treaty, the respondent may raise objections to the Court's jurisdiction *ratione temporis*, or to the admissibility of the application.

In the case concerning *Jurisdictional Immunities of the State* (*Germany* v. *Italy: Greece intervening*), Germany requested the Court to find that Italy had failed to respect the jurisdictional immunity which Germany enjoyed under international law by allowing civil claims to be brought against it in the Italian courts for damage caused to Italy by the German Reich in WWII and by taking measures of constraint against German State property located in Italy.[58] Italy raised no objection of any kind regarding the jurisdiction of the Court and the admissibility of the application. Pursuant to its jurisprudence,[59] the Court nevertheless examined *proprio motu* the question of jurisdiction.

The jurisdictional basis on which Germany relied was Article 1 of the European Convention for the Peaceful Settlement of Disputes (the European Convention). The scope of Article 1 is as broad as that of Article 36, paragraph

55 *Ibid.*, pp. 122–123.

56 *Ibid.*, p. 123.

57 See Article 28 of the Vienna Convention on the Law of Treaties of 1969 on non-retroactivity of treaties.

58 *Jurisdictional Immunities of the State* (*Germany* v. *Italy: Greece intervening*), *Judgment, I.C.J. Reports 2012*, p. 99.

59 See *Appeal relating to the Jurisdiction of the ICAO Council* (*India* v. *Pakistan*), *Judgment, I.C.J. Reports 1972*, p. 52, para. 13. According to that jurisprudence, the Court "must … always be satisfied that it has jurisdiction, and must if necessary go into the matter *proprio motu.*"

2, of the Statute. The Convention entered into force between the parties on 18 April 1961 and remained valid at the time when the case was filed in the Court. Therefore, as far as jurisdiction *ratione personae* and jurisdiction *ratione materiae* were concerned, the Court was competent. However, Article 27, subparagraph (a), of the same Convention provided that the Convention shall not apply to "disputes relating to facts or situations prior to the entry into force of this Convention as between the parties to the dispute." Accordingly, any dispute relating to facts or situations between the parties before 18 April 1961 would not fall within the scope of the Court's jurisdiction *ratione temporis*. In this case, the Court therefore had to decide whether Germany's claims did or did not relate to such facts or situations. If the answer was in the affirmative, the Court would lack jurisdiction *ratione temporis* to adjudicate the dispute.

The Court identified the "facts or situations" of the case that had given rise to the dispute before the Court as Italian judicial decisions that denied Germany the jurisdictional immunity which it claimed, and measures of constraint applied to property belonging to Germany. Those acts which took place between 2004 and 2011 clearly fell within the ambit of the Court's jurisdiction. To dispel any confusion of the present dispute with the question of reparation for the injury caused by the actions of the German armed forces in 1943–1945, the Court further elaborated the subject-matter of the current application. It emphasized that Germany's complaint before the Court was not about the "treatment of that subject-matter" in the judgments of the Italian courts, but about alleged violations of Germany's "immunities from jurisdiction and enforcement."[60] Substantively, the Court here was discussing the subject-matter of the dispute and the jurisdiction *ratione materiae* of the Court, but logically that issue had a direct bearing on the applicability *ratione temporis* of the compromissory clause of the European Convention.

During the proceedings, Italy drew a link between the question of Germany's performance of its obligation to make reparation to the victims and that of the jurisdictional immunity which Germany might rely on before the foreign courts to which those victims applied, in the sense that a State which failed to perform its obligation to make reparation to the victims of grave violations of international humanitarian law, and which offered those victims no effective means of claiming the reparation to which they may be entitled, would be deprived of the right to invoke its jurisdictional immunity before the courts of the State of the victims' nationality. Italy contended that, although its counterclaim on the same facts was dismissed by the Court, that decision none the

60 *Jurisdictional Immunities of the State* (*Germany* v. *Italy: Greece intervening*), *Judgment, I.C.J. Reports 2012*, pp. 118–119, para. 44.

less did not prevent it from using the same argument as a defence against Germany's claim in the main proceedings.[61]

Germany, for its part, argued that the question of reparation claims as stated by Italy fell outside the jurisdiction of the Court by virtue of Article 27 of the European Convention. In its view, "reparation claims do not fall within the subject-matter of the present dispute and do not form part of the present proceedings."[62] Italy's counter-claim that had been dismissed by the Court was based on precisely the same facts that occurred in 1943–1945. Based on the limitation *ratione temporis* of Article 27, Germany argued that Italy's claim should be rejected.

The Court did not directly rule on the question *ratione temporis*, but implicitly took Italy's claim as a defence against Germany' claim, as it proceeded to the merits to address the question raised by Italy: whether the failure of a State to perform completely a duty of reparation which it allegedly bore was capable of having an effect, in law, on the existence and scope of that State's jurisdictional immunity before foreign courts. The Court stated that only when it had drawn a positive conclusion on that question, would it then consider whether, in the specific circumstances of the case, taking account in particular of Germany's conduct on the issue of reparation, the Italian courts had sufficient grounds for setting aside Germany's immunity.[63]

Having identified the scope of customary international law on State immunity, with regard to *acta jure imperii* in general and acts of foreign armed forces in particular, and other claims raised by Italy,[64] the Court concluded that the question whether Germany still had a responsibility towards Italy, or individual Italians, in respect of war crimes and crimes against humanity committed by it during WWII did not affect Germany's entitlement to immunity. Similarly, the Court's ruling on the issue of immunity could have no effect on whatever responsibility Germany may have.[65]

The Court, by drawing a distinction between the issue of whether Germany had a duty of reparation towards the Italian victims of the crimes committed by the German Reich during WWII and the issue of whether a failure to fulfil the duty of reparation should deprive a State of jurisdictional immunities in foreign courts, managed to get around the question of its jurisdiction *ratione*

61 *Ibid.*, pp. 119–120, paras. 45, 47.

62 *Ibid.*, p. 119, para. 46.

63 *Ibid.*, p. 120, para. 50.

64 In this case, the Court also examined Italy's claims relating to the gravity of the violations, the "last resort" argument, and the combined effects of the circumstances.

65 *Jurisdictional Immunities of the State* (Germany v. *Italy: Greece intervening*), *Judgment, I.C.J. Reports 2012*, p. 145, para. 108.

materiae. In a way it shows that the temporal issue is often interwoven with the subject-matter of the case.

Another complicated case is *Croatia* v. *Serbia*.[66] After Croatia instituted proceedings in the Court against Serbia for a dispute relating to Serbia's alleged violations of its obligations under the Genocide Convention, Serbia raised a number of preliminary objections to the jurisdiction of the Court and the admissibility of the application. In its second preliminary objection, Serbia argued that Croatia's claims based on acts and omissions which took place prior to the date when Serbia proclaimed to be a State, were beyond the jurisdiction of the Court and inadmissible.

The title of jurisdiction relied on by Croatia was Article IX of the Genocide Convention. Serbia advanced two reasons to object to the Court's jurisdiction *ratione temporis* and the admissibility of the claim. One was that the Convention entered into force between the parties only on 27 April 1992; the other was that the Convention could not apply to Serbia before it came into existence as a State. Consequently those alleged acts were not attributable to Serbia.[67]

Croatia contended that, even though Serbia came into existence on 27 April 1992, acts prior to that date could still be attributed to it. It referred to Article 10, paragraph 2, of the International Law Commission's Articles on State responsibility regarding insurrectional movement and the principle that "a state in *statu nascendi* is responsible for conduct carried out by its officials and organs or otherwise under its direction and control."[68]

Serbia's objection actually concerned both the question of jurisdiction *ratione temporis* and the issue of admissibility. On these two elements, the Court recalled its observation in the *Oil Platforms* case, where it stated that,

> Objections to admissibility normally take the form of an assertion that, even if the Court has jurisdiction and the facts stated by the applicant State are assumed to be correct, nonetheless there are reasons why the Court should not proceed to an examination of the merits.[69]

In examining the claims of the parties, the Court found that Serbia's second preliminary objection *ratione temporis* presented two inseparable issues. One was the question of applicability of the obligations of the Genocide Convention

66 *Application of the Convention on the Prevention and Punishment of the Crime of Genocide (Croatia* v. *Serbia), Preliminary Objections, Judgment, I.C.J. Reports 2008*, p. 412.

67 *Ibid.*, p. 457, para. 121.

68 *Ibid.*, pp. 458–459, para. 125.

69 *Oil Platforms (Islamic Republic of Iran* v. *United States of America), Judgment, I.C.J. Reports 2003*, p. 177, para. 29.

to Serbia before it came into existence; the other was the admissibility of the claim in relation to the alleged acts. The Court did not consider that it had sufficient evidence before it at the preliminary stage to determine those two questions without to some degree determining issues properly pertaining to the merits. In light of that consideration, the Court concluded that Serbia's preliminary objection *ratione temporis* did not possess, in the circumstances of the case, an exclusively preliminary character.[70] Thus Croatia's claim was left to the merits phase.

In the merits phase, based on the principle of treaty law enshrined in Article 28 of the Vienna Convention on the Law of Treaties, the Court held that "the substantive provisions of the Convention do not impose upon a State obligations in relation to acts said to have occurred before that State became bound by the Convention," and that Serbia was "bound by the Genocide Convention only with effect from 27 April 1992."[71] However, the Court ultimately rejected Serbia's second jurisdictional objection and founded its jurisdiction on the basis of State succession to responsibility under Article IX of the Genocide Convention.[72]

In the two cases above, the question *ratione temporis*, in one way or another, was merged with the merits. In the former case, the temporal limitation of the compromissory clause was overcome by a narrow definition of the subject-matter of the dispute, while in the latter, validity in time of the title of jurisdiction was given different interpretation.[73] The objection *ratione temporis* was considered together with the admissibility of the claim.

---

70 *Application of the Convention on the Prevention and Punishment of the Crime of Genocide (Croatia* v. *Serbia), Preliminary Objections, Judgment, I.C.J. Reports 2008*, p. 460, paras. 129–130.

71 *Application of the Convention on the Prevention and Punishment of the Crime of Genocide (Croatia* v. *Serbia), Merits, Judgment*, paras. 100, 105.

72 *Ibid.*, paras. 106–117. Article IX of the Genocide Convention reads: "Disputes between the Contracting Parties relating to the interpretation, application or fulfilment of the present Convention, including those relating to *the responsibility of a State* for genocide or any of the other acts enumerated in Article 3, shall be submitted to the International Court of Justice at the request of any of the parties to the dispute." (Emphasis added.)

73 The Court reiterated its finding in 1996 regarding the temporal limit of the Genocide Convention by stating that there was no express provision in the Genocide Convention limiting its jurisdiction *ratione temporis*. This is an interesting point, because, with or without such a provision, the treaty status and the legal effect, *ratione temporis*, of a treaty on a State is governed by the law of treaties, i.e., Article 28 of the Vienna Convention on the Law of Treaties.

CHAPTER VIII

Objections to Jurisdiction and Admissibility

As is discussed in Chapter 2, the question of jurisdiction is a matter of substance as well as procedure. A decision on jurisdiction is no less important than a decision on the merits. According to the Charter and the Statute, the jurisdiction of the Court must be founded on the consensual basis of the parties. In the case concerning *Appeal Relating to the Jurisdiction of the ICAO Council* brought up by India against Pakistan in 1971, the Court gave a notable account of the importance of jurisdiction:

(a) Although a jurisdictional decision does not determine the "ultimate merits" of the case, it is a decision of a substantive character, inasmuch as it may decide the whole affair by bringing it to an end, if the finding is against the assumption of jurisdiction. A decision which can have that effect is of scarcely less importance than a decision on the merits, which it either rules out entirely or, alternatively, permits by endorsing the existence of the jurisdictional basis which must form the indispensable foundation of any decision on the merits. A jurisdictional decision is therefore unquestionably a constituent part of the case, viewed as a whole, and should, in principle, be regarded as being on a par with decisions on the merits as regards any right of appeal that may be given.

(b) Nor should it be overlooked that for the party raising a jurisdictional objection, its significance will also lie in the possibility it may offer of avoiding, not only a decision, but even a hearing, on the merits,—a factor which is of prime importance in many cases. An essential point of legal principle is involved here, namely, that a party should not have to give an account of itself on issues of merits before a tribunal which lacks jurisdiction in the matter, or whose jurisdiction has not yet been established.

(c) At the same time, many cases before the Court have shown that although a decision on jurisdiction can never directly decide any question of merits, the issues involved may be by no means divorced from the merits. A jurisdictional decision may often have to touch upon the latter or at least involve some consideration of them. This illustrates the importance of the jurisdictional stage of a case, and the influence it may have on

 | DOI 10.1163/9789004342767_009

> the eventual decision on the merits, if these are reached—a factor well known to parties in litigation.[1]

In dealing with objections to the jurisdiction, the Court must uphold the rules and principles as provided in the Statute and the Rules of Court. This chapter will discuss the procedural aspects of preliminary objections.

1 Jurisdiction as a Matter for the Court to Decide

To institute proceedings in the Court is also called "to seise the Court." After an application is properly received in the Court, and the named respondent State is notified, it is still necessary to have the consent of the latter to accept the jurisdiction of the Court. Only when that happens, can it be said that the Court is validly seised. If, in the event of *forum prorogatum*, the named State does not consent to the jurisdiction of the Court in the case, the case will not enter the General List of the Court.

In the Statute there is no provision referring to preliminary objections, except for Article 36, paragraph 6, which provides that: "In the event of a dispute as to whether the Court had jurisdiction, the matter shall be settled by the decision of the Court." This self-prescribed power is described in scholarly writings as "jurisdiction as to jurisdiction" (in French, compétence de la compétence). That is to say, the Court has the competence to decide whether it has jurisdiction in a case, if the matter is disputed by the parties. This competence can only be exercised in the particular context of each case.

The power of a court to decide on its own competence was originally recognized in the practice of international arbitrations.[2] The idea could be traced back to the Jay Treaty of 1794, under which the arbitration committees appointed therefor were entrusted to determine their own jurisdiction.[3] Later, in

---

1 *Appeal Relating to the Jurisdiction of the ICAO Council (India* v. *Pakistan), Judgment, I.C.J. Reports 1972*, p. 56, para. 18.

2 At the first Hague Conference, the Report of the Rapporteur Baron Descamps stated on this point: "The more arbitration assumes the character of an institution of international common law, the more the power of the arbitrator to decide upon this matter appears to be of the very essence of the arbitral function and one of the inherent requirements for the exercise of this function." Shabtai Rosenne, *The Law and Practice of the International Court, 1920–2005, Vol. II, Jurisdiction*, 4th edition, Martinus Nijhoff Publishers, 2006, p. 814. It is clear that this common law tradition is the root of this practice.

3 Shabtai Rosenne records that when the issue arose for the first time in the modern era in the case of the Betsey (under the Jay Treaty of 1794 between Great Britain and the United States), the British Lord Chancellor, Lord Loughborough, used characteristically forthright language:

the *Alabama Claims* Arbitration, the practice was affirmed. In the *Nottebohm* case, the Court recalled that since the *Alabama* case, it had been a long established rule for an international tribunal to be given the power to decide on its jurisdiction in case there was a dispute between the parties over the jurisdiction of the court, unless the contrary was expressly reserved in advance.[4] Since there exists no superior power to make a decision in case of a dispute on jurisdiction, it would be impossible for any international tribunal to take on its functions without such empowerment; the authority of the judicial organ would be greatly weakened, if not paralysed.[5]

According to Article 38, paragraph 2, of the Rules of Court, an application shall specify as far as possible the legal grounds upon which the jurisdiction of the Court is said to be based, the State against which the claim is brought, and the subject of the dispute. Accordingly, upon receiving the notification of the Registrar, the named State would be in a position to make a preliminary assessment of the fact and law of the case. If the State does not consider that the jurisdictional grounds as claimed by the applicant apply to the present case and therefore the Court has no jurisdiction, or if it disagrees with the applicant on the existence of a dispute relating to the subject-matter of the application, or if it does not deem that the parties have satisfied the preconditions for the seisin of the Court, or if it does not think that the claims submitted in the application are admissible, it may raise objections to the jurisdiction of the Court or to the admissibility of the application.

As is discussed previously, jurisdiction is a matter for the Court to decide. In any event, the Court shall, first of all, satisfy itself that the case in question is set on a solid and sound jurisdictional basis. However, when the respondent State raises objections to the jurisdiction of the Court and the admissibility of the application, the Court has to deal with it according to a special set of rules.

"The doubt respecting the authority of the commissioners to settle their own jurisdiction, was absurd ... they must necessarily decide upon cases being within, or without, their competency." Shabtai Rosenne, *ibid.*, pp. 813–814. See also Chapter 1, pp. 4–5.

4 The Court stated that: "Since the Alabama case, it has been generally recognized, following the earlier precedents, that, in the absence of any agreement to the contrary, an international tribunal has the right to decide as to its own jurisdiction and has the power to interpret for this purpose the instruments which govern that jurisdiction." *Nottebohm case (Liechtenstein v. Guatemala) (Preliminary Objection), Judgment of November 18th, 1953: I.C.J. Reports 1953*, p. 119.

5 See Christian Tomuschat, "Article 36," in Andreas Zimmermann, Karin Oellers-Frahm, Christian Tomuschat, and Christian J. Tams (eds.), *The Statute of the International Court of Justice: A Commentary*, Oxford University Press, 2006, p. 694; see also Shabtai Rosenne, *op. cit. supra* footnote 2, *Vol. II, Jurisdiction*, pp. 813–814.

The respondent may either raise the issue in its Counter-Memorial or raise it separately as preliminary objections.

The Court's Rules on preliminary objections have undergone several stages during the time of the Permanent Court and the current Court.[6] In 2001, the Court, based on its 1976 and 1978 Rules, adopted a complete set of rules on preliminary objections as reflected in the text of Article 79 of the Rules of Court.[7]

Under Article 79, paragraph 2, after the filing of the application but before the time-limits for the written pleadings of the parties are fixed, the Court may, in consultation with the parties, decide to address the questions of jurisdiction and admissibility in the first place and ask the parties to prepare and submit their written pleadings only in that regard. In other words, the Court, *proprio motu*, sets a preliminary stage. In the two cases concerning *Obligations concerning Negotiations relating to Cessation of the Nuclear Arms Race and to Nuclear Disarmament* (*Marshall Islands* v. *India*) (*Marshall Islands* v. *Pakistan*), India and Pakistan, the respondents in the two cases respectively, in their communications with the Court expressed their objections to the jurisdiction of the Court and to the admissibility of the claims raised by the Marshall Islands. Given the views of the parties, the Court decided to resolve first of all the questions of the Court's jurisdiction and the admissibility of the applications before proceeding to the merits. In the Order of 16 June 2014 for the *Marshall Islands* v. *India* case and the Order of 10 July 2014 for the *Marshall Islands* v. *Pakistan* case,[8] the Court instructed the parties to confine their first written pleadings only to the questions of jurisdiction and admissibility.[9]

The power of the Court on the question of jurisdiction can also be observed in the non-appearance cases. When a respondent chooses not to appear before the Court, its position can be regarded by the Court as an objection to the

6 See Shabtai Rosenne, *op. cit. supra* footnote 2, *Vol. II, Jurisdiction*, pp. 829–855.

7 Article 79 of the 1978 Rules was revised substantially, with two new paragraphs, i.e., paragraphs 2 and 3, added to the Article.

8 *Obligations concerning Negotiations relating to Cessation of the Nuclear Arms Race and to Nuclear Disarmament* (*Marshall Islands* v. *India*), *Order of 16 June 2014, I.C.J. Reports 2014*, p. 464; *Obligations concerning Negotiations relating to Cessation of the Nuclear Arms Race and to Nuclear Disarmament* (*Marshall Islands* v. *Pakistan*), *Order of 10 July 2014, I.C.J. Reports 2014*, p. 471.

9 It is interesting to note that in the case brought up by the Marshall Islands against the United Kingdom for the same subject-matter, by the agreement of the parties, the Court did not limit the Memorial of the Marshall Islands only to the question of jurisdiction and admissibility. See *Obligations concerning Negotiations relating to Cessation of the Nuclear Arms Race and to Nuclear Disarmament* (*Marshall Islands* v. *United Kingdom*), *Order of 16 June 2014, I.C.J. Reports 2014*, p. 468.

jurisdiction of the Court, although, more often than not, the respondent would nevertheless communicate with the Court, explicitly stating its objections to the jurisdiction of the Court. The Court may take the non-appearance or the communication of the objecting party as an objection to the jurisdiction of the Court. Pursuant to Article 53, paragraph 2, of the Statute, the Court must satisfy itself that it has jurisdiction in accordance with Articles 36 and 37 of the Statute in the event that a party does not appear, or fails to defend its case. In the two *Fisheries Jurisdiction* (*United Kingdom* v. *Iceland*) (*Federal Republic of Germany* v. *Iceland*) cases, for example, Iceland informed the Court that it was not willing to confer jurisdiction on the Court and would not appoint an Agent. The Court decided to first of all resolve the question of jurisdiction and asked the parties to address the question of jurisdiction in their first written pleadings. In its judgment of 2 February 1973, the Court observed that:

> It is to be regretted that the Government of Iceland has failed to appear in order to plead the objections to the Court's jurisdiction which it is understood to entertain. Nevertheless the Court, in accordance with its Statute and its settled jurisprudence, must examine *proprio motu* the question of its own jurisdiction to consider the Application... Furthermore, in the present case the duty of the Court to make this examination on its own initiative is reinforced by the terms of Article 53 of the Statute of the Court. According to this provision whenever one of the parties does not appear before the Court, or fails to defend its case, the Court, before finding upon the merits, must satisfy itself that it has jurisdiction.[10]

Upon examination of all the documents available, the Court finally came to the conclusion that it had jurisdiction in the two cases.

The same situation happened in the *Nuclear Tests* cases, where after France indicated that it would not accept the Court's jurisdiction in the cases, the Court proceeded to address first of all the questions of jurisdiction and admissibility.[11]

In the incidental proceedings, the question of jurisdiction and admissibility may also arise. When a counter-claim is raised by the respondent, the applicant may object to the jurisdiction of the Court over the subject-matter of

10 *Fisheries Jurisdiction* (*United Kingdom* v. *Iceland*), *Jurisdiction of the Court, Judgment, I.C.J. Reports 1973*, p. 7, para. 12; *Fisheries Jurisdiction* (*Federal Republic of Germany* v. *Iceland*), *Jurisdiction of the Court, Judgment, I.C.J. Reports 1973*, p. 54, para. 13.

11 *Nuclear Tests* (*Australia* v. *France*), *Judgment, I.C.J. Reports 1974*, p. 253; *Nuclear Tests* (*New Zealand* v. *France*), *Judgment, I.C.J. Reports 1974*, p. 457.

the counter-claim. When a request for the indication of provisional measures is submitted, the respondent may object to granting such measures on the ground that the Court has no jurisdiction in the case or the request is inadmissible. In the case where a third State requests to intervene as a party, the parties to the principal case may not give their consent to the jurisdiction of the Court in that regard. In these cases, it is always for the Court to decide on the question of jurisdiction.

2 Preliminary Phase—Possible Bifurcation of the Proceedings

In practice, the respondent may raise its objections either in the Counter-Memorial, or separately before it submits the Counter-Memorial.[12] In the former case, the Court will first dispose of the issue of jurisdiction by dealing with the objections at the beginning of the proceedings, either in the main proceedings or in a separate phase. Should the Court find that it has no jurisdiction in the case, the whole case would be dismissed right there. In the latter situation, the respondent should, pursuant to Article 79, paragraph 1, of the Rules of Court, raise its objections in writing. Such objections are characterized as preliminary objections.

Procedurally, the moment the Registrar receives the written preliminary objections, the proceedings on the merits shall be suspended, which means that the case enters a special phase—preliminary proceedings;[13] the main proceedings as a result are bifurcated. However, if the parties reach an agreement that the preliminary objections raised by the respondent be heard and determined within the framework of the merits, the Court will give effect to such agreement.[14]

On the timing for the submission of preliminary objections, Article 79, paragraph 1, as it currently stands, provides that a preliminary objection shall

12 If the respondent submits the Counter-Memorial, it does not forfeit its right to raise jurisdictional issues during the merits phase, but the proceedings will not be suspended to yield to a special phase on preliminary objections. This approach can shorten the process, and is thus more economical. If the respondent does not raise any objection to jurisdiction, the Court may take it that it has accepted the jurisdiction of the Court.

13 Article 79, paragraph 5, provides that: "Upon receipt by the Registry of a preliminary objection, the proceedings on the merits shall be suspended and the Court, or the President if the Court is not sitting, shall fix the time-limit within which the other party may present a written statement of its observations and submissions; documents in support shall be attached and evidence which it is proposed to produce shall be mentioned."

14 See Article 79, paragraph 10, of the Rules of Court.

be submitted "as soon as possible, and not later than three months after the delivery of the Memorial." Under the 1978 Rules, it is only required that an objection be made within the time-limit fixed for the delivery of the Counter-Memorial. The 2001 amendment reduces the maximum time frame for raising an objection, encouraging the respondent to respond in a swifter manner so as to speed up the whole process of litigation.

Normally after receiving the application from the Court, the respondent would be able to assess and evaluate the case and decide whether it would raise objections, because the application is required to state the subject-matter of the case and specify the legal grounds on which the jurisdiction of the Court is based. In order to have a full view of the case, the respondent may wish to wait till it reads the Memorial so as to appreciate better the factual and legal background of the case before its move. Besides, the preparation of preliminary objections may require some substantial amount of time. Three months after the delivery of the Memorial is a reasonable time limit for the respondent to submit its written pleadings on preliminary objections.

The time limit under Article 79, paragraph 1, is nevertheless not rigid. In the case concerning *Question of the Delimitation of the Continental Shelf between Nicaragua and Colombia beyond 200 Nautical Miles from the Nicaraguan coast*, by the Order of 9 December 2013, the Court fixed 9 December 2014 as the time-limit for the filing of the Memorial of Nicaragua and 9 December 2015 for the filing of the Counter-Memorial of Colombia.[15] On 14 August 2014, before the expiry of the time-limit for the filing of the Memorial of Nicaragua, Colombia raised preliminary objections to the jurisdiction of the Court and to the admissibility of the application. Nicaragua, although surprised at the fact that Colombia's objections were raised four months before the expiry of the time-limit for the filing of its Memorial, did not oppose it, but requested the Court to give it sufficient time to prepare a written statement of its observations and submissions on these objections. Subsequently, the Court, by the Order of 19 September 2014, fixed 19 January 2015 as the time-limit for the presentation by Nicaragua of its written statement of observations.[16]

Under normal circumstances, the respondent would likely put itself at a disadvantage for not waiting to read the Memorial before producing its preliminary objections. Article 79, paragraph 1, requires the respondent to raise its objections "as soon as possible," but it only fixes the maximal time limit, not

15 *Question of the Delimitation of the Continental Shelf between Nicaragua and Colombia beyond 200 Nautical Miles from the Nicaraguan Coast* (*Nicaragua* v. *Colombia*), *Order of 9 December 2013, I.C.J. Reports 2013*, p. 396.

16 *Ibid., Order of 19 September 2014, I.C.J. Reports 2014*, p. 479.

the minimal period. This leaves certain flexibility for the respondent. Nicaragua asked for sufficient time to prepare its statement for fear that Colombia's action might adversely affect the time-limit for itself to prepare the written statement of its observations on the objections. Pursuant to the principle of equality of the parties, the Court must ensure that the amount of time allocated to the parties for the preparation of their pleadings, both written and oral, should always be equal.

In practice, the objecting party could also be the applicant rather the respondent. In that case, by virtue of Article 79, paragraph 1, of the Rules,[17] such objection should be filed within the time-limit fixed for the delivery of its Memorial. A good example is the *Monetary Gold* case.[18] In handling a certain quantity of monetary gold removed by the Germans from Rome in 1943, France, the United Kingdom and the United States agreed to submit the matter to arbitration for the determination of the ownership of the monetary gold. They agreed that, should the arbitrator decide that the gold belonged to Albania, it would be used for partial satisfaction of the judgment in the *Corfu Channel* case. As Italy also claimed the gold,[19] the three Powers agreed that the gold should be transferred to the United Kingdom unless within 90 days from the date of the communication of the arbitrator's opinion to Italy and Albania, either Albania or Italy made an application to the ICJ for the determination of who was entitled to the gold. After the arbitrator gave his opinion that the gold in question belonged to Albania in 1943, Italy in due course declared that it accepted the jurisdiction of the Court in respect of the dispute concerning the monetary gold in question and filed an application against France, the United Kingdom and the United States in the Court.

Before its filing of the Memorial, Italy submitted to the Court a declaration requesting it to address a "Preliminary Question." It doubted that the Court had jurisdiction to adjudicate upon such a question without the consent of Albania. In light of this new development, the Court suspended the proceedings on the merits and fixed the time-limits for the parties to submit documents in support of their positions on the question raised by Italy.[20]

17 The last sentence of Article 79, paragraph 1, of the Rules reads: "Any such objection made by a party other than the respondent shall be filed within the time-limit fixed for the delivery of that party's first pleading."

18 *Case of the Monetary gold removed from Rome in 1943* (*Italy* v. *France, United Kingdom and United States of America*) (*Preliminary Question*), *Judgment of June 15th, 1954: I.C.J. Reports 1954*, p. 19.

19 Italy claimed the gold for the partial satisfaction of the damage caused to Italy by the Albanian law of 13 January 1945. *Ibid.*, p. 22.

20 *Ibid.*, pp. 22–23.

In the preliminary stage, Italy submitted that, as the agreement among the three respondents did not constitute a sufficient basis for the Court to adjudicate the subject-matter contained in Italy's first submission, the Court was consequently without jurisdiction to adjudicate on the merits of the case. The United Kingdom argued that given Italy's objection to the competence of the Court, its application should accordingly be invalid and void, so that there was no longer "an application" before the Court for the determination of the question relating to the agreement among the three States.

Regarding Italy's contention, the Court stated the following,

> The Court cannot consider itself as lacking jurisdiction to adjudicate upon the validity, withdrawal or cancellation of an application which has been submitted to it: to adjudicate upon such questions with a view to deciding upon the effect to be given to the Application falls within the purview of its judicial task.[21]

The Court observed that it was very unusual that a State who submitted an application to the Court of its own accord should subsequently challenge the jurisdiction of the Court.[22] However, as the Rules of Court did not preclude the party other than the respondent to raise preliminary questions, the Court did not consider that Italy's preliminary question was contrary to the Rules of Court. Besides, Italy's application, once properly deposited, had to be considered "as real and as remaining real unless it is formally withdrawn."[23]

On the question raised by Italy, the Court ultimately decided that, in the absence of the consent of Albania, it had no jurisdiction to adjudicate the merits of the case. Procedurally the *Monetary Gold* judgment provides a very atypical case for studying preliminary questions. It shows that the Court, while leaving considerable discretion to the parties to raise preliminary objections, maintains the last word on the question of jurisdiction.

The preliminary procedure, as the principal proceedings, consists of two parts: written and oral. According to Article 79 of the Rules, normally there is only one round of written pleadings at the preliminary phase. If the Court decides to deal first of all with the question of jurisdiction, it may order the objecting party to produce a Memorial, and the other party a Counter-Memorial

21 *Ibid.*, p. 28.

22 *Ibid.*

23 *Ibid.*, p. 29.

with respect to the preliminary questions, irrespective of its previous order on the written pleadings for the main proceedings.[24]

If the objecting party in due course presents its preliminary objection, the Court shall fix the time limit for the other party to submit the written statement of its observations on the objection. The preliminary objection shall contain the following contents: the facts and the law on which the objection is based, the submissions and a list of the documents in support. Moreover, the objecting party shall mention any evidence which it may desire to adduce. Copies of the supporting documents shall be attached.[25] Likewise, the written statement of observations shall respond to the claims in the preliminary objection, with documents in support thereof, its submissions and the evidence it wishes to produce.[26]

Under Article 79, paragraph 6, of the Rules, there should be oral proceedings with regard to the question of jurisdiction and admissibility, a formal procedure similar to the main proceedings. Unless otherwise decided by the Court or demanded by the parties, oral hearings shall be public.

According to Article 79, paragraph 7, of the Rules, all the statements and evidence presented in both written and oral proceedings must be confined to the matters that are relevant to the objection.[27] They shall not deal with the merits of the case. This is because, before the Court has properly established the jurisdiction in the case, the subject-matter in question does not fall within the purview of the Court. As the Court pointed out in the case concerning *Appeal Relating to the Jurisdiction of the ICAO Council* (*India* v. *Pakistan*), "a party should not have to give an account of itself on issues of merits before a tribunal which lacks jurisdiction in the matter, or whose jurisdiction is not yet established".[28] The preliminary objection is expected to serve "the purpose of excluding an examination by the Court of the merits of the case," and to be "one upon which the Court can give a decision without in any way adjudicating upon the merits."[29]

---

24 That is to say, in the two different phases, there are two sets of written pleadings. See Article 79, paragraph 3, of the Rules of Court.

25 See Article 79, paragraph 4, of the Rules of Court.

26 See Article 79, paragraph 5, of the Rules of Court.

27 Article 79, paragraph 7, reads as follows: "The statement of facts and the law in the pleadings referred to in paragraphs 4 and 5 of this Article, and the statements and evidence presented at the hearings contemplated by paragraph 6, shall be confined to those matters that are relevant to the objection."

28 *Appeal Relating to the Jurisdiction of the ICAO Council* (*India* v. *Pakistan*), *Judgment, I.C.J. Reports 1972*, p. 56, para. 18.

29 See *Panevezys-Saldutiskis Railway, Judgment, 1939, P.C.I.J., Series A/B, No. 76*, p. 22.

3 Decisions on Preliminary Questions

In order to satisfy itself that it has jurisdiction in the case, the Court may put questions to the parties and ask them to argue all the issues of law and fact and adduce all the evidence, which bear on the question of jurisdiction. At the end of the preliminary stage, the Court shall decide whether to uphold or reject the objection. If the objecting party has raised several objections, the Court has to rule on each of them. The decision of the Court shall be made in the form of a judgment, not an order. It shall state the reasons on which its decision is based. The extent to which the Court upholds or rejects the objections will determine whether or not the Court has jurisdiction in the case, and if so, the scope of its jurisdiction in the merits phase. That means that, if the Court upholds some objections, but rejects others, the Court's jurisdiction will not extend to the issues upon which the Court found at the preliminary phase that it was without jurisdiction to adjudicate. For instance, in the *Alleged Violations* (*Nicaragua* v. *Colombia*) case, the Court found that the parties, at the time of the filing of the application, had a dispute only relating to Nicaragua's first claim, but not to its second claim.[30] Consequently, in the merits phase, the Court's jurisdiction will be confined to Nicaragua's first claim.

According to the jurisprudence of the Court, when preliminary objections are exclusively preliminary, they have to be decided upon immediately at the preliminary stage. As the Court pointed out in the *Military and Paramilitary Activities* case,

> practice has shown that there are certain kinds of preliminary objections which can be disposed of by the Court at an early stage without examination of the merits. Above all, it is clear that a question of jurisdiction is one which requires decision at the preliminary stage of the proceedings.[31]

In practice, however, there are certain objections that do not possess an exclusively preliminary character. During the PCIJ period, the Court had the discretion in handling such preliminary objections. It had the power to join an objection to the merits "whenever the interests of the good administration of justice require it."[32] This power of joinder, however, was not free from

30 *Alleged Violations of Sovereign Rights and Maritime Spaces in the Caribbean Sea* (*Nicaragua* v. *Colombia*), *Preliminary Objections, Judgment*, para. 79.

31 *Military and Paramilitary Activities in and against Nicaragua* (*Nicaragua* v. *United States of America*), *Merits, Judgment, I.C.J. Reports 1986*, pp. 30–31, para. 41.

32 *Panevezys-Saldutiskis Railway, Order of 30 June 1938, P.C.I.J., Series A/B, No. 75*, p. 56.

problems. In the *Barcelona Traction* case (New Application), the Court was faced with a situation where, if the Court was to decide on an objection raised by Spain, it would run the risk of adjudicating on questions relating to the merits of the case and therefore of prejudging their solution. After hearing full arguments of the parties on the merits, the Court ultimately concluded that, in the particular circumstances of the present case, it did not consider that *jus standi* was conferred on the Belgian Government by considerations of equity. Consequently, the applicant did not have a right of protection in respect of its nationals, shareholders in Barcelona Traction.[33] The case went through two stages, but finally ended up with a decision on the preliminary question. This result was criticized "as an unnecessary prolongation of an expensive and time-consuming procedure."[34] This experience led to the advocacy that all the preliminary objections should be immediately decided on at the preliminary stage and no joinder to the merits should be possible.

The Court, however, did not fail to see that such approach may not be able to meet all situations that may arise at the preliminary stage. It observed that:

> To find out, for instance, whether there is a dispute between the parties or whether the Court has jurisdiction, does not normally require an analysis of the merits of the case. However that does not solve all questions of preliminary objections, which may, as experience has shown, be to some extent bound up with the merits.[35]

The Court therefore was of the view that there should be some flexibility reserved for the Court to deal with such objections, but the Court's exercise of that power should be limited by laying down stricter conditions.[36] In the 1972 Rules, the power of joinder was removed, and instead, a provision of what Article 79, paragraph 9, currently stands was included. It was maintained in the 1978 Rules and further amended in 2001.[37] It provides that the Court may

33 *Barcelona Traction, Light and Power Company, Limited (New Application: 1962) (Belgium* v. *Spain), Judgment, I.C.J. Reports 1970*, p. 50, para. 101.

34 *Military and Paramilitary Activities in and against Nicaragua (Nicaragua* v. *United States of America), Merits, Judgment, I.C.J. Reports 1986*, p. 30, para. 39.

35 *Ibid.*, p. 30. para. 40.

36 *Questions of Interpretation and Application of the 1971 Montreal Convention arising from the Aerial Incident at Lockerbie (Libyan Arab Jamahiriya* v. *United Kingdom), Preliminary Objections, Judgment, I.C.J. Reports 1998*, p. 28, para. 49.

37 Article 79, paragraph 9, reads: "After hearing the parties, the Court shall give its decision in the form of a judgment, by which it shall either uphold the objection, reject it, or declare that the objection does not possess, in the circumstances of the case, an exclusively

declare that an objection does not possess an exclusively preliminary character and, as a result, the objection will be moved on to the merits phase when the Court is in a position to decide on it with more evidence and facts.

Since the adoption of Article 79, paragraph 9, of the Rules of Court, there have been three cases, in which the Court applied the provision and decided that the objection raised by the respondent did not possess an exclusively preliminary character.

In the *Military and Paramilitary Activities* case, the United States, relying on the reservation to its declaration made under Article 36, paragraph 2, of the Statute,[38] claimed that Nicaragua invoked four multilateral treaties in its application.[39] The dispute was therefore one "arising under" those multilateral treaties, and consequently fell outside the jurisdiction of the Court. The United States explained that the rationale of its reservation was to protect the United States and third States from the inherently prejudicial effects of partial adjudication of complex multiparty disputes. It identified Nicaragua's three Central American neighbours, Honduras, Costa Rica and El Salvador as States which would be "affected by the decision of the Court."[40]

The Court noted that the United States did not clarify who was to determine whether the States would be "affected." The Court could only make a determination when the general lines of the judgment to be given became clear. At any rate, the Court considered that this was a question concerning matters of substance relating to the merits of the case, but not in itself a jurisdictional problem. By invoking Article 79, paragraph 9,[41] the Court declared that the objection based on the multilateral treaty reservation of the United States Declaration of Acceptance did not possess, in the circumstances of the case, an exclusively preliminary character, and that consequently it did not

---

preliminary character. If the Court rejects the objection or declare that it does not possess an exclusively preliminary character, it shall fix time-limits for the further proceedings."

38 The United States' reservation stated that the United States' acceptance of the Court's compulsory jurisdiction shall not extend to "disputes arising under a multilateral treaty, unless (1) all parties to the treaty affected by the decision are also parties to the case before the Court, or (2) the United States of America specially agrees to jurisdiction."

39 The four treaties include: the Charter of the United Nations, the Charter of the Organization of American States, the Montevideo Convention on Rights and Duties of States of 26 December 1933, and the Havana Convention on the Rights and Duties of States in the Event of Civil Strife of 20 February 1928.

40 *Military and Paramilitary Activities in and against Nicaragua* (*Nicaragua* v. *United States of America*), *Jurisdiction and Admissibility, Judgment, I.C.J. Reports 1984*, pp. 422–424, paras. 69–72.

41 At that time the provision was Article 79, paragraph 7. It was amended in 2001.

constitute an obstacle for the Court to entertain the proceedings instituted by Nicaragua.[42]

At the merits phase, having examined the facts of the case and the law, the Court found that El Salvador, as a party to the United Nations Charter and to the Charter of the Organization of American States, was a State which would be "affected" by the decision which the Court would have to take on the claims by Nicaragua against the United States. Accordingly, the Court concluded that the jurisdiction conferred upon it by the United States declaration under Article 36, paragraph 2, of the Statute did not permit the Court to entertain the claims relating to multilateral treaties.[43]

The second relevant case is the *Lockerbie* (*Libyan Arab Jamahiriya* v. *United Kingdom*) case. At the preliminary stage, the Court declared in its decision that the objection raised by the United Kingdom according to which Security Council resolutions 748 (1992) and 883 (1993) had rendered the claims of Libya without object did not, in the circumstances of the case, have an exclusively preliminary character.[44]

In reaching that conclusion, the Court did not accept the argument advanced by the United Kingdom that its objection was of an exclusively preliminary character. It observed that, should the objection be upheld, there would be no ground for proceeding to a judgment on the merits. It would effectively prevent, *in limine*, any consideration of the case.[45] Regarding the contestation between the parties on the character of the objection, namely, whether or not it was exclusively preliminary, the Court considered that the objection related to many aspects of the dispute. It pointed out that,

---

42 *Military and Paramilitary Activities in and against Nicaragua* (*Nicaragua* v. *United States of America*), *Jurisdiction and Admissibility, Judgment, I.C.J. Reports 1984*, pp. 425–426, paras. 74–76.

43 *Military and Paramilitary Activities in and against Nicaragua* (*Nicaragua* v. *United States of America*), *Merits, Judgment, I.C.J. Reports 1986*, p. 38, para. 56.

44 *Questions of Interpretation and Application of the 1971 Montreal Convention arising from the Aerial Incident at Lockerbie* (*Libyan Arab Jamahiriya* v. *United Kingdom*), *Preliminary Objections, Judgment, I.C.J. Reports 1998*, p. 29, para. 50. See also *Questions of Interpretation and Application of the 1971 Montreal Convention arising from the Aerial Incident at Lockerbie* (*Libyan Arab Jamahiriya* v. *United States of America*), *Preliminary Objections, Judgment, I.C.J. Reports 1998*, p. 134, para. 49.

45 *Questions of Interpretation and Application of the 1971 Montreal Convention arising from the Aerial Incident at Lockerbie* (*Libyan Arab Jamahiriya* v. *United Kingdom*), *Preliminary Objections, Judgment, I.C.J. Reports 1998*, p. 27, para. 47. See also *Questions of Interpretation and Application of the 1971 Montreal Convention arising from the Aerial Incident at Lockerbie* (*Libyan Arab Jamahiriya* v. *United States of America*), *Preliminary Objections, Judgment, I.C.J. Reports 1998*, p. 132, para. 46.

> by requesting such a decision, the United Kingdom is requesting, in reality, at least two others which the decision not to proceed to judgment on the merits would necessarily postulate: on the one hand a decision establishing that the rights claimed by Libya under the Montreal Convention are incompatible with its obligations under the Security Council resolutions; and, on the other hand, a decision that those obligations prevail over those rights by virtue of Articles 25 and 103 of the Charter.[46]

The Court therefore held that Libya's rights on the merits would not only be affected by such a decision at the preliminary stage, but also in many respects constituted the "very subject-matter" of such decision. The United Kingdom's objection had the character of a defence on the merits. In its view, that objection was "inextricably interwoven" with the merits.[47]

In the case concerning *Application of the Convention on the Prevention and Punishment of the Crime of Genocide* (*Croatia* v. *Serbia*), as discussed in the previous chapter, Serbia raised a preliminary objection to the temporal jurisdiction of the Court and the admissibility of Croatia's claims against Serbia with regard to the alleged acts which occurred prior to the date of the FRY's proclamation of independence on 27 April 1992.[48] In that regard, the Court decided that, "[i]n order to be in a position to make any findings on each of these issues [raised by Serbia], the Court will need to have more elements before it."[49]

These cases demonstrate that if an objection contains both preliminary aspects and other aspects of substance relating to the merits of the case, and any decision of the Court at the preliminary stage may touch upon the elements of the merits, or prejudge the solution, the Court may postpone its consideration of the objection to the merits phase, when the facts and law of the case are fully presented. This approach will discourage the unnecessary prolongation of proceedings at the jurisdictional stage. Of course, from the three above-mentioned cases, it can also be observed that the Court in applying Article 79, paragraph 9, of the Rules of Court, has to give sufficient reasoning for its decision.

46 *Questions of Interpretation and Application of the 1971 Montreal Convention arising from the Aerial Incident at Lockerbie* (*Libyan Arab Jamahiriya* v. *United Kingdom*), *Preliminary Objections, Judgment, I.C.J. Reports 1998*, p. 29, para. 50.

47 *Ibid.* The cases were eventually discontinued by the agreement of the parties in 2003.

48 *Application of the Convention on the Prevention and Punishment of the Crime of Genocide* (*Croatia* v. *Serbia*), *Preliminary Objections, Judgment, I.C.J. Reports 2008*, p. 412.

49 *Ibid.*, p. 460, para. 129.

Conclusion

Since the establishment of the Permanent Court of International Justice, the World Court has gone a long way in promoting judicial settlement of international disputes. Although the role of the first World Court in addressing the main political issues of its day was perceived as no more than a "footnote,"[1] it laid down the foundation for the World Court to develop—permanent institution, election mechanism of salaried judges with fixed term of office, and statutory rules of the Court. Its initial practice proved the usefulness of the judicial mechanism in the pacific settlement of international disputes.

Historically, it was not by accident that the proposal to impose compulsory jurisdiction in the design of international courts and arbitral tribunals never succeeded; scepticism in selecting impartial and independent judges, coupled with mistrust in the judicial role in resolving international disputes, was prevailing at that time. Nation States under the European Westphalian system were the dominant players in international affairs. Of course, such States did not include those still under colonial rule or foreign domination. That historical deficiency explains the limited role of the PCIJ.

The 70 years of judicial practice of the ICJ have witnessed the fundamental change of international relations. In many ways, the ICJ cannot be considered a successor of the PCIJ, although its Statute was drafted on the basis of the Statute of the PCIJ and the PCIJ's jurisprudence is carried on till today. The ICJ, as the principal judicial organ and one of the six major organs of the United Nations, has a much more visible and expected role to play in international affairs entrusted to the United Nations. Either during the Cold War period or afterwards, the Court has, through discharging its two functions, settling contentious cases and providing advisory opinions, made commendable contributions to the peaceful settlement of international disputes and the development of international law. Its settled jurisprudence and legal practice provide guidance for other international courts and tribunals.

Jurisdiction is a central matter of the third-party mechanism. Among the basic principles and rules introduced in this Special Course, the principle of consent is the cornerstone. This consensual basis reflects the nature and function of the International Court and the limits of the third party settlement mechanism in resolving international disputes. It permeates almost every aspect of the judicial process.

1 Ole Spiermann, *International Legal Argument in the Permanent Court of International Justice: The Rise of the International Judiciary,* Cambridge University Press, 2009, p. 132.

 | DOI 10.1163/9789004342767_010

Jurisdiction is essentially a substantive matter. It bears on the sovereign decision of a State as to the means of settlement it considers suitable for the resolution of an international dispute with another State; the recourse it chooses would have a direct impact on the outcome of the resolution. Therefore, its decision to submit a dispute to a third party for settlement can be just as important as the judgment itself, if not more. What the State would take into account in making such a decision often goes far beyond the legal issues involved. Before the Court determines that it has jurisdiction in a case, it does not have the competence to address the merits.

Jurisdiction as a necessary shield keeps away matters that do not fall within judicial purview. Either for judicial economy or for the good administration of justice, the Court shall not exercise its jurisdiction when the case is without object. It shall, according to the Statute, exercise its jurisdiction to the fullest extent, while refraining from pronouncing on any matter that does not fall within its jurisdiction.

There are several ways by which a State may give consent to the jurisdiction of the Court. A State may accept the jurisdiction of the Court by a Special Agreement, a compromissory clause, a declaration accepting the compulsory jurisdiction of the Court, an exchange of Notes, or by *forum progogatum*. The extent of consent thus conferred is determined by the specific terms of each particular instrument. Even in accepting compulsory jurisdiction of the Court, a State may still attach certain reservations, exclusions and conditions to its declaration, specifically defining the scope of its consent. This gives a substantial discretion to States in considering resort to the Court. Notwithstanding that discretion, however, once an application is filed in the Court, it is for the Court to interpret the relevant legal instruments and determine whether the case falls or not within its jurisdiction and the application is or not admissible.

The jurisdiction of the Court in contentious cases is built on mutuality and reciprocity. The Court is only competent to entertain cases where a dispute exists between two States, even when the subject-matter of the dispute involves multiple applicants or multiple respondents, since the question of jurisdiction has to be examined and determined in the mutual relationship of the two parties in each specific case; a reservation attached by one party to its declaration accepting the compulsory jurisdiction of the Court may be used against it by the other party on the basis of reciprocity. In other words, the consent of the parties to the jurisdiction of the Court must coincide in scope in each case.

The preliminary objection procedure under Article 79 of the Statute is a unique judicial practice of international adjudication. It serves to guarantee both the principle of consent and the integrity of the judicial system. In determining its jurisdiction, the Court shall make an objective determination based on law and fact. It must satisfy itself, even in the absence of one of the parties, that conditions for the exercise of its jurisdiction are met and the Court has the full competence with respect to the parties, the subject-matter of the case and within the time limit of the jurisdiction.

The Court's contribution to the development of international law through its advisory function is equally significant. Its advisory jurisdiction is subject to certain conditions. Only the UN General Assembly and the Security Council, as well as duly authorized organs and specialized agencies may submit a request. As in contentious cases, the Court also has to first of all determine that it has the competence to deal with a request submitted to it.

In the post-Cold War era, the workload of the Court is noticeably on the rise, so is the call from States and the international community to increase the effectiveness and efficiency of the judicial institution. More fundamentally, the Court, challenged by a proliferation of international courts and tribunals, needs to reinforce, and perhaps redefine, its role as the principal judicial organ of the United Nations.

Notwithstanding that expectation, one cannot but observe an increasingly litigious tendency in international dispute settlement. Instead of conducting direct negotiations and consultations, more States find themselves in the Court in an adversarial process. The Court's jurisprudence on the questions of jurisdiction and admissibility also, understandably, moves in a direction that militates in favour of jurisdiction.

This Special Course introduces the basic rules and principles governing the jurisdiction of the ICJ on the basis of the existing practice of the Court. It should be pointed out that judicial practice is an evolving process. No one should take such practice as static. What should be closely followed is how the Court interprets and applies these rules and principles in practice. While maintaining consistency of its jurisprudence, the Court, through judicial interpretation, will inevitably develop the law. Judicial activism may from time to time test the vitality of the principle of consent.

Bibliography

Books

American Law Institute, *Restatement of the Law, Second (1965): Foreign Relations Law of the United States*, American Law Institute Publishers, 1965.

Basdevant, J. (ed.), *Dictionnaire de la terminologie du droit international*, Sirey, 1960.

Bello, E.G., and B.A. Ajibola (eds.), *Essays in Honour of Judge Taslim Olawale Elias, Vol. I*, Martinus Nijhoff Publishers, 1992.

Cheng, B., *General Principles of Law as Applied by International Courts and Tribunals*, Cambridge University Press, 1953.

Dinstein, Y. (ed.), *International Law at a Time of Perplexity: Essays in Honour of Shabtai Rosenne*, Kluwer Academic Publishers, 1989.

Hobér, K., *Essays on International Arbitration*, Huntingdon and JurisNet, LLC, 2006.

Hudson, M.O., *International Tribunals: Past and Future*, Carnegie Endowment for International Peace, 1944.

Jayakumar, S., and T. Koh, *Pedra Branca: The Road to the World Court*, NUS Press, 2009.

Kawano, M., "The Role of Judicial Procedures in the Process of the Pacific Settlement of International Disputes", *Recueil des cours*, Vol. 346, 2009.

Kolb, R., *The International Court of Justice*, Hart Publishing, 2013.

Lamm, V., *Compulsory Jurisdiction in International Law*, Edward Elgar, 2014.

MacDonald, R.St.J. (ed.), *Essays in Honour of Wang Tieya*, Martinus Nijhoff Publishers, 1994.

McWhinney, E., *The International Court of Justice and the Western Tradition of International Law*, Martinus Nijhoff, 1987.

Registry of the International Court of Justice, *The International Court of Justice*, United Nations, 2006.

Registry of the International Court of Justice, *The Permanent Court of International Justice: 1922–2012*, 2012.

Rosenne, S., *The Law and Practice of the International Court, 1920–2005, Vol. I, The Court and the United Nations*, 4th edition, Martinus Nijhoff Publishers, 2006.

Rosenne, S., *The Law and Practice of the International Court, 1920–2005, Vol. II, Jurisdiction*, 4th edition, Martinus Nijhoff Publishers, 2006.

Rosenne, S., *The World Court, What It Is and How It Works*, 5th completely revised edition, Martinus Nijhoff Publishers, 1995.

Spiermann, O., *International Legal Argument in the Permanent Court of International Justice: The Rise of the International Judiciary*, Cambridge University Press, 2005.

Thirlway, H., *The Law and Procedure of the International Court of Justice: fifty years of jurisprudence*, Vol. I, Oxford University Press, 2013.

Walker, D. (ed.), *The Oxford Companion to Law*, Oxford University Press, 1980.

Winiarski, B., "Quelques réflexions sur le soi-disant forum prorogatum en droit international", *Festschrift für Jean Spiropoulos*, 1957.

Zimmermann, A., *et al.* (eds.), *The Statute of the International Court of Justice: A Commentary*, 2nd edition, Oxford University Press, 2012.

Zimmermann, A., C. Tomuschat and K. Oellers-Frahm (eds.), *The Statute of the International Court of Justice: A Commentary*, Oxford University Press, 2006.

Book Chapters

Brown, C., "Article 59", in A. Zimmermann *et al.* (eds.), *The Statute of the International Court of Justice: A Commentary*, 2nd edition, Oxford University Press, 2012.

Dupuy, P., "Article 34", in A. Zimmermann *et al.* (eds.), *The Statute of the International Court of Justice: A Commentary*, 2nd edition, Oxford University Press, 2012.

Fassbender, B., "Article 9", in A. Zimmermann, C. Tomuschat and K. Oellers-Frahm (eds.), *The Statute of the International Court of Justice: A Commentary*, Oxford University Press, 2006.

Jennings, Sir.R., "Reflections on the Term 'Dispute'", in R.St.J. MacDonald (ed.), *Essays in Honour of Wang Tieya*, Martinus Nijhoff Publishers, 1994.

Jiménez de Aréchaga, E., "The Compulsory Jurisdiction of the International Court of Justice under the Pact of Bogotá and the Optional Clause", in Y. Dinstein (ed.), *International Law at a Time of Perplexity: Essays in Honour of Shabtai Rosenne*, Kluwer Academic Publishers, 1989.

McWhinney, E., "'Internationalizing' the International Court: the Quest for Ethno-cultural and Legal-systemic Representativeness", in E.G. Bello and B.A. Ajibola (eds.), *Essays in Honour of Judge Taslim Olawale Elias*, Martinus Nijhoff Publishers, 1992.

Tomuschat, C., "Article 36", in A. Zimmermann *et al.* (eds.), *The Statute of the International Court of Justice: A Commentary*, 2nd edition, Oxford University Press, 2012.

Zeuner, A. and H. Koch, "Effects of Judgments (*Res Judicata*)" in M. Cappelletti (chief ed.), *Volume XVI Civil Procedure, International Encyclopedia of Comparative Law*, 2012, pp. 3–84.

Zimmermann, A., "Article 35", in A. Zimmermann *et al.* (eds.), *The Statute of the International Court of Justice: A Commentary*, 2nd edition, Oxford University Press, 2012.

Zuckerman, A., "Civil Procedure", in A. Zuckerman (ed.), Halsbury's Laws of England, Volume 12, Fifth Edition, LexisNexis, 2015.

Journal Articles

American Society of International Law, "Statement of Department of State on US Withdrawal from Nicaragua Proceedings, 18 January 1985", in "Contemporary Practice of the United States", *American Journal of International Law*, Vol. 79, 1985.

Bingham, T. "Alabama Arbitration", *Max Planck Encyclopedia of Public International Law*, October 2006, http://opil.ouplaw.com/view/10.1093/law:epil/9780199231690/law-9780199231690-e89?prd=EPIL, 8 April 2016.

Chayes, A., "Nicaragua, The United States, and the World Court", *Columbia Law Review*, Vol. 85, 1985, pp. 1445–1482.

Cortado, R.R., "Central American Court of Justice (1907–18)", *Max Planck Encyclopedia of Public International Law*, http://opil.ouplaw.com/view/10.1093/law:epil/9780199231690/law-9780199231690-e15, 7 April 2016.

Fraser, H.S., "Sketch of the History of International Arbitration", *Cornell Law Quarterly*, Vol. 11, 1925–1926, pp. 179–208.

Kattan, V., "Decolonizing the International Court of Justice: The Experience of Judge Sir Muhammad Zafrulla Khan in the South West Africa Cases", *Asian Journal of International Law*, Vol. 5, issue 2, July 2015, pp. 310–355.

McWhinney, E., "Judicial Opinion-Writing in the World Court and the Western Sahara Advisory Opinion", *Heidelberg Journal of International Law*, Vol. 37, 1977, pp. 1–42.

Reichler, P., "Holding America to Its Own Best Standards: Abe Chayes and Nicaragua in the World Court", *Harvard International Law Journal*, Vol. 42, 2001, pp. 15–46.

Schwebel, S., "Celebrating a Fraud on the Court", *American Journal of International Law*, Vol. 106, 2012, pp. 102–105.

Schwebel, S., "The *Nicaragua* Case: A Response to Paul Reichler", *American Journal of International Law*, Vol. 106, 2012, pp. 582–583.

Thirlway, H., "The Law and Procedure of the International Court of Justice 1960–1989: Part Nine", *British Yearbook of International Law*, Vol. 69, 1998, pp. 1–83.

Thirlway, H., "The International Court of Justice 1989–2009: At the Heart of the Dispute Settlement System?", *Netherlands International Law Review*, Vol. 57, 2010, pp. 347–395.

Documents

PCIJ Documents

Annual Report of the Permanent Court of International Justice (1 January 1922–15 June 1925), P.C.I.J., Series E, No. 1.

UN documents

Security Council resolution, The International Court of Justice, S/Res/9, 15 October 1946.

Security Council resolution, The International Court of Justice, S/Res/11, 15 November 1946.

General Assembly resolution, Conditions on which Switzerland may become a Party to the International Court of Justice, UN doc. A/Res/91(I), 11 December 1946.

Security Council resolution, The Corfu Channel incidents, S/Res/22, 9 April 1947.

General Assembly resolution, Conditions under which a State, a party of the Statute of the International Court of Justice but not a member of the United Nations, may participate in the elections of members of the Court, UN doc. A/Res/264(III), 8 October 1948.

General Assembly resolution, Scale of assessment for the apportionment of the expenses of the United Nations, UN doc. A/Res/1308(XIII), 10 December 1958.

General Assembly resolution, Legal action to ensure the fulfillment of the obligations assumed by the Union of South Africa in respect of the Territory of South West Africa, UN doc. A/Res/1361(XIV), 17 November 1959.

General Assembly resolution, Declaration on the Granting of Independence to Colonial Countries and Peoples, UN doc. A/Res/1514(XV), 14 December 1960.

General Assembly resolution, The future of the Trust Territory of the Cameroons under United Kingdom administration, UN doc. A/Res/1608(XV), 21 April 1961.

General Assembly resolution, Question of equitable representation on the Security Council and the Economic and Social Council, UN doc. A/Res/1991(XVIII), 17 December 1963.

General Assembly resolution, Question of South West Africa, UN doc. A/Res/2145(XXI), 27 October 1966.

Security Council resolution, The Situation in Namibia, S/Res/264, 20 March 1969.

General Assembly resolution, Participation of States which are parties to the Statute of the International Court of Justice, but are not Members of the United Nations, in the procedure for effecting amendments to the Statute, UN doc. A/Res/2520(XXIV), 4 December 1969.

Security Council resolution, The Situation in Namibia, S/Res/276, 30 January 1970.

Security Council resolution, Namibia, S/Res/284, 29 July 1970.

General Assembly resolution, United Nations Decade of International Law, UN doc. A/Res/45/40, 28 November 1990.

Security Council resolution, Libyan Arab Jamahiriya, S/Res/748, 31 March 1992.

"Letter dated 6 May 1992 from the Chargé d'affaires a.i. of the Permanent Mission of Yugoslavia to the United Nations addressed to the Secretary-General", UN doc. A/46/915, 7 May 1992.

Security Council resolution, Federal Republic of Yugoslavia, S/Res/777, 19 September 1992.

General Assembly resolution, Recommendation of the Security Council of 19 September 1992, UN doc. A/Res/47/1, 22 September 1992.

Security Council resolution Libyan Arab Jamahiriya, S/Res/883, 11 November 1993.
General Assembly resolution, Request for an advisory opinion from the International Court of Justice on the legality of the threat or use of nuclear weapons, UN doc. A/Res/49/75 K, 15 December 1994.
"Letter dated 27 October 2000 from the President of the Federal Republic of Yugoslavia to the Secretary-General", Annex to "Application of the Federal Republic of Yugoslavia for admission to membership in the United Nations", UN doc. A/55/528-S2000/1043, 30 October 2000.
General Assembly resolution, 2005 World Summit Outcome, UN doc. A/RES/60/1, 24 October 2005.
General Assembly resolution, The rule of law at the national and international levels, UN doc. A/Res/61/39, 18 December 2006.
International Court of Justice, *Yearbook 2006–2007*, No. 61.
General Assembly resolution, The rule of law at the national and international levels, UN doc. A/Res/62/70, 8 January 2008.
General Assembly resolution, The rule of law at the national and international levels, UN doc. A/Res/63/128, 15 January 2009.
General Assembly resolution, The rule of law at the national and international levels, UN doc. A/Res/64/116, 15 January 2010.
General Assembly resolution, The rule of law at the national and international levels, UN doc. A/Res/65/32, 10 January 2011.
General Assembly resolution, The rule of law at the national and international levels, UN doc. A/Res/66/102, 13 January 2012.
General Assembly resolution, Declaration of the high-level meeting of the General Assembly on the rule of law at the national and international levels, UN doc. A/Res/67/1, 30 November 2012.
International Court of Justice, *Yearbook 2012–2013*, No. 67.
General Assembly resolution, The rule of law at the national and international levels, UN doc. A/Res/67/97, 14 January 2013.
General Assembly resolution, The rule of law at the national and international levels, UN doc. A/Res/68/116, 18 December 2013.
General Assembly resolution, The rule of law at the national and international levels, UN doc. A/Res/69/123, 18 December 2014.
UN OLA, *United Nations Reports of International Arbitral Awards*, Vol. III.
UN OLA, *United Nations Reports of International Arbitral Awards*, Vol. VI.

Treaties, Conventions and Statutes

Statute of the Permanent Court of International Justice, 16 December 1920 (entered into force 20 August 1921), 6 *LNTS* 389.
Rules of Court, Permanent Court of International Justice, Series D, No.1, fourth edition, April 1940, p. 44.

Statute of the International Court of Justice, 26 June 1945 (entered into force 24 October 1945), 33 UNTS 933.

Rules of Court, International Court of Justice, 14 April 1978 (entered into force 1 July 1978), Amendment entered into force on 14 April 2005.

American Treaty on Pacific Settlement (Pact of Bogotá), 30 April 1948 (entered into force 6 May 1949), 30 *UNTS* 55.

International Convention for the Pacific Settlement of International Disputes, 29 July 1899 (entered into force 4 September 1900), (1899–99) 187 CTS 410.

Covenant of the League of Nations, 28 June 1919 (entered into force 10 January 1920), 225 CTS 195.

Charter of the United Nations, 26 June 1945 (entered into force 24 October 1945), 1 *UNTS* XVI.

Treaty of Amity, Economic Relations, and Consular Rights of 1955 between the United States and Iran, 15 August 1955 (entered into force 16 June 1957), 284 *UNTS* 93.

International Convention on the Elimination of All Forms of Racial Discrimination, 7 March 1966 (entered into force 4 January 1969), 660 *UNTS* 195.

Convention against Torture and Other Cruel, Inhuman or Degrading Treatment or Punishment, 10 December 1984 (entered into force 26 June 1987), 1465 *UNTS* 85.

Convention on the Prevention and Punishment of the Crime of Genocide, 9 December 1948 (entered into force 12 January 1951), 78 *UNTS* 277.

Treaty of Friendship, Commerce and Navigation between the United States of America and the Republic of Nicaragua signed at Managua, 21 January 1956 (entered into force 24 May 1958), 367 *UNTS* 3.

The Montevideo Treaty concerning the boundary constituted by the River Uruguay, 7 April 1961 (entered into force 19 January 1966), 635 *UNTS* 98.

Vienna Convention on the Law of Treaties of 1969, 23 May 1969 (entered into for 27 January 1980), 1155 *UNTS* 331.

European Convention for the Peaceful Settlement of Disputes (the European Convention), 29 April 1957 (entered into force 30 April 1958), 320 *UNTS* 243.

Charter of the Organization of American States, 30 April 1948 (entered into force 13 December 1951), 119 *UNTS* 3.

Montevideo Convention on Rights and Duties of States of 26 December 1933, 26 December 1933 (entered into force 26 December 1934), 165 *LNTS* 19.

Havana Convention on the Rights and Duties of States in the Event of Civil Strife of 20 February 1928, 20 February 1928 (entered into force 21 May 1929), 134 *LNTS* 45.

Other Resources

Annuaire De l'Institut de Droit International, Vol. 45, 1954, Part II, p. 296, Part I.

Corte Centroamericana de Justicia, "Historia del Tribunal", http://portal.ccj.org.ni/ccj2/Historia/tabid/57/Default.aspx, 30 September 2016.

"Declarations recognizing as compulsory the jurisdiction of the International Court of Justice under Article 36, paragraph 2, of the Statute of the Court", United Kingdom of Great Britain and Northern Ireland, 31 December 2014, *Multilateral Treaties Deposited with the Secretary-General*, United Nations, New York (ST/LEG/SER.E), https://treaties.un.org/Pages/ParticipationStatus.aspx, 30 September 2016.

PCA, "Member States", https://pca-cpa.org/en/about/introduction/member-states/, 30 September 2016.

The International Court of Justice: Handbook, 6th edition, http://legal.un.org/avl/pdf/rs/other_resources/manuel_en.pdf, 30 September 2016.

List of Cases

ICJ Contentious Cases

Corfu Channel (United Kingdom of Great Britain and Northern Ireland* v. *Albania)

Corfu Channel case, Judgment on Preliminary Objection: I.C.J. Reports 1948, p. 15.
Corfu Channel case, Judgment of April 9th, 1949: I.C.J. Reports 1949, p. 4.
Corfu Channel case, Judgment of December 15th, 1949: I.C.J. Reports 1949, p. 244.

Rights of Nationals of the United States of America in Morocco (France* v. *United States of America)

Case concerning rights of nationals of the United States of America in Morocco, Judgment of August 27th, 1952: I.C.J. Reports 1952, p. 176.

Request for Interpretation of the Judgment of 20 November 1950 in the Asylum Case (Colombia* v. *Peru)

Request for interpretation of the Judgment of November 20th, 1950, in the asylum case, Judgment of November 27th, 1950: I.C.J. Reports 1950, p. 395.

Haya de la Torre (Colombia* v. *Peru)

Haya de la Torre Case, Judgment of June 13th, 1951: I.C.J. Reports 1951, p. 71.

Anglo-Iranian Oil Co. (United Kingdom* v. *Iran)

Anglo-Iranian Oil Co. Case, Order of July 5th, 1951: I.C.J. Reports 1951, p. 89.
Anglo-Iranian Oil Co. Case, Order of July 5th, 1951: I.C.J. Reports 1951, Dissenting opinion of Judges Winiarski and Badawi Pasha, p. 96.
Anglo-Iranian Oil Co., Pleadings, Part IV, Correspondence, p. 700.
Anglo-Iranian Oil Co. case (jurisdiction), Judgment of July 22nd, 1952: I.C.J. Reports 1952, p. 93.

Nottebohm (Liechtenstein* v. *Guatemala)

Nottebohm case (Preliminary Objection), Judgment of November 18th, 1953: I.C.J. Reports 1953, p. 111.

Monetary Gold Removed from Rome in 1943 (Italy* v. *France, United Kingdom of Great Britain and Northern Ireland and United States of America)

Case of the monetary gold removed from Rome in 1943 (Preliminary Question), Judgment of June 15th, 1954: I.C.J. Reports 1954, p. 19.

***Certain Norwegian Loans* (*France* v. *Norway*)**

Case of Certain Norwegian Loans, Judgment of July 6th, 1957: I.C.J. Reports 1957, p. 9.

***Right of Passage over Indian territory* (*Portugal* v. *India*)**

Case concerning right of passage over Indian territory (Preliminary Objections), Judgment of November 26th, 1957: I.C.J. Reports 1957, p. 125.

***Temple of Preah Vihear* (*Cambodia* v. *Thailand*)**

Case concerning the Temple of Preah Vihear (Cambodia v. *Thailand), Preliminary Objections, Judgment of 26 May 1961: I.C.J. Reports 1961*, p. 17.

Case concerning the Temple of Preah Vihear (Cambodia v. *Thailand), Merits, Judgment of 15 June 1962: I.C.J. Reports 1962*, p. 6.

***South West Africa* (*Ethiopia* v. *South Africa; Liberia* v. *South Africa*)**

South West Africa Cases (Ethiopia v. *South Africa; Liberia* v. *South Africa), Preliminary Objections, Judgment of 21 December 1962: I.C.J. Reports 1962*, p. 319.

South West Africa Cases (Ethiopia v. *South Africa; Liberia* v. *South Africa), Preliminary Objections, Judgment of 21 December 1962: I.C.J. Reports 1962*, Dissenting opinion of Judge Morelli, p. 564.

South West Africa, Second Phase, Judgment, I.C.J. Reports 1966, p. 6.

South West Africa, Second Phase, Judgment, I.C.J. Reports 1966, Dissenting opinion of Vice-President Wellington Koo, p. 216.

South West Africa, Second Phase, Judgment, I.C.J. Reports 1966, Dissenting opinion of Judge Jessup, p. 325.

***Northern Cameroons* (*Cameroon* v. *United Kingdom*)**

Case concerning the Northern Cameroons (Cameroon v. *United Kingdom), Preliminary Objections, Judgment of 2 December 1963: I.C.J. Reports 1963*, p. 15.

***Barcelona Traction, Light and Power Company, Limited* (*Belgium* v. *Spain*) (*New Application: 1962*)**

Barcelona Traction, Light and Power Company, Limited, Preliminary Objections, Judgment, I.C.J. Reports 1964, p. 6.

Barcelona Traction, Light and Power Company, Limited, Judgment, I.C.J. Reports 1970, p. 3.

***North Sea Continental Shelf* (*Federal Republic of Germany/Denmark; Federal Republic of Germany/Netherlands*)**

North Sea Continental Shelf (Federal Republic of Germany/Denmark; Federal Republic of Germany/Netherlands), Pleadings, Oral Arguments, Documents, Vol. I, 1968.

***Appeal Relating to the Jurisdiction of the ICAO Council* (*India* v. *Pakistan*)**

Appeal Relating to the Jurisdiction of the ICAO Council (India v. *Pakistan), Judgment, I.C.J. Reports 1972*, p. 46.

***Fisheries Jurisdiction* (*United Kingdom of Great Britain and Northern Ireland* v. *Iceland*)**

Fisheries Jurisdiction (United Kingdom v. *Iceland), Jurisdiction of the Court, Judgment, I.C.J. Reports 1973*, p. 3.

***Fisheries Jurisdiction* (*Federal Republic of Germany* v. *Iceland*)**

Fisheries Jurisdiction (Federal Republic of Germany v. *Iceland), Jurisdiction of the Court, Judgment, I.C.J. Reports 1973*, p. 49.

Fisheries Jurisdiction (Federal Republic of Germany v. *Iceland), Merits, Judgment, I.C.J. Reports 1974*, p. 175.

***Nuclear Tests* (*Australia* v. *France*)**

Nuclear Tests (Australia v. *France), Judgment, I.C.J. Reports 1974*, p. 253.

***Nuclear Tests* (*New Zealand* v. *France*)**

Nuclear Tests (New Zealand v. *France), Judgment, I.C.J. Reports 1974*, p. 457.

***Aegean Sea Continental Shelf* (*Greece* v. *Turkey*)**

Aegean Sea Continental Shelf, Judgment, I.C.J. Reports 1978, p. 3.

***Continental Shelf* (*Tunisia/Libyan Arab Jamahiriya*)**

Continental Shelf (Tunisia/Libyan Arab Jamahiriya), Judgment, I.C.J. Reports 1982, p. 18.

***United States Diplomatic and Consular Staff in Tehran* (*United States of America* v. *Iran*)**

United States Diplomatic and Consular Staff in Tehran (United States of America v. *Iran), Provisional Measures, Order of 15 December 1979, I.C.J. Reports 1979*, p. 4.

United States Diplomatic and Consular Staff in Tehran, Judgment, I.C.J. Reports 1980, p. 3.

***Delimitation of the Maritime Boundary in the Gulf of Maine Area* (*Canada/United States of America*)**

Delimitation of the Maritime Boundary in the Gulf of Maine Area, Judgment, I.C.J. Reports 1984, p. 246.

Continental Shelf (Libyan Arab Jamahiriya/Malta)

Continental Shelf (Libyan Arab Jamahiriya/Malta), Application to Intervene, Judgment, I.C.J. Reports 1984, p. 3.

Frontier Dispute (Burkina Faso/Republic of Mali)

Frontier Dispute, Judgment, I.C.J. Reports 1986, p. 554.

Military and Paramilitary Activities in and against Nicaragua (Nicaragua v. *United States of America)*

Military and Paramilitary Activities in and against Nicaragua (Nicaragua v. *United States of America), Provisional Measures, Order of 10 May 1984, I.C.J. Reports 1984*, p. 169.

Military and Paramilitary Activities in and against Nicaragua (Nicaragua v. *United States of America), Jurisdiction and Admissibility, Judgment, I.C.J. Reports 1984*, p. 392.

Military and Paramilitary Activities in and against Nicaragua (Nicaragua v. *United States of America), Merits, Judgment, I.C.J. Reports 1986*, p. 14.

Military and Paramilitary Activities in and against Nicaragua (Nicaragua v. *United States of America), Merits, Judgment, I.C.J. Reports 1986*, Separate Opinion of Judge Lachs, p. 158.

Military and Paramilitary Activities in and against Nicaragua (Nicaragua v. *United States of America), Merits, Judgment, I.C.J. Reports 1986*, Dissenting opinion of Judge Oda, p. 212.

Military and Paramilitary Activities in and against Nicaragua (Nicaragua v. *United States of America), Merits, Judgment, I.C.J. Reports 1986*, Dissenting opinion of Judge Schwebel, p. 259.

Border and Transborder Armed Actions (Nicaragua v. *Honduras)*

Border and Transborder Armed Actions (Nicaragua v. *Honduras), Jurisdiction and Admissibility, Judgment, I.C.J. Reports 1988*, p. 69.

Border and Transborder Armed Actions (Nicaragua v. *Honduras), Jurisdiction and Admissibility, Judgment, I.C.J. Reports 1988*, Separate opinion of Judge Shahabuddeen, p. 133.

Land, Island and Maritime Frontier Dispute (El Salvador/Honduras: Nicaragua intervening)

Land, Island and Maritime Frontier Dispute (El Salvador/Honduras), Application to Intervene, Judgment, I.C.J. Reports 1990, p. 92.

Land, Island and Maritime Frontier Dispute (El Salvador/Honduras: Nicaragua intervening), Judgment, I.C.J. Reports 1992, p. 351.

Elettronica Sicula S.p.A. (ELSI) (United States of America v. Italy)

Elettronica Sicula S.p.A. (ELSI), Judgment, I.C.J. Reports 1989, p. 15.

Maritime Delimitation in the Area between Greenland and Jan Mayen (Denmark v. Norway)

Maritime Delimitation in the Area between Greenland and Jan Mayen, Judgment, I.C.J. Reports 1993, p. 38.

Certain Phosphate Lands in Nauru (Nauru v. Australia)

Certain Phosphate Lands in Nauru (Nauru v. *Australia), Preliminary Objections, Judgment, I.C.J. Reports 1992*, p. 240.

Certain Phosphate Lands in Nauru (Nauru v. *Australia), Preliminary Objections, Judgment, I.C.J. Reports 1992*, Dissenting opinion of President Jennings, p. 301.

East Timor (Portugal v. Australia)

East Timor (Portugal v. *Australia), Judgment, I.C.J. Reports 1995*, p. 90.

Passage through the Great Belt (Finland v. Denmark)

Passage through the Great Belt (Finland v. *Denmark), Provisional Measures, Order of 29 July 1991, I.C.J. Reports 1991*, p. 12.

Questions of Interpretation and Application of the 1971 Montreal Convention arising from the Aerial Incident at Lockerbie (Libyan Arab Jamahiriya v. United Kingdom)

Questions of Interpretation and Application of the 1971 Montreal Convention arising from the Aerial Incident at Lockerbie (Libyan Arab Jamahiriya v. *United Kingdom), Preliminary Objections, Judgment, I.C.J. Reports 1998*, p. 9.

Questions of Interpretation and Application of the 1971 Montreal Convention arising from the Aerial Incident at Lockerbie (Libyan Arab Jamahiriya v. United States of America)

Questions of Interpretation and Application of the 1971 Montreal Convention arising from the Aerial Incident at Lockerbie (Libyan Arab Jamahiriya v. *United States of America), Preliminary Objections, Judgment, I.C.J. Reports 1998*, p. 115.

Oil Platforms (Islamic Republic of Iran v. United States of America)

Oil Platforms (Islamic Republic of Iran v. *United States of America), Preliminary Objection, Judgment, I.C.J. Reports 1996*, p. 803.

Oil Platforms (Islamic Republic of Iran v. *United States of America), Counter-Claim, Order of 10 March 1998, I.C.J. Reports 1998*, p. 190.
Oil Platforms (Islamic Republic of Iran v. *United States of America), Judgment, I.C.J. Reports 2003*, p. 161.

Application of the Convention on the Prevention and Punishment of the Crime of Genocide (Bosnia and Herzegovina v. *Serbia and Montenegro)*

Application of the Convention on the Prevention and Punishment of the Crime of Genocide, Preliminary Objections, Judgment, I.C.J. Reports 1996, p. 595.
Application of the Convention on the Prevention and Punishment of the Crime of Genocide, Counter-claims, Order of 17 December 1997, I.C.J. Reports 1997, p. 243.
Application of the Convention on the Prevention and Punishment of the Crime of Genocide (Bosnia and Herzegovina v. *Serbia and Montenegro), Judgment, I.C.J. Reports 2007*, p. 43.

Land and Maritime Boundary between Cameroon and Nigeria (Cameroon v. *Nigeria: Equatorial Guinea intervening)*

Land and Maritime Boundary between Cameroon and Nigeria, Preliminary Objections, Judgment, I.C.J. Reports 1998, p. 275.
Land and Maritime Boundary between Cameroon and Nigeria, Preliminary Objections, Judgment, I.C.J. Reports 1998, Dissenting opinion of Judge Koroma, p. 377.
Land and Maritime Boundary between Cameroon and Nigeria, Application to Intervene, Order of 21 October 1999, I.C.J. Reports 1999, p. 1029.
Land and Maritime Boundary between Cameroon and Nigeria (Cameroon v. *Nigeria: Equatorial Guinea intervening), Judgment, I.C.J. Reports 2002*, p. 303.

Fisheries Jurisdiction (Spain v. *Canada)*

Fisheries Jurisdiction (Spain v. *Canada), Jurisdiction of the Court, Judgment, I.C.J. Reports 1998*, p. 432.

Request for an Examination of the Situation in Accordance with Paragraph 63 of the Court's Judgment of 20 December 1974 in the Nuclear Tests (New Zealand *v.* France) *Case (New Zealand* v. *France)*

Request for an Examination of the Situation in Accordance with Paragraph 63 of the Court's Judgment of 20 December 1974 in the Nuclear Tests (New Zealand *v.* France) *Case, I.C.J. Reports 1995*, p. 288.

Request for Interpretation of the Judgment of 11 June 1998 in the Case concerning the Land and Maritime Boundary between Cameroon and Nigeria (Cameroon *v.* Nigeria)

Request for Interpretation of the Judgment of 11 June 1998 in the Case concerning the Land and Maritime Boundary between Cameroon and Nigeria (Cameroon *v.* Nigeria), Preliminary Objections (*Nigeria* v. *Cameroon*), *Judgment, I.C.J. Reports 1999*, p. 31.

Sovereignty over Pulau Ligitan and Pulau Sipadan (*Indonesia/Malaysia*)

Sovereignty over Pulau Ligitan and Pulau Sipadan (*Indonesia/Malaysia*), *Application for Permission to Intervene, Judgment, I.C.J. Reports 2001*, p. 575.

Sovereignty over Pulau Ligitan and Pulau Sipadan (*Indonesia/Malaysia*), *Application for Permission to Intervene, Judgment, I.C.J. Reports 2001*, Dissenting opinion of Judge Oda, p. 609.

Sovereignty over Pulau Ligitan and Pulau Sipadan (*Indonesia/Malaysia*), *Application for Permission to Intervene, Judgment, I.C.J. Reports 2001*, Separate opinion of Judge *ad hoc* Weeramantry, p. 630.

Sovereignty over Pulau Ligitan and Pulau Sipadan (*Indonesia/Malaysia*), *Judgment, I.C.J. Reports 2002*, p. 625.

Ahmadou Sadio Diallo (*Republic of Guinea* v. *Democratic Republic of the Congo*)

Ahmadou Sadio Diallo (*Republic of Guinea* v. *Democratic Republic of the Congo*), *Preliminary Objections, Judgment, I.C.J. Reports 2007*, p. 582.

LaGrand (*Germany* v. *United States of America*)

LaGrand (*Germany* v. *United States of America*), *Provisional Measures, Order of 3 March 1999, I.C.J. Reports 1999*, p. 9.

LaGrand (*Germany* v. *United States of America*), *Judgment, I.C.J. Reports 2001*, p. 466.

Legality of Use of Force (*Yugoslavia* v. *United States of America*)

Legality of Use of Force (*Yugoslavia* v. *United States of America*), *Provisional Measures, Order of 2 June 1999, I.C.J. Reports 1999*, p. 916.

Legality of Use of Force (*Serbia and Montenegro* v. *Belgium*)

Legality of Use of Force (*Serbia and Montenegro* v. *Belgium*), *Preliminary Objections, Judgment, I.C.J. Reports 2004*, p. 279.

Legality of Use of Force (*Serbia and Montenegro* v. *United Kingdom*)

Legality of Use of Force (*Serbia and Montenegro* v. *United Kingdom*), *Preliminary Objections, Judgment, I.C.J. Reports 2004*, p. 1307.

Legality of Use of Force (Serbia and Montenegro v. *United Kingdom), Preliminary Objections, Judgment, I.C.J. Reports 2004*, Joint declaration of Vice-President Ranjeva, Judges Guillaume, Higgins, Kooijmans, Al-Khasawneh, Buergenthal and Elaraby, p. 1353.

Armed Activities on the Territory of the Congo (Democratic Republic of the Congo v. *Uganda)*

Armed Activities on the Territory of the Congo (Democratic Republic of the Congo v. *Uganda), Order of 29 November 2001, I.C.J. Reports 2001*, p. 660.

Application of the Convention on the Prevention and Punishment of the Crime of Genocide (Croatia v. *Serbia)*

Application of the Convention on the Prevention and Punishment of the Crime of Genocide (Croatia v. *Serbia), Preliminary Objections, Judgment, I.C.J. Reports 2008*, p. 412.

Application of the Convention on the Prevention and Punishment of the Crime of Genocide (Croatia v. *Serbia), Preliminary Objections, Judgment, I.C.J. Reports 2008*, Joint declaration of Judges Ranjeva, Shi, Koroma and Parra-Aranguren, p. 472.

Application of the Convention on the Prevention and Punishment of the Crime of Genocide (Croatia v. *Serbia), Merits, Judgment of 3 February 2015.*

Arrest Warrant of 11 April 2000 (Democratic Republic of the Congo v. *Belgium)*

Arrest Warrant of 11 April 2000 (Democratic Republic of the Congo v. *Belgium), Judgment, I.C.J. Reports 2002*, p. 3.

Certain Property (Liechtenstein v. *Germany)*

Certain Property (Liechtenstein v. *Germany), Preliminary Objections, Judgment, I.C.J. Reports 2005*, p. 6.

Territorial and Maritime Dispute (Nicaragua v. *Colombia)*

Territorial and Maritime Dispute (Nicaragua v. *Colombia), Preliminary Objections, Judgment, I.C.J. Reports 2007*, p. 832.

Armed Activities on the Territory of the Congo (New Application: 2002) (Democratic Republic of the Congo v. *Rwanda)*

Armed Activities on the Territory of the Congo (New Application: 2002) (Democratic Republic of the Congo v. *Rwanda), Provisional Measures, Order of 10 July 2002, I.C.J. Reports 2002*, p. 219.

Armed Activities on the Territory of the Congo (New Application: 2002) (Democratic Republic of the Congo v. *Rwanda), Jurisdiction and Admissibility, Judgment, I.C.J. Reports 2006*, p. 6.

Avena and Other Mexican Nationals(Mexico v. *United States of America)*

Avena and Other Mexican Nationals(Mexico v. *United States of America), Judgment, I.C.J. Reports 2004*, p. 12.

Certain Criminal Proceedings in France (Republic of the Congo v. *France)*

Certain Criminal Proceedings in France (Republic of the Congo v. *France), Provisional Measure, Order of 17 June 2003, I.C.J. Reports 2003*, p. 102.

Certain Criminal Proceedings in France (Republic of the Congo v. *France), Order of 16 November 2010, I.C.J. Reports 2010*, p. 635.

Pulp Mills on the River Uruguay (Argentina v. *Uruguay)*

Pulp Mills on the River Uruguay (Argentina v. *Uruguay), Provisional Measures, Order of 13 July 2006, I.C.J. Reports 2006*, p. 113.

Pulp Mills on the River Uruguay (Argentina v. *Uruguay), Judgment, I.C.J. Reports 2010*, p. 14.

Certain Questions of Mutual Assistance in Criminal Matters (Djibouti v. *France)*

Certain Questions of Mutual Assistance in Criminal Matters (Djibouti v. *France), Judgment, I.C.J. Reports 2008*, p. 177.

Request for Interpretation of the Judgment of 31 March 2004 in the Case concerning Avena and Other Mexican Nationals (Mexico *v*. United States of America) *(Mexico* v. *United States of America)*

Request for Interpretation of the Judgment of 31 March 2004 in the Case concerning Avena and Other Mexican Nationals (Mexico v. United States of America) *(Mexico* v. *United States of America), Judgment, I.C.J. Reports 2009*, p. 3.

Application of the International Convention on the Elimination of All Forms of Racial Discrimination (Georgia v. *Russian Federation)*

Application of the International Convention on the Elimination of all Forms of Racial Discrimination (Georgia v. *Russian Federation), Provisional Measures, Order of 15 October 2008, I.C.J. Reports 2008*, p. 353.

Application of the International Convention on the Elimination of All Forms of Racial Discrimination (Georgia v. *Russian Federation), Preliminary Objections, Judgment, I.C.J. Reports 2011*, p. 70.

Application of the International Convention on the Elimination of All Forms of Racial Discrimination (Georgia v. *Russian Federation), Preliminary Objections, Judgment, I.C.J. Reports 2011*, Separate opinion of Judge Abraham, p. 224.

Jurisdictional Immunities of the State (Germany* v. *Italy: Greece intervening)

Jurisdictional Immunities of the State (Germany v. *Italy: Greece intervening), Judgment, I.C.J. Reports 2012*, p. 99.

Questions relating to the Obligation to Prosecute or Extradite (Belgium* v. *Senegal)

Questions relating to the Obligation to Prosecute or Extradite (Belgium v. *Senegal), Judgment, I.C.J. Reports 2012*, p. 422.

Whaling in the Antarctic (Australia* v. *Japan: New Zealand intervening)

Whaling in the Antarctic (Australia v. *Japan: New Zealand intervening), Judgment, I.C.J. Reports 2014*, p. 226.

Frontier Dispute (Burkina Faso/Niger)

Frontier Dispute (Burkina Faso/Niger), Judgment, I.C.J. Reports 2013, p. 44.

Certain Activities carried out by Nicaragua in the Border Area (Costa Rica* v. *Nicaragua)

Certain Activities Carried Out by Nicaragua in the Border Area (Costa Rica v. *Nicaragua), Provisional Measures, Order of 8 March 2011, I.C.J. Reports 2011*, p. 6.

Certain Activities Carried Out by Nicaragua in the Border Area (Costa Rica v. *Nicaragua); Construction of a Road in Costa Rica along the San Juan River (Nicaragua* v. *Costa Rica), Counter-Claims, Order of 18 April 2013, I.C.J. Reports 2013*, p. 200.

Certain Activities Carried Out by Nicaragua in the Border Area (Costa Rica v. *Nicaragua); Construction of a Road in Costa Rica along the San Juan River (Nicaragua* v. *Costa Rica), Order of 16 July 2013, Provisional Measures, I.C.J. Reports 2013*, p. 230.

***Request for Interpretation of the Judgment of 15 June 1962 in the Case concerning the* Temple of Preah Vihear (Cambodia *v.* Thailand) (Cambodia *v.* Thailand)**

Request for Interpretation of the Judgment of 15 June 1962 in the Case concerning the Temple of Preah Vihear (Cambodia *v.* Thailand) *(Cambodia* v. *Thailand), Judgment, I.C.J. Reports 2013*, p. 281.

Request for Interpretation of the Judgment of 15 June 1962 in the Case concerning the Temple of Preah Vihear (Cambodia *v.* Thailand) *(Cambodia* v. *Thailand), Judgment, I.C.J. Reports 2013*, Joint declaration of Judges Owada, Bennouna and Gaja, p. 320.

***Construction of a Road in Costa Rica along the San Juan River* (*Nicaragua* v. *Costa Rica*)**

Construction of a Road in Costa Rica along the San Juan River (Nicaragua v. *Costa Rica), Joinder of Proceedings, Order of 17 April 2013, I.C.J. Reports 2013*, p. 184.

***Obligation to Negotiate Access to the Pacific Ocean* (*Bolivia* v. *Chile*)**

Obligation to Negotiate Access to the Pacific Ocean (Bolivia v. *Chile), Preliminary Objection, Judgment of 24 September 2015.*

***Question of the Delimitation of the Continental Shelf between Nicaragua and Colombia beyond 200 nautical miles from the Nicaraguan Coast* (*Nicaragua* v. *Colombia*)**

Question of the Delimitation of the Continental Shelf between Nicaragua and Colombia beyond 200 Nautical Miles from the Nicaraguan Coast (Nicaragua v. *Colombia), Order of 9 December 2013, I.C.J. Reports 2013*, p. 395.

Question of the Delimitation of the Continental Shelf between Nicaragua and Colombia beyond 200 Nautical Miles from the Nicaraguan Coast (Nicaragua v. *Colombia), Preliminary Objections, Judgment of 17 March 2016.*

Question of the Delimitation of the Continental Shelf between Nicaragua and Colombia beyond 200 Nautical Miles from the Nicaraguan Coast (Nicaragua v. *Colombia), Preliminary Objections, Judgment of 17 March 2016*, Joint dissenting opinion of Vice-President Yusuf, Judges Cançado Trindade, Xue, Gaja, Bhandari, Robinson and Judge *ad hoc* Brower.

Question of the Delimitation of the Continental Shelf between Nicaragua and Colombia beyond 200 Nautical Miles from the Nicaraguan Coast (Nicaragua v. *Colombia), Preliminary Objections, Judgment of 17 March 2016*, Separate opinion of Judge Owada.

***Alleged Violations of Sovereign Rights and Maritime Spaces in the Caribbean Sea* (*Nicaragua* v. *Colombia*)**

Alleged Violations of Sovereign Rights and Maritime Spaces in the Caribbean Sea (Nicaragua v. *Colombia), Preliminary Objections, Judgment of 17 March 2016.*

***Obligations concerning Negotiations relating to Cessation of the Nuclear Arms Race and to Nuclear Disarmament* (*Marshall Islands* v. *India*)**

Obligations concerning Negotiations relating to Cessation of the Nuclear Arms Race and to Nuclear Disarmament (Marshall Islands v. *India)*, Counter-Memorial of India.

Obligations concerning Negotiations relating to Cessation of the Nuclear Arms Race and to Nuclear Disarmament (Marshall Islands v. *India), Order of 16 June 2014, I.C.J. Reports 2014*, p. 464.

Obligations concerning Negotiations relating to Cessation of the Nuclear Arms Race and to Nuclear Disarmament (Marshall Islands v. *India), Preliminary Objections, Judgment of 5 October 2016.*

Obligations concerning Negotiations relating to Cessation of the Nuclear Arms Race and to Nuclear Disarmament (Marshall Islands v. *Pakistan)*

Obligations concerning Negotiations relating to Cessation of the Nuclear Arms Race and to Nuclear Disarmament (Marshall Islands v. *Pakistan), Order of 10 July 2014, I.C.J. Reports 2014*, p. 471.

Obligations concerning Negotiations relating to Cessation of the Nuclear Arms Race and to Nuclear Disarmament (Marshall Islands v. *Pakistan), Preliminary Objections, Judgment of 5 October 2016.*

Obligations concerning Negotiations relating to Cessation of the Nuclear Arms Race and to Nuclear Disarmament (Marshall Islands v. *United Kingdom)*

Obligations concerning Negotiations relating to Cessation of the Nuclear Arms Race and to Nuclear Disarmament (Marshall Islands v. *United Kingdom), Order of 16 June 2014, I.C.J. Reports 2014*, p. 468.

Obligations concerning Negotiations relating to Cessation of the Nuclear Arms Race and to Nuclear Disarmament (Marshall Islands v. *United Kingdom), Preliminary Objections, Judgment of 5 October 2016.*

ICJ Advisory Opinions

Conditions of Admission of a State to United Nations (Charter, Art. 4)

Conditions of Admission of a State to United Nations (Charter, Art. 4), Advisory Opinion: I.C.J. Reports 1948, p. 57.

Reparation for injuries suffered in the service of the United Nations

Reparation for injuries suffered in the service of the United Nations, Advisory Opinion: I.C.J. Reports 1949, p. 174.

Interpretation of Peace Treaties with Bulgaria, Hungary and Romania

Interpretation of Peace Treaties with Bulgaria, Hungary and Romania, First Phase, Advisory Opinion: I.C.J. Reports 1950, p. 65.

International status of South-West Africa

International status of South-West Africa, Advisory Opinion: I.C.J. Reports 1950, p. 128.

Reservations to the Convention on the Prevention and Punishment of the Crime of Genocide

Reservations to the Convention on the Prevention and Punishment of the Crime of Genocide, Advisory Opinion: I.C.J. Reports 1951, p. 15.

Effect of Awards of Compensation Made by the United Nations Administrative Tribunal

Effect of Awards of Compensation Made by the United Nations Administrative Tribunal, Advisory Opinion, I.C.J. Reports 1954, p. 47.

Judgments of the Administrative Tribunal of the ILO upon complaints made against the Unesco

Judgments of the Administrative Tribunal of the ILO. upon complaints made against the Unesco, Advisory Opinion of October 23rd, 1956: I.C.J. Reports 1956, p. 77.

Certain expenses of the United Nations (Article 17, paragraph 2, of the Charter)

Certain expenses of the United Nations (Article 17, paragraph 2, of the Charter), Advisory Opinion of 20 July 1962: I.C.J. Reports 1962, p. 151.

Legal consequences for States of the continued presence of South Africa in Namibia

Legal consequences for States of the continued presence of South Africa in Namibia (South West Africa) notwithstanding Security Council resolution 276 (1970), Advisory Opinion, I.C.J. Reports 1971, p. 16.

Interpretation of the Agreement of 25 March 1951 between the WHO and Egypt

Interpretation of the Agreement of 25 March 1951 between the WHO and Egypt, Advisory Opinion, I.C.J. Reports 1980, p. 73.

Applicability of the Obligation to Arbitrate under Section 21 of the United Nations Headquarters Agreement of 26 June 1947

Applicability of the Obligation to Arbitrate under Section 21 of the United Nations Headquarters Agreement of 26 June 1947, Advisory Opinion, I.C.J. Reports 1988, p. 12.

Applicability of Article VI, Section 22, of the Convention on the Privileges and Immunities of the United Nations, Advisory Opinion

Applicability of Article VI, Section 22, of the Convention on the Privileges and Immunities of the United Nations, Advisory Opinion, I.C.J. Reports 1989, p. 177.

Legality of the Use by a State of Nuclear Weapons in Armed Conflict

Legality of the Use by a State of Nuclear Weapons in Armed Conflict, Advisory Opinion, I.C.J. Reports 1996, p. 66.

Legality of the Threat or Use of Nuclear Weapons

Legality of the Threat or Use of Nuclear Weapons, Advisory Opinion, I.C.J. Reports 1996, p. 226.

Legality of the Threat or Use of Nuclear Weapons, Advisory Opinion, I.C.J. Reports 1996, p. 226, Dissenting opinion of Judge Oda, p. 330, Dissenting opinion of Judge Weeramantry, p. 429.

Legal Consequences of the Construction of a Wall in the Occupied Palestinian Territory

Legal Consequences of the Construction of a Wall in the Occupied Palestinian Territory, Advisory Opinion, I.C.J. Reports 2004, p. 136.

PCIJ Cases

S.S. "Wimbledon"

S.S. "Wimbledon", Judgments, [16 January] 1923, P.C.I.J., Series A, No. 1, p. 15.

Status of Eastern Carelia

Status of Eastern Carelia, Advisory Opinion [of July 23rd], 1923, Series B, No. 5, p. 7.

Mavrommatis Palestine Concessions

Mavrommatis Palestine Concessions, Judgment No. 2, 1924, P.C.I.J., Series A, No. 2, p. 5.

Polish Postal Service in Danzig

Polish Postal Service in Danzig, Advisory Opinion [of May 16th], 1925, P.C.I.J., Series B, No. 11, p. 5.

Certain German Interests in Polish Upper Silesia

Certain German Interests in Polish Upper Silesia, Jurisdiction, Judgment No. 6, [25 August] 1925, P.C.I.J., Series A, No. 6, p. 3.

Certain German Interests in Polish Upper Silesia, Judgment No. 7, 1926, P.C.I.J., Series A, No. 7, p. 3.

Interpretation of Judgments Nos. 7 and 8 (Factory at Chorzów)

Interpretation of Judgments Nos. 7 and 8 (Factory at Chorzów), Judgment No. 11, 1927, P.C.I.J., Series A, No. 13, p. 27.

Rights of Minorities in Upper Silesia (Minority Schools)

Rights of Minorities in Upper Silesia (Minority Schools), Judgment No. 12, [26 April] 1928, P.C.I.J., Series A, No. 15, p. 3.

Factory at Chorzów

Factory at Chorzów, Merits, Judgment No. 13, [13 September] 1928, P.C.I.J., Series A, No. 17, p. 3.

Free Zones of Upper Savoy and the District of Gex

Free Zones of Upper Savoy and the District of Gex [(second phase)], Order of 6 December 1930, P.C.I.J., Series A, No. 24, p. 3.

Free Zones of Upper Savoy and the District of Gex [(second phase)], Judgment [of June 7th], 1932, P.C.I.J., Series A/B, No. 46, p. 95.

Panevezys-Saldutiskis Railway

Panevezys-Saldutiskis Railway, Order of 30 June 1938, P.C.I.J., Series A/B, No. 75, p. 52.

Panevezys-Saldutiskis Railway, Judgment [of February 28th], 1939, P.C.I.J., Series A/B, No. 76, p. 3.

Electricity Company of Sofia and Bulgaria

Electricity Company of Sofia and Bulgaria, Judgment [of April 4], 1939, P.C.I.J., Series A/B, No. 77, p. 63.

Société commerciale de Belgique

Société commerciale de Belgique, Judgment [of June 15th], 1939, P.C.I.J., Series A/B, No. 78, p. 159.

Arbitration Cases

Alabama Claims Arbitration, China Navigation Co., Ltd. (Great Britain) *v.* United States (*Newchwang* case), 9 December 1921, *United Nations Reports of International Arbitral Awards*, Vol. VI, p. 64.

Société Française de Banque et de Dépôts case, the Franco-German Mixed Arbitral Tribunal (See Bin Cheng, p. 371.).

Trail Smelter case (United States of America, Canada), *United Nations Reports of International Arbitral Awards*, Vol. III, p. 1905.

Other Cases

U.S. Supreme Court decision in *Banco Nacional de Cuba* v. *Sabbatino*, 376 U.S. 398 (1964).

Index